The
Transformation
of
Urban Housing

A WORLD BANK RESEARCH PUBLICATION

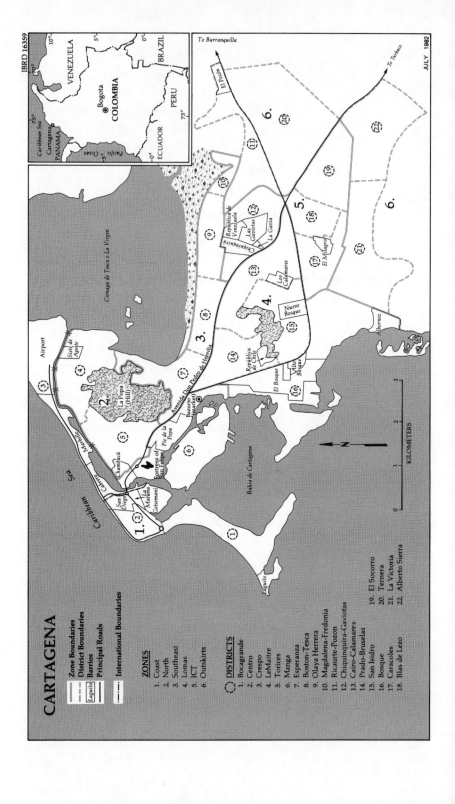

CARTAGENA

Zone Boundaries
District Boundaries
Laguito Barrios
Principal Roads

International Boundaries

ZONES

1. Coast
2. North
3. Southeast
4. Lomas
5. ICT
6. Outskirts

DISTRICTS

1. Bocagrande
2. Centro
3. Crespo
4. LeMaitre
5. Torices
6. Manga
7. Esperanza
8. Boston-Tesca
9. Olaya Herrera
10. Magdalena-Fredonia
11. Ricaurte-Pozon
12. Chiquinquira-Gaviotas
13. Cairo-Calamares
14. Prado-Bruselas
15. San Isidro
16. Bosque
17. Caracoles
18. Blas de Lezo
19. El Socorro
20. Ternera
21. La Victoria
22. Alberto Sierra

IBRD 16359

JULY 1982

The
Transformation
of
Urban Housing

*The Experience
of Upgrading
in Cartagena*

W. Paul Strassmann

Published for The World Bank

THE JOHNS HOPKINS UNIVERSITY PRESS

Baltimore & London

The Johns Hopkins University Press
Baltimore, Maryland 21218, U.S.A.

EDITOR   Virginia deHaven Hitchcock
MAP   Julio Ruiz and Larry A. Bowring
BOOK DESIGN   Christine Houle
BINDING DESIGN   Joyce C. Eisen

Library of Congress Cataloging in Publication Data

Strassmann, W. Paul (Wolfgang Paul), 1926-
   The transformation of urban housing.

   Bibliography: p.
   Includes index.
   1. Housing—Colombia—Cartagena (Province)
2. Urban renewal—Colombia—Cartagena (Province)
   I. World Bank.   II. Title
HD7325.C4S77   1982   363.5'8   81-48176
ISBN 0-8018-2805-8   AACR2

Contents

Tables

Acknowledgments

THIS STUDY OF URBAN HOUSING WOULD HAVE BEEN IMPOSSIBLE without the help of numerous people. Most important numerically and otherwise were the 293 families of Cartagena who were willing to answer 100 questions, some personal, others rather absurd. Gratitude is also due to the smaller sample of landlords. The high rate of successful responses to interview attempts—86 percent—was due to the energy, skill, and dedication of four interviewers from the School of Social Work of the University of Cartagena: Samia Rosa Francis, Lylia Marina Jaquín Sánchez, Elena Lepesqueur de Guerrero, and Margarita Mejía Guerrero. Our drivers, Napoleon Baena and Antonio Cardona, did not spare their vehicles from remote and rugged journeys and helped with encyclopedic knowledge of the city. They all worked together with Norma L. Botero M. whose tact and organizing skill enabled the interviews to be completed in a mere fourteen days, July 5–18, 1978. Norma's creativity, diligence, and good humor kept the entire study on course.

The work in Cartagena began with practical advice from Hector Trujillo, Ester de Alvear, Gilda de Calvo, and Lácydes Cortés Díaz of the Planning Commission for the North of Bolívar. At the University of Cartagena, Libardo Castro Reyes explained economic conditions, and Gustavo Pacheco gave us crucial details about demographic trends and population densities. At the University Jorge Tadeo Lozano, Tova Solo, an ingenious architect, and Carlos Marnet, a fellow economist, were most helpful. Policies of the Banco Central Hipotecario were patiently explained by Diego Salgado.

The Territorial Credit Institute (ICT) plays an important role in low cost housing, and we could have accomplished little without the patience and interest of their leading officials, Dionisio Velez, Fernando Navarro, Delly de Barrios, Melba de Chávez, and Edgardo Martínez. Their information was supplemented by that of Antonio Acuña and Lisímaco Durán of the Oficina Departamental de Rehabilitación de Tugurios (Slum Rehabilitation).

For further background information we sought the help of Jorge Payares Bossa of the Chamber of Commerce, Hernando Sarmiento Castillo of the municipal treasury (Catastro), Alberto Flórez Rojas of the national statistical service (DANE), Camilo Abadío of the Chamber of Construction, Jorge Ochoa Covo of the National Association of Industrialists, Oscar Gómez of the Municipal Planning Office, Raúl Quintero of Municipal Public Enterprises, Juan Carlos Lemaitre and David Escudero of the National Vocational Training Service (SENA), and Omar Díaz Granados and Aníbal Pérez of the Cartagena branch of the Banco de la República. All provided important clues, were generous with time, and gave us a library of documents.

To make sure we were on the right track from the point of view of people living in Southeast Zone, we often compared notes with Angel Palacio, president of Communal Action in Olaya Herrera. (One day the collapse of a neighboring shack killed a man and his wife, and Angel adopted their surviving children.) Eric Hoffman, a former Peace Corps volunteer who still lives in La Magdalena, also helped with his thorough knowledge of the area. Our last interview, as reported in the last chapter, was in Fredonia with two indomitable former nuns, Cruz Elena Ramírez P. and Teresa de Jesús Gonzáles V., "Sister Amparo."

To put findings from Cartagena into an appropriate context of national trends and policies, we had ten days of interviews in Bogotá. Especially helpful were Lucia Cruz de Schlesinger and Daniel Schlesinger Ricaurte of the Banco de la República and Augusto Cano of the University of the Andes, all former graduate students of Michigan State University. Others who made important suggestions were Augusto Alfredo Solarte and Lauchlin Currie of the National Planning Department; Gustavo Jiménez of ICT; Elsie de Alcalá of the Caja de Vivienda Popular (CVP); Jorge Torres of the National Center for Construction Studies (CENAC); Miriam Ordoñez, Carlos Velásquez, Noel Olaya, and Moises Rojas of DANE, Martha Baquero and Carlos Zorro of the University of the Andes; and Ramiro Cardona, José Fernando Pineda, Guillermo Rojas, and Alvaro López of the Centro de Cooperación Regional de Población.

This project was initiated at the World Bank with counsel from John Courtney, Orville Grimes, Gregory Ingram, Friedrich Kahnert, Anupam Khanna, Nicolas Lethbridge, and Alastair Stone.

Colleagues at Michigan State University who gave advice on the questionnaire and project design were Aaron Gurwitz, Carl Liedholm, and Daniel Saks. Three thousand pages of questionnaires were ingeniously transformed into computer printout by Chris Wolf, who was helped by Cathy Caswell, Cheryl Wilkins, Mary Moeller, and others. For typing all these names, pages, and numbers in tables correctly, I am thankful to Ty Dao, Pat Trommater, Kelli Sweet, and Miae Evans.

My wife, Betty, accompanied me on some of the interviews, to some of the tugurios, to the eradication of La Carbonera, and finally read some early drafts of chapters and conscientiously found embarrassing mistakes. For all this and more, much thanks.

W. PAUL STRASSMANN

Acronyms

BCH Banco Central Hipotecario
  (Central Mortgage Bank)
CAMACOL Cámara de Construcción
  (Colombian Chamber of Construction)
CAV Corporación de Ahorro y Vivienda
  (Corporation for Saving and Housing)
CEDE Centro de Estudios sobre Desarrollo Económico
  (Center for Economic Development Studies)
CENAC Centro Nacional de Estudios de la Construcción
  (National Center for Construction Studies)
CVP Caja de Vivienda Popular de Bogotá
  (Low-Cost Housing Bank of Bogota)
DANE Departamento Administrativo Nacional de Estadistica
  (National Statistics Department)
ECIEL Estudios Conjuntos sobre Integración Economica Latino-
  americana
  (Joint Studies of Latin American Economic Integration)
EPM Empresas Publicas Municipales
  (Municipal Public Enterprises)
ICT Instituto de Crédito Territorial
  (Territorial Credit Institute)
INSFOPAL Instituto Nacional de Fomento Municipal
  (National Institute for Urban Development)
SENA Servicio Nacional de Aprendizaje
  (National Apprenticeship Service)
ZFIC Zona Franca Industrial y Comercial de Cartagena
  (Duty-free Industrial and Commercial Zone of Cartagena)

The
Transformation
of
Urban Housing

1

Introduction and Summary

IN A MATERIAL SENSE, economic development means a better countryside and better cities. New seeds, new pumps, new engines, new shoes, and countless other new goods are supposed to replace the worn-out and obsolete. Even new cities have been built, but these have turned out to be too expensive and dreary.[1] In the urban setting, therefore, the main task is to improve the old appealing cities and the present housing stock, rather than to replace it. This book is about the transformation of housing.

The Role of Housing in Economic Development

Because of population growth and migration, old cities will need many new dwellings, but these, like others, will have to be transformed, expanded, and modified over the years to play their part in the development process. Housing transformation must not only be expected and tolerated but should even be fostered as a good way to raise an important type of production, to generate employment, and to improve equity in distribution. For example, employment naturally accompanies small-scale improvements of dwellings: labor-intensive, conventional building methods are still more efficient than capital-intensive prefabrication in almost all settings.[2]

With respect to equity, most young families in developing countries cannot obtain any type of newly built two-room dwelling with a kitchen and bathroom if they pay only one-fifth of their income for fifteen years at an unsubsidized real interest rate of around 12 percent.[3] Subsidies that bring such housing within reach of the poor are inequitable because they can be given to only a small minority unless investment in all other sectors is wholly neglected. The poor should have access to their share of finance plus a widely dispersed, hence modest, subsidy. With that they can easily acquire a utility-serviced site, an incomplete but expandable core house, or an existing substandard dwelling that can be upgraded.

3

The case for an urban strategy that stresses such lending is strong. In recent years this strategy has been recommended by several national housing agencies and by international lenders, such as the World Bank and the U.S. Agency for International Development.[4] Not only does this upgrading strategy provide more improved housing than the costly alternative of eradicating slums, subsidizing the middle class, and hoping that the benefits will filter downward, but it also leads to more employment and to entrepreneurial opportunities for the poor.[5]

Casual observation and studies of specific projects and neighborhoods have shown that many of the poor are already upgrading their dwellings, despite obstacles and institutional constraints. Instruction on technical details might be useful, but massive campaigns such as those for better nutrition or family planning will not be needed. What has been lacking instead is knowledge by urban authorities of how upgrading transforms the use of the entire housing stock by a growing population with changing incomes. Without such knowledge, policies dealing with finance, land, and infrastructure will generate an inadequate and misdirected volume of construction.

The upgrading or the transformation of housing must be understood in terms of the changing housing market as a whole. The demand for new dwellings or for improvements depends on population growth, household formation, migration, personal income growth, income distribution, access to land and finance, the availability of competing goods and services, the characteristics of the old housing stock, and various regulations. Analysis of supply is even more complex because of the diversity of actors that are involved: workers, builders, utility providers, materials suppliers, financiers, and often designers, landlords, and others. Some perform multiple functions. It would be misleading, however, to assume that all the financial and entrepreneurial institutions of advanced countries exist in cities in developing countries. When the focus is on housing by and for the poor, complex theories based on irrelevant settings are not helpful.[6]

Poor households will save and work to transform dwellings progressively in a variety of ways. They can use current income, liquidate past savings, borrow from relatives, or take out materials or general construction loans. Some countries have informal credit societies or money-lending clubs.[7] Construction work can be performed by the family, by friends and neighbors, by artisan contractors from the informal sector, as well as by registered builders.[8]

One pattern is obvious: constraints of any type inhibit the transformation of housing.[9] In some countries occupants must follow predetermined housing designs, whereas in others they must simply convince inspectors that they are building in a structurally sound manner. A few countries prohibit renting, subletting, or selling the serviced site with its newly built or upgraded dwelling for several years to anyone other than the supervising or lending institution. These restrictions are meant to prohibit real estate speculation and transfers to higher income groups. Presumably if "trickle-down" policies left the poor out in the past, "trickle-up" policies might be equally bad. And yet this may be the very way that self-help builders can become entrepreneurs with increasing skills. They can become the suppliers of middle-income housing by living on the premises during construction.[10] Thus the 1950s squatter settlement called 27 de Octubre across the Rimac River from Lima, Peru, had become the partly middle-class area of San Martín de Porras by the 1970s.[11] In the World Bank Dandora project at Nairobi, Kenya, occupants were encouraged to finance expansions by taking in lodgers. Partly as a result, the average dwelling was completed within eight instead of eighteen months.[12] Afterward entire dwellings were sublet or sold to richer households. Integrating informal building with the rest of the urban economy in this manner reduces dualism, a reduction that some take as synonymous with development. The poor are not hurt if they are allowed to develop specialized talents and to use them most productively. Someone has to build middle-income housing—why not the poor, organized in their own fashion?

Obviously, immediate resale of serviced sites or core houses, perhaps drawn by poor families through a lottery, would be an awkward way of giving the poor income instead of better housing. Some say that income is indeed what poor families lack, so why not let them allocate it in terms of their own priorities?[13] Urban planners and development economists, however, have a longer perspective than specific poor individuals and are concerned with the functioning of the city and the economy for decades ahead. Policies should not only mitigate poverty within the next few years but also prevent eventual urban breakdowns and raise the productivity of the poor.[14] The best way to raise their productivity is to give them work experience in a sector with an expanding market. Resale should be discouraged for a year and be limited to substantially improved dwellings.

An Overview of the Study

The ideas reviewed in the preceding section are by no means new, but in 1978 they had never been empirically tested in a comprehensive manner for an entire city. The Urban Projects Department of the World Bank therefore asked the author to study the determinants of the supply and demand for housing among different socioeconomic groups, the current and potential resource allocating mechanisms, and the role of institutional, policy, and material constraints, with a case study of one city, Cartagena, Colombia. As described in the next chapter, Cartagena had been a leading South American city in Spanish colonial times, but its fortunes had varied after its liberation in 1821. In the 1970s the World Bank, together with local and national agencies, was financing a commercial and industrial duty-free district and was upgrading the city's Southeast Zone. One-fifth of the population lived there in 1978 with monthly incomes of US$20 per capita, half the average in the remaining city (although that included other sizable slums). In the rest of the city about 70 percent of households had indoor piped water and means of sanitary disposal better than latrines, whereas in the Southeast Zone only about 30 percent had those facilities. With luck, a study of Cartagena could be relevant to further projects in that city and could provide guidelines for policymakers elsewhere.

A questionnaire with 100 items was developed, tested, and used during July 5–18, 1978, in interviews with 296 households (out of 340 attempts). The sample and procedure are described in Appendix A, and the questionnaire reproduced in English in Appendix B. There were also interviews with local authorities and experts, as well as with others in Bogotá. Furthermore, a substantial number of published and unpublished reports about urban conditions in Colombia were consulted.

Chapter 2 gives the general background to the study and provides some history (omitting heroes and battles), a review of demographic and economic trends, a description of employment and the labor force, two paragraphs about the free port, and other information that helps to set the stage.

Chapters 3 and 4 are about demand and related public institutions. One chapter deals with housing in terms of physical needs; the other is about effective demand, hence income levels, income distribution, credit systems, and access to land as they affect households of different sizes and at different stages of their life cycles. Tenants and owners are treated separately.

Housing supply is discussed in two parts. Chapter 5 surveys two conventional matters, the old housing stock and new construction. Hedonic price indexes show how specific physical characteristics account for the overall value of a dwelling. A number of cross-tabulations show what kind of household has settled in what type of dwelling. Other sections deal with construction costs, employment effects, and innovations. Since the housing market is fractured, as in most third world cities, a comprehensive model of rational behavior is not applied. The implication is not that builders, landlords, and occupants are "irrational," but rather that they are rational in a very imperfect context. For example, we found that most adult occupants know how to appraise the value of their own dwelling rather shrewdly. Detailed training in price indexing and patterns of urbanization would not greatly improve their estimates. We found that the permanent income hypothesis holds: unexpected lump sum receipts from a lottery, an inheritance, smuggling, or a remittance from Venezuela are not squandered but saved and invested in housing or durables.

Improvement and conversion of the existing housing stock are discussed in Chapter 6. Downgrading through subdivision and poor maintenance are also possibilities but not of comparable significance in developing countries. In the face of rapid population growth and urban expansion, usually only a small portion of the old housing stock is a candidate for subdivision. Doubling up of several generations of middle-class or impoverished upper-class families occurs if there are constraints on building. Subdivision for tenants is often illegal, hence clandestine, in public housing. Such subdivision goes on primarily in very large cities without opportunities for squatting at accessible locations. There is much subdivision in Bogotá, little in Cartagena. Squatting usually takes place on public land with tacit official tolerance.[15]

Thirteen different types of improvements can be made, but added rooms get the most attention. A variety of econometric tests all suggest that with access to indoor piped water, households will improve their dwellings much more than otherwise. Landlords make improvements but only when their rented premises happen to be vacant.

Following these chapters on demand and supply is another on their interaction. Demand and supply interact when an existing dwelling is improved by the occupants or when a family moves from one dwelling to another. Chapter 7 reports why households in Cartagena had moved, and why some were thinking of moving again. From figures about housing values and characteristics during a single month, we could not, however, deduce much about price changes and stock adjustments as ways of clearing the housing market with all its imperfections. It is easier to project what will have to be built by 1990 if households in each income bracket are to have at least the same level of housing quality as they had in 1978.

The concluding chapter lists a few topics that merit further examination. Recommendations are made for upper-, middle-, and low-income housing. Outside support for upgrading is favored if it is designed to meet the occupants' priorities and capabilities. Utopian thinking, paternalism, and paper-intensive delivery systems will not work.

The experience of Cartagena seems to support all these recommendations, because opportunities for transforming the housing stock were unusually good in that city during the 1970s. Many families received transitory incomes, and the principal housing agency had financed incomplete, expandable dwellings. Eradication of squatter settlements was no longer official policy. The response of owner-occupants to these opportunities was energetic. The poor were just as likely to add a room as the rich. Everyone's additions and improvements made housing nearly twice as good as might have been predicted on the basis of income alone. Rooms per dwelling increased by 24 percent for the city during 1973–78, and value per dwelling rose even more. Access to public utilities, especially water, was a significant spur to modernization and elaboration. More could have been done, but at least the policies that stressed public utilities and unfinished housing were justified.

Notes to Chapter 1

1. Bertrand Renaud has concluded that new towns "constitute the most expensive way of financing urban development." *National Urbanization Policy in Developing Countries* (New York: Oxford University Press, 1981), p. 114. See also Ved Prakash, *New Towns in India* (Durham, N.C.: Duke University Program in Comparative Studies on Southern Asia, 1969). John F. C. Turner tells about "the architects and planners who preserve some of the slums that are cleared to make way for their schemes, in order to have somewhere pleasant to live themselves" in *Housing by People: Towards Autonomy in Building Environments* (New York: Pantheon Books, 1976), p. 3.

2. W. Paul Strassmann, *Housing and Building Technology in Developing Countries*, MSU International Business and Economic Studies (East Lansing, Mich.: Michigan State University, 1978), is a survey of the literature on appropriate technology and employment in building.

3. Orville F. Grimes, *Housing for Low-Income Urban Families* (Baltimore, Md.: Johns Hopkins University Press, 1976), especially pp. 61–81. Barbara Ward, *The Home of Man* (Toronto: McClelland and Stewart, 1976), pp. 192–233, and works of the United Nations Foundation for Human Settlements also show how the emphasis in this field has shifted toward housing for the poor. See also Anthony A. Churchill and Margaret Lycette, *Shelter*, Poverty and Basic Needs Series (Washington, D.C.: World Bank, 1980). Johannes Linn, *Cities in the Developing World: Policies for Their Equitable and Efficient Growth* (New York: Oxford University Press, 1982), explores in detail the issues raised in these introductory pages.

4. World Bank, *Housing Sector Policy Paper* (Washington, D.C: World Bank, 1975); Agency for International Development, Comptroller General, *Agency for International Development's Housing Investment Guaranty Program*, report to the Congress (Washington, D.C.: U.S. General Accounting Office, September 6, 1978); also, Agency for

International Development, Office of Housing, *Tunisia: Shelter Sector Assessment* (Washington, D.C., January 1979), and similar reports for other countries.

5. Geoffrey K. Payne, *Urban Housing in the Third World* (London: Leonard Hill, 1977), pp. 194–99, 211–16.

6. Rakesh Mohan, *Urban Economic and Planning Models: Assessing the Potential for Cities in Developing Countries* (Baltimore, Md.: Johns Hopkins University Press, 1979).

7. Marguerite Jellicoe, "Credit and Housing Associations among Luo Immigrants in Kampala," in *Urban Challenge in East Africa*, ed. John Hutton (Nairobi: East Africa Publishing House, 1970); Bernard Gallin, *Hsin Hsing, Taiwan: A Chinese Village in Change* (Berkeley, Calif.: University of California Press, 1966), pp. 74–75.

8. David Drakakis-Smith, "Low-Cost Housing Provision in the Third World," *Housing in Third World Countries*, ed. H. S. Murison and J. P. Lea (New York: St. Martin's Press, 1979), pp. 22–30.

9. Sally Cameron, "Local Participation in Bank-Supported Urban Development Projects" (Washington, D.C., World Bank, Urban Projects Department, 1978; processed). Linn, *Cities in the Developing World*.

10. Carlos Zorro Sánchez and Edgar Reveiz Roldán, *Estudio sobre los Inquilinatos (Vivienda Compartida en Arrendamiento) en Bogotá* (Bogotá: Centro de Estudios sobre Desarrollo Económico, University of the Andes, Etapa I, February 1974 and Segunda Parte, June 1976).

11. David Collier, *Squatters and Oligarchs: Authoritarian Rule and Policy Change in Peru* (Baltimore, Md.: Johns Hopkins University Press, 1976), p. 91.

12. M. S. Muller, "House Building in Site and Services Schemes: Some Observations" (University of Nairobi, Housing Research and Development Unit, June 1977; processed); Mazingira Institute, "Post-Habitat Evaluation Report on Human Settlements" (Nairobi, July 1978; processed); Bureau of Educational Research, "The Residents of Umoja Housing Estate" (University of Nairobi, March 1978; processed).

13. Ira S. Lowry, Mack Ott, and Charles Noland, "Housing Allowances and Household Behavior," Rand Corporation note prepared for the Department of Housing and Urban Development (Santa Monica, Calif., March 1973; processed).

14. Leland S. Burns and Leo Grebler, *The Housing of Nations: Analysis and Policy in a Comparative Framework* (London: Macmillan, 1977).

15. Collier, *Squatters and Oligarchs*, pp. 40–54; A. A. Laquian, "Squatters and Slum Dwellers," in *Housing Asia's Millions*, ed. Stephen H. K. Yeh and A. A. Laquian (Ottawa: International Development Research Center, 1979), pp. 51–65. Payne, *Urban Housing in the Third World*, p. 198, refers to similar policies in Turkey.

2

Cartagena

CARTAGENA DE INDIAS IS COLOMBIA'S MAIN CENTER for two rather contradictory activities: tourism and the production of chemicals, especially petrochemicals. The city also remains an important naval base, capital of the Department of Bolivar, and the commercial center for a cattle-raising hinterland. The influx of tourists, sailors, students, smugglers, migrants from the interior, as well as workers back from Venezuela makes demography guesswork in Cartagena, but a population of 429,000 seemed reasonable for 1978.

Evolution of the City

Tourists are attracted by the city's pleasant configuration of peninsulas and islands between a large bay of the Caribbean Sea and a series of lagoons (see map, frontispiece). During the colonial era, this configuration made Cartagena the fortified port best suited for collecting gold from all Nueva Granada until enough was at hand for a convoy of galleons. The date of the Spanish founding of Cartagena is 1533; that of the preceding Indian settlement of Calamary is a problem for archeologists. African slaves built an elaborate (and now photogenic) series of fortifications for the Spaniards and dug the Canal del Dique, a 115-kilometer diversion of the Magdalena River. In 1851 the slaves were freed. Just before national independence in 1811, the population of Cartagena was estimated at 18,000 and just afterward at 12,000, indicating the hazards of liberation.

In the latter half of the nineteenth century, the economy of Cartagena was stimulated by a brief tobacco boom and the steady growth of coffee exports. Some of the fortifications were razed at La Matuna so that a railway could reach the docks at the Bahía de Animas. This railway and its freightyards split the former enlisted men's quarter of Getsemaní from the more aristocratic quarters along the ocean and around the cathedral. The population rose from 9,700 in 1905 to 36,600 in 1912.

The boom ended when coffee shipments were diverted to Buenaventura on the Pacific Coast after the opening of the Panama Canal in 1914. When the port of Barranquilla at the mouth of the Magdalena was properly dredged in the 1930s, Cartagena lost additional shipping. A somewhat premature oil refinery had been set up in 1908 and was closed in 1921. In the early 1950s the railway and its station, called La Machina, were dismantled, leaving space for a sector of high-rise banks and offices that would finance and organize the tourism and chemical industries.

The population rose from 85,000 in 1938, to 129,000 in 1951, and to 242,000 in 1964. The migrants of the 1950s included many refugees from the anarchic civil war in the interior, La Violencia. The first squatters appropriated the former garbage dump of San Francisco in 1955, just as a new one was being started at Albornoz. These squatters were rounded up in trucks and locked in the athletic stadium while their shacks were knocked down. The second great eradication of 4,000 dwellings on 9 hectares at Chambacú proceeded more gently from the late 1960s to 1973 with sociological guidance and compensation. If Cartagena was to become enchanting to tourists, a vast encampment of shacks was simply intolerable between the giant fortress of San Felipe and the crenellated walls of San Diego.

Meanwhile the central city behind its fortifications was declared a historical monument, except for La Matuna, and only whitewashed colonial houses could be built or renovated here. Balconies and patios were now cultural shrines, together with the Palace of the Inquisition. The national government appropriated money for a sewerage system that opened in March 1968. Rich old families had already moved from the Centro to Manga and to Bocagrande. Until the 1970s there had been only one large tourist hotel in Bocagrande, low-rise and elegant but unairconditioned, built in 1948. Now high-rise hotels and condominiums appeared along the beach, and mansions were converted to pensions, pizza parlors, and discotheques. The displaced rich, by no means impoverished by the change, have built new mansions for themselves, in some cases 12 kilometers west of town on the hills of Turbaco. The chemical plants and refineries are located 12 kilometers south of town at Mamonal. Fortunately the tradewinds blow from the north.

They blow hardest from December through March, the dry season. On the coolest January mornings the temperature falls to 19 degrees (C), the annual minimum. As one might expect at 10 degrees of latitude north of the equator, the August maximum averages 32 degrees, but the temperature can reach 36 degrees. The rainy season is May to October and generates an annual 885 millimeters of rainfall. Average humidity is 88 percent.

Cartagena is governed by three levels of government—national, departmental, and municipal—and autonomous public agencies. The national president appoints the governor who appoints the mayor, who works with an elected municipal council. The national government plays a predominant role in health, welfare, education, and housing. Among four autonomous municipal agencies, the Empresas Publicas Municipales (EPM) is most important since it supplies water, provides refuse collection and sewerage disposal, builds some and maintains all streets and parks, fights fires, and administers the slaughterhouse and municipal markets. Most streets and roads, however, are built by the Valorization Department, which finances its work with special assessments. Private firms carry out the actual construction. Coordination of all this is complex and subject to frequent changes.[1]

Population and the Economy during the 1970s

From 1964 to 1978 the population of Cartagena grew at an annual rate of 4.2 percent and reached 429,000, excluding tourists and temporary military personnel. The 1973 census is considered very inaccurate, off by 10 to 50 percent, so that it is preferable to use a variety of local statistical interpolations.[2] Perhaps some 123,000 people were economically active. In recent years unemployment has been estimated at around 19 percent. About two-thirds of employment is informal, that is, in activities not registered with the Colombian Social Security Institute. The distribution of employment in the municipality in 1975 is shown in Table 2-1.

Labor force participation was 70 percent among men and 25 percent among women. Men had a life expectancy of 58.6 years; women, 62.5 years. Adjusted infant mortality was 111 per thousand. The 1973 gross birth rate (adjusted by the Chandrasekar-Deming method) was urban, 3.0 percent; semi-urban, 3.8 percent; and rural Bolívar, 4.9 percent. Rural women were likely to have completed families of 9.9 children; urban women had 2.9 children. Women with no education had 4.8 children, those with only primary education 2.7 children, those with secondary education 1.3 children, and those with higher education only 0.5 children.[3]

The distribution of employment and income among four general categories of workers according to the census of 1973 is shown in Table 2-2. Most striking is that 65 percent of workers earned 1,500 pesos or less

Table 2-1. *Distribution of Employment, 1975*

Sector	Number of employees	Percent
Agriculture, forestry, fishing	2,600	3.0
Mining	300	0.4
Manufacturing	12,000	12.8
Construction	5,600	6.5
Electricity, gas, water	1,100	1.3
Commerce	20,100	20.0
Finance	2,300	2.7
Personal services	30,600	31.0
Government	10,500	11.1
Military and police	2,100	2.4
Transport	7,400	7.5
Communications	1,100	1.3
Total	95,700	100.0

Source: Department of Economic Research of the University of Cartagena.

per month, which is less than about 6,000 1978 pesos (US$154). In our survey we found that only 39.2 percent of households earned less than 6,000 pesos. A total of 65 percent earned up to 9,400 pesos. Only 29 percent of all households received their income only from the earnings of one person.

One could go on with other statistics. For example, some 100,000 children, nearly one-fourth of the population, were enrolled in primary and secondary education. Vocational programs enrolled about 17,000 workers, and an additional 4,500 students were in the three institutions of higher learning: the University of Cartagena, the Corporacion Tecnológica de Bolivar, and the Cartagena branch of the University Jorge Tadeo Lozano. Fifteen hospitals had more than 1,000 beds.

In 1976, 1,044 ships docked in the Bay of Cartagena, not quite three daily. Compared with the 700 tourists and other visitors who arrived by ship, about 200,000 came by air. To swell their numbers further, in July 1978 the cornerstone was laid for an International Convention Center at the Bahía de Animas. It will accommodate 4,000 delegates in two auditoriums connected by closed circuit television.

In August 1978 a new urban physical development plan was issued to prevent the encroachment on one another of tourists, industries, and housing. Of the 5,310 hectares that were considered part of the urban area of Cartagena, half were under water in rivers, channels, bays,

Table 2-2. *Distribution of Income, for Employed Workers Ten Years Old and Over, by Occupational Category, 1973*
(percent)

Occupation	Income (pesos per month)							
	1–1,500	1,501–3,000	3,001–6,000	6,001–10,000	10,001–20,000	20,000+	No income	Total
Office workers	16.3	44.4	58.4	81.6	60.0	50.0	5.1	26.9
	(39.2)	(33.5)	(16.4)	(7.3)	(2.7)	(0.2)	(0.7)	(100.0)
Commercial and service workers	40.0	18.6	22.1	6.1	32.0	50.0	30.8	33.0
	(78.2)	(11.4)	(5.0)	(0.4)	(1.2)	(0.2)	(3.6)	(100.0)
Other non-agricultural workers	38.2	35.8	18.2	12.3	4.0	—	38.6	35.1
	(70.3)	(20.6)	(3.9)	(0.8)	(0.1)	—	(4.9)	(100.0)
Agricultural workers	5.5	1.2	1.3	—	4.0	—	25.6	5.0
	(72.3)	(5.0)	(2.0)	—	(1.0)	—	(19.8)	(100.0)
Total	100.0	100.0	100.0	100.0	100.0	100.0	100.0	
	(64.7)	(20.3)	(7.5)	(2.4)	(1.2)	(0.1)	(3.8)	

Note: Excluded are 21,058 workers about whom there is no information or who have poorly defined jobs. US$1.00 = Col$23.70.
— None.
Source: Advance census sample cited in Ramiro Cardona, *Migración y Fuerza de Trabajo en el Departamento de Bolívar*, vol. 2 (Bogotá: Consorcio de Ingenierías e Investigaciones, Consultores, August 1977), p. 66.

lagoons, and marshes. Some of these were being filled in by families seeking land for squatting, as described in this study. The primary fill area was the Southeast Zone that extended for 7 kilometers along the southern shore of the Cienga de Tesca. The families that moved here had good access to employment, markets, and schools. Filling in land was easy because even in the wet season, the water was no more than from 20 to 40 centimeters deep. However, periodic damage came with storm-water runoff from nearby hills and from tidal incursions that could reach 80 centimeters. Seven drainage ditches and several minor canals ran through the area but were not enough to keep trickles from kitchens and outhouses from meandering about. Nevertheless, in 1975 it was decided not to eradicate this zone, and in November 1977 a program began of large-scale filling in with limestone and general upgrading. Total cost was estimated to be $35 million, including a foreign exchange component of $10 million that came primarily from a World Bank loan.[4]

Of the 2,650 hectares of dry Cartagena land, about 81 percent is suitable for urbanization, being neither too high nor too steep. By contrast with other cities, it has not been increasingly difficult to find land for expansion of the city. Since the 1950s the density of settlement has remained fairly stable at around 160 people per hectare. Of course, growth has meant greater investments in roads and infrastructure. But the city has been expanding away from the confinements of islands and peninsulas below the steep hills toward open country. It has been moving southwest toward the industrial areas of Mamonal and Pasacaballos, and even a few of the rich have migrated southwestward toward Turbaco.

Plans for the land have been followed by plans for the water, in the form of measures to halt further pollution of the bay. As a first step, 30 million pesos (US$770,000) was allocated to coordinate national and international pollution studies.

Employment in the Formal Sector

The formal economic sector of Cartagena can be defined as enterprises affiliated with the Instituto de Seguros Sociales (Social Security). According to the Institute, in December 1977, 2,100 such enterprises employed 32,300 workers (15.4 workers per firm) and paid them an average of 4,070 pesos (US$105) monthly. Compared with the previous year, employment had risen by 4.7 percent, and the average wage by 23.2 percent. Since the cost of living for workers (Barranquilla) rose by 46 percent, real wages declined by about 15 percent.

Income distribution in the formal sector was:

Income (pesos)	Percentage of workers
0–2,040	1.0
2,040–2,819	50.9
2,820–3,779	15.4
3,780–5,039	14.0
5,040–8,399	11.7
8,400–16,000	5.5
16,000+	1.6

According to the Institute, workers were distributed among the sectors as follows:

Economic sector	Percentage of formal employment
Manufacturing	30.9
Construction	4.1
Electricity, water	2.3
Commerce, banking, insurance	25.3
Transport, communications	6.8
Other services	26.0
Miscellaneous	4.6

The 30.9 percent of workers in manufacturing was a much higher share than the 13 percent of the labor force as a whole. The number of workers in construction had fallen from 2,400 in 1976 to 1,300. The government had tightened credit to offset inflationary pressures from the boom in coffee and illegal marijuana exports. The Banco de la República exchanged dollars for pesos without asking questions at the *ventanilla siniestra.*

Women made up 29.5 percent of the workers in the formal sector. About 8,900 men and women, or 28.9 percent, belonged to trade unions in 1976. Since the labor force of the formal sector was 32.3 percent of employment in 1975, trade unions made up only 9 percent of the total.

Within the formal sector, the largest twenty-five enterprises employed an average of 255 workers, for a total of 6,400 at the end of 1977. Largest of all was the chemical firm, Alcalis de Colombia, with 1,600 workers and sales of 800 million pesos (US$21 million). First in output was the government refinery, Ecopetrol, with 2.6 billion pesos (US$67 million) and 380 workers. Other employers of more than 100 workers packed fish; made chewing gum; processed vegetable oil; bottled soft drinks; made soap, polymers, chemicals, and petrochemicals; and worked on ships. Less important were dairies, bakeries, and plants making textiles, paper products, shoes, and furniture. Altogether the largest twenty-five firms produced an output of 9.3 billion pesos (US$237 million) of which they exported one-third in 1977. Output per worker in these capital-intensive plants was 1.45 million pesos (US$37,000). Without the refinery, output per worker was 1.1 million pesos (US$28,000).

Cartagena's share of national industrial output was 3.8 percent in 1975, not remarkably high and unchanged since 1966. Striking, however, was its 17 percent share of chemicals. Together with petroleum products, this sector produced 70 percent of the manufacturing output, required 84 percent of the investment, and therefore employed only 26 percent of manufacturing workers. The rest of the formal sector employed 43 percent, and handicraft manufacturing employed 31 percent. To attract more medium-sized, nonchemical industries, the National Association of Industrialists backed plans for a free port with an industrial park. They hoped that some firms might set up headquarters in Cartagena rather than Bogotá and that manufacturing employment would rise to the national average of 14.6 percent.[5]

The Free Port and Export Processing Zone

Plans for the Cartagena free port or Zona Franca Industrial y Comercial de Cartagena (ZFIC) began in 1973 with the experience of Shannon Airport in Ireland as a model. South of Mamonal (the existing industrial complex) 104 hectares had been set aside for eighty-six industrial sites near the fishing village of Pasacaballos. The cost of the first stage of about 640 million pesos (US$16 million) was primarily financed with a World Bank loan. Represented on the board of ZFIC were the State of Bolivar, the City of Cartagena, and such branches of the national government as SENA (vocational training), ICT (low-cost housing and urbanization), the Corporación Financiera Popular (small enterprise promotion), and the Instituto Colombiano de Bienestar Familiar (family welfare). Industrial development was to be combined with tourist facilities and social programs for thirteen nearby communities. Nevertheless, as a dependency of the Ministry of Development, the main purpose of ZFIC was economic. By 1987 some sixty primarily foreign-owned plants are supposed to employ 20,000 workers and export 80 percent of US$150 million (1976 U.S. dollars) in goods. Umbrellas, plastic plumbing fixtures, and inflatable boats were expected to lead the way in the earliest plants. To avoid a crass and destabilizing difference between activities associated with the free port and existing communities, the new was to be integrated with the old, for example, through the extension of public services. At the beginning further steps were still a matter of research, and several surveys were under way.[6] Environmental considerations were included to avoid such past mistakes as destroying the oyster mangroves of Cartagena Bay through pollution.

The broader goals of the Free Zone related to all aspects of economic and social development.[7] Consequently there were nutritional programs, educational programs, and health programs, including improvement of water and sewerage systems. The area seemed suitable for a neighborhood development center (Centro de Desarrollo Vecinal). By late 1976 a communal enterprise for making building materials (Empresa Comunitaria de Producción de Materiales para Construcción) had been set up with support of the Corporacion Financiera Popular, a government bank for small firms. The twenty-one founding members were various types of construction workers with an average age of twenty-two. Because of delays in the rest of the project, this enterprise failed, but it may be revived. A restaurant was the second such enterprise, but it was limited to serving subsidized food to primary school children. Both firms will be needed when buildings in the Free Zone are under construction.

A Tour of the City

For most outsiders, a drive around the city was likely to begin at a hotel in Bocagrande, the narrow peninsula that was redesigned by a Dutch engineer a generation ago. Tourism had intruded on Bocagrande's pastel villas among luxurious gardens and had brought in hotels, ice cream parlors, and horse carriage stands like those in resorts throughout the world. On the bay side was the naval station with its marines in camouflage uniforms drilling on the parade ground. Going north, Avenida San Martin became Avenida Venezuela where the ramparts of the historical center ended and the high-rise banks of La Matuna began. A bridge led to a large empty stretch below the Fortress of San Felipe de Barajas. Here the great slum of Chambacú (population 8,000) was eradicated in the late 1960s and early 1970s, and here preparations for the construction of luxury apartments had begun but were then stalled for years.

Continuing north one saw a number of quarters between the wooded promontory of La Popa (the poopdeck) and the sea. The income level varied sharply from block to block, even from house to house. The condition of streets varied from poor to impassable swamp. The city ended with a settlement for noncommissioned military personnel in a triangle between the shore and the airport. Streets were unpaved because the city considered that a task for the navy, but the navy left it to the city.

The airport runways were so close to the muddy lagoon, Cienaga de Tesca o la Virgen, that no squatters were found along this shore. But they had settled along the Caño Juan De Angola that drained this lagoon. Huts were made of odd-size pieces of old lumber and were surrounded by bamboo fencing. As symbol of persistence, one settlement was defiantly called Cara del Perro. Smoke showed that the squatters were cooking with wood. Their neighbors used kerosene bought from one of the two-barreled, two-wheeled donkey carts that one passed on the streets. (The middle and upper classes cooked with bottled propane.) Little cardboard huts were not really latrines along the Caños and Cienagas because at night the excrement was dumped into the water. Stacks of enormous cement pipes showed that these northern districts might eventually get a sewerage system.

To reach the eastern districts after seeing the northern Crespo and Le Maitre, one had to drive back along the Paseo Bolivar to the Fortress of San Felipe and turn left on Avenida Don Pedro de Heredia, a noisy route crowded with trucks and buses. It passed just below the highest point of La Popa with its Augustine monastery. Squatter shacks on the slopes were spreading fast but might be eradicated for reforestation to prevent erosion. Besides, they were above the 25-meter limit for pumping water in Cartagena.

Beyond the football stadium, the bull ring, and the baseball field came the public housing developments of ICT (the Territorial Credit Institute)—first, Chiquinquirá, then República de Venezuela. Here 800 Chambacú households who had been owners were resettled. They had owned their Chambacú houses for an average of seventeen years. These families were too demoralized by the confiscation to improve their new minimal 42-square-meter concrete block houses. The new houses indeed looked raw and uncared for, with nothing planted. Settlers from other parts of Cartagena, usually richer, had plastered, painted, and added iron grills, glass windows, and tile floors. A few occupants had even built a precarious second story and an occasional carved wooden balcony of the sort seen in the historical center. In 1980 tensions still existed among those from Chambacú and other residents of Chiquinquirá, making community action programs impossible.[8]

Between the ICT and other developments were large empty stretches of weedy terrain reputedly held by speculators. Over the crest of an uninhabited hill one came suddenly into a valley with shacks among banana leaves and thick foliage, an invasion of squatters, called El Milagro (the miracle) because it sprang up almost overnight. ICT was helping these people get loans for legal title to their land, provided they would relocate in a systematic fashion. A new water treatment plant was to be built nearby, but for the time being trucks delivered water at ten times the normal price.

El Milagro in the eastern hills was quite different from the vast squatter settlement along the southern shore of the Cienaga de Tesca o la Virgen. In this Southeast Zone the taxi let one off in 1978 where the road became an impassable trail with hilly and marshy places. Shacks were close together, and the salty earth discouraged even tropical vegetation, hence shade. Some houses had short spiral-fluted white columns that supported roofs over small terraces. A few were unpainted, but others were pink or turquoise or had mosaics of sailboats or fish. Fancy signs gave house numbers, often unauthorized and just randomly chosen by the owner. So many children were about that each house seemed like a school during recess. In the doorways air stirred a little, perhaps cooling a very young girl standing there in some stage of pregnancy. Dogs were abundant and seemed to be suffering with the heat or disease.

Most corner houses had a business, such as selling fried snacks or soft drinks. Tailors and furniture makers had their terms of credit painted on the walls. Some sold water out of 2-meter-square cement cisterns that were filled when water was available (in 1978 between 2:00 AM and 5:00 AM). Few houses had a connection, and by dawn all the water had been sold.

Near the shoreline, the last huts became utterly rudimentary without any decorative touch. The path dipped gradually into a morass of sewerage, and what the map showed as a street was just a few rotting boards between mounds built during the dry season by squatters. The last mound was an island with a framework for the latest hut, but no one was about except three muddy pigs, signs of wealth. A ramshackle outhouse was on a little peninsula. Patches of short mangrove were nearby, and a solid mangrove stretch shuts off the horizon a few hundred yards away. White herons and other waterfowl stalked about in the lagoon, proving how shallow it was. Pelicans came in for landing, then flew off.

By December 1980 the Southeast Zone was dry, since most of the drainage ditches were in operation and yellow clay had been dumped in and spread throughout the area as part of the ICT–World Bank project. The little huts appeared to be sitting in holes. Their owners now had to shovel in dirt through the doors and, in some cases, raise the roofs. A few blocks away the water sellers could now turn on the taps as early as 10:00 PM.

A drive around Cartagena would be incomplete without a visit to the outskirts of Turbaco on a plateau a dozen kilometers away. Here a few wealthy Cartagenians introduced something new to their society: commuting. With red tile roofs and elaborate balconies, their mansions showed nostalgia for the historical, fortified center, and even the multi-car garages were in the colonial style. The cost of water depended on the depth of wells and on the size of lawns to be watered in the dry season. Pumping it up depended on uncertain electric power. The urge to commute from these lonesome heights was overestimated by developers, however, and in late 1980 the empty network of streets and lightposts had almost disappeared among tropical weeds and shrubs and resembled an unexplored archeological site with remnants of some lost civilization.

Notes to Chapter 2

1. Johannes Linn made a thorough analysis of the situation in the mid-1970s in "Urban Public Finances in Developing Countries: A Case Study of Cartagena, Colombia," Urban and Regional report no. 77-1 (Washington, D.C.: World Bank, January 1975; processed).

2. Regulo Ahumada Sulbaran, "A Medias Quedó el Censo de Cartagena," *El Espectador* (August 11, 1978). In this study we have used the detailed estimates of Gustavo Pacheco, demographer at the University of Cartagena. They were generally preferred by local experts.

3. Ramiro Cardona, *Migración y Fuerza de Trabajo en el Departamento de Bolivar*, vol. 1 (Bogotá: Consorcio de Ingenierías e Investigaciones, Consultores, August 1977), p. 71.

4. World Bank data.

5. Asociación Nacional de Industriales, *Monografía Industrial de Cartagena, 1976* (Cartagena, 1977), pp. 22–23.

6. Ministerio de Desarrollo Económico, "Zona Franca Industrial y Comercial de Cartagena: Una Visión Nueva de Una Región en Desarrollo" (Cartagena, August 1976).

7. Humberto Serna Gomez and Francisco Rodriguez Urrego, *Area de Promoción Humana y Desarrollo Tecnológico, Informe Segunda Etapa* (Bogotá: Ministerio de Desarrollo Económico, September 1976).

8. Robert V. Farrell and Lácydes Cortés, "Four Walls Are Not Enough: A Case Study of Education and Housing in Cartagena, Colombia," *International Journal for Housing Science and Its Applications*, vol. 4, no. 5 (1980), pp. 425–26.

3

Physical Need for Housing, Water, and Waste Disposal

STUDIES AND POLICY RECOMMENDATIONS ON HOUSING usually take "need" in some physical sense as a point of departure. Intense sun, rain, wind, or cold make some form of shelter necessary for physical survival in many parts of the world, so it is tempting to put housing in a class with water, food, sanitation, and medicine as a "basic need." After disasters such as typhoons or earthquakes, tents are usually among the goods that are sent in as emergency relief; but for more than short-term survival, they will be inadequate. Improvement in housing quality, however, has trouble competing with primary education and job-oriented investment for special public favors. One cannot really specify a minimum amount of space per person or a maximum number of persons per room with as much confidence as the need for water within 200 meters or a minimum of 2,350 calories per adult male. Since access to water reinforces the desire for more space and other improvements, basic and secondary needs cannot be unraveled in practice. The term "basic need" loses most of its physical connotation if it is defined as that which is the minimum socially acceptable.

Flows and Standards

But if things are, in fact, complex, nothing is lost when an over-simplification is abandoned. A dwelling performs more functions than a tent or an umbrella. The location of each dwelling is unique and gives access to work, to public amenities such as schools and parks or police and hospitals, and to various neighborhood benefits of a physical and social nature. Each of these is obtained not once, but steadily over a period of time: they are a flow of services that are received for outbidding or out-maneuvering other claimants for a particular site. The size of the site and the implied density of settlement also matter and give rise to flows of benefits. Flows from the structure itself come not only from the roof and walls but also from the lock on the door, the decorations, work space, rental income from lodgers, the chance for long-term capital gains, and the plumbing. Even vacant units raise the flow of benefits from the existing housing stock because they facilitate moves from one unit to another.

It is costly to provide each of these flows. The installation has to be built; the component must be added, and often land must be diverted from other productive uses. Since a society's values can diverge from its performance, the minimum socially acceptable can easily cost more than society can afford. If all families are to reach the minimum level for housing, such a large share of GNP may have to be spent on construction that nutrition, health, and education will fall drastically below their own socially acceptable minimum level. Housing standards can be both a safeguard and a spur to action if they are somewhat in advance of economic possibilities; but when they rise to unrealistic levels, they will be simply ignored as curiosities in the archives.

There are two implications. One is that minimum socially acceptable standards are not absolute but will rise in the course of economic development. The other is that different standards can be applied to different income groups—that more can be asked of the rich than of the poor. In other words, the subject of this chapter—need and physical standards—cannot be separated from that of the next—income, finance, and effective demand.

Economic factors primarily affect the quality of the dwelling because that depends on each household's ability to pay rent, to build, or to finance a loan. The number of units that must be built depends on the rate of population growth, specifically the rate of household formation. Although they are not independent, these demographic and sociological factors can be discussed separately from income trends.

The provision of streets, drainage, water, and sewerage systems does mainly depend on the sheer numbers that have to be served and involves so many economies of scale and externalities that they will often be subsidized or provided at public expense. Such subsidies should nevertheless be avoided as much as possible. The provision of infrastructure also helps to determine the density of settlement and therefore the type of structure and neighborhood.

Density standards vary with income, transport technology, and the number of people in a city. Improvements in income and transport tend to improve density standards by raising the space per household. Population growth works in the opposite direction. Households in a prospering but rapidly proliferating city may therefore have to change their concept of what is a minimally acceptable density. Instead of having a free-standing dwelling, they may have to learn to share walls with neighbors and ultimately to share buildings, perhaps in the form of a condominium. As buses came to Cartagena, the density fell from 294 people per hectare in 1916 to 163 in 1956. After that the density nearly stabilized and was estimated as 157 in 1976. Luxury apartments have found a market in prestigious neighborhoods such as Laguito in Bocagrande, but middle- and lower-income groups still resist the distasteful risks of sharing buildings with strangers. They believe that they can never be pressured into that.

Housing Needs and Zones

Reports of housing needs in Cartagena resemble those made for other cities. Studies describe and project population growth and density. Changes in household formation, family structure, and age distribution modify expectations, but not necessarily in a precise way. Even more vague and subjective are surveys of deficiencies of existing houses and the "qualitative gap." More precise are estimates of needs for public utilities that will allow dwellings to have washbasins, sinks, showers, and toilets. What it takes to make better neighborhoods beyond that still eludes specification.

If we accept Gustavo Pacheco's estimate of the Cartagena population as being 428,800 in 1978 and if the average family had seven members, then 61,300 dwellings were needed (not counting a stock of useful vacancies). If population is projected to grow 4.4 percent per year up to 1990 (perhaps a maximum), it will reach 721,000 people. If the average household size remains the same, then 103,000 units will be needed in 1990. In each of the twelve intervening years approximately 3,475 dwellings will have to be build if the housing backlog is not to worsen.

The changing density of settlement can be seen from Table 3-1, which gives Pacheco's 1978 and 1990 estimates in terms of twenty-two principal districts. Pacheco divides each of these further into anywhere from two to seventeen barrios. Our sample of 300 interviews was selected on the basis of these barrio densities. Although the total population rises by only 68 percent, most of the western districts (numbers 10–22) double, triple, and more in population.

In presenting data geographically in this study, the twenty-two districts have been combined into six zones with distinct characteristics (see map, frontispiece). Zone 1, the Coast, is the high-income part of the city along the Caribbean and part of the bay and includes districts 1, 2, 3, and 6. As with all zones, within it are some barrios that are different—in this case, the poorer areas of Getsemaní and Militar. Zone 2, the North, includes the old districts 4 and 5, Canapote-Le Maitre and Torices. Zone 3 is the Southeast Zone, districts 7–10 along the Cienaga de Tesca (see Appendixes F, G, and H). Around the hills with the water reservoir are districts 13–16, Lomas, or Zone 4. Zone 5 can be called the ICT Zone because in districts 12, 17, 18, and 19 are the principal ICT developments. In Zone 6 the remaining districts, 11, 20, 21, and 22, are simply called the

Table 3-1. *Estimated Population for 1978 and Projections for 1990, by District*

District number and name	Population		Interviews	
	1978	*1990*	*Planned*	*Acceptable*
1. Bocagrande (excluding naval base)	19,410	32,610	14	9
2. Centro	19,780	26,505	14	11
3. Crespo	8,375	13,380	6	6
4. Le Maitre	38,210	40,870	27	27
5. Torices	40,470	44,125	28	28
6. Manga	27,670	41,135	19	18
7. Esperanza	38,600	65,355	27	31
8. Boston-Tesca	11,920	24,520	8	8
9. Olaya Herrera	24,710	42,075	17	17
10. Magdalena-Fredonia	9,980	14,430	7	7
11. Ricaurte-Pozón	8,175	44,410	6	6
12. Chiquinquirá-Gaviotas	17,255	40,125	12	12
13. Cairo-Calamares	24,530	42,900	17	15
14. Prado-Bruselas	24,560	44,625	17	17
15. San Isidro	10,380	31,370	7	7
16. Bosque	28,165	38,055	20	20
17. Caracoles	12,410	18,090	9	9
18. Blas de Lezo	26,210	33,210	18	18
19. El Socorro	19,010	41,040	13	13
20. Ternera	10,265	37,870	7	7
21. La Victoria	3,700	31,815	3	3
22. Alberto Sierra	5,050	8,760	4	4
Total	428,835	720,965	300	293

Source: Gustavo Pacheco, demographer, University of Cartagena. Excluded are the naval base, the fishing village of La Boquilla, and eastern rural areas.

Outskirts. The population in 1978 and numbers of households in our sample were:

Zone	Population (thousands of persons)	Sample (number of interviews)
1. Coast	75.3	44
2. North	78.7	55
3. Southeast	85.2	63
4. Lomas	88.0	59
5. ICT	74.9	52
6. Outskirts	27.3	20
Total	429	293

Further details about the sample are discussed in Appendix A.

If Pacheco's estimates are correct, and knowledgeable Cartagenians believe so, then the 1973 population was close to 350,000, not 304,000 as reported by the census of that year—a 15 percent underestimate. But if the population grew by 4.2 percent, and the housing stock grew by an annual 4.0 percent, then the deficit worsened more than reported by the National Center of Construction Studies (CENAC).

CENAC projected growth rates of families and housing to 1980. For the Department of Bolivar it was thus assumed that each household consisted of 1.18 families—a ratio attained only by the other Caribbean Departments of Sucre and Cordoba and exceeded by Atlantico with 1.24. The number of Cartagena families was expected to rise to 67,100 and the housing stock to 52,800. Hence the deficit would go to 14,300. These figures imply nothing about the changing deficit in qualitative terms. Moreover, given the erratic quality of the 1973 census, the projections are open to a large margin of error. Before giving more details from the 1973 census, the concept of household and family structure should be examined.

Family Structure

According to definitions used for the 1973 census, members of a household live in the same dwelling and share at least one meal daily. They may be related or not. CENAC defined a family as a group of related people living together, including grandparents, uncles, and aunts. If any of these has a spouse present, however, the household is defined as consisting of two or more family units.

These definitions do not apply well to the way of life in Cartagena. For the poor, the recognized head of the household, the owner of the dwelling and provider of most income, may be a woman working in Venezuela as a cook. For the rich, the head may be a father or brother who manages a cattle ranch in the interior. In between are many variations.

A detailed analysis was made by Lácydes Cortés Díaz in 1971.[1] The population was divided into categories: 5 percent upper class, 10 percent middle class, and 85 percent lower class. In general, the upper class lived in the three barrios of Bocagrande and in Crespo. The middle class lived in the other oceanfront barrios of the Centro, San Diego, Cabrero, and Marbello, as well as in Militar, Pie de la Popa, Manga, Alto Bosque, and Nuevo Bosque. The poor lived everywhere else, with some much poorer than others. The pattern of settlement was extremely heterogeneous, however, with rich and poor, ancient and upstart families intermingled in several parts of the city.

According to Cortés, in 1971 the wealth and achievements of some had not yet become equivalent to the ancient name inherited by a group of poorer and relatively undistinguished people.[2] This group stressed intermarriage within itself or with outsiders of European ancestry and thus set a model of racial prejudice for the rest of the population. According to a survey by Triana y Antorveza, about 70 percent of poor Cartagenians considered whites superior and preferred to marry them either to "preserve" or to "improve" their family stock.[3] Household income of the three classes, according to Cortés, ranged from a monthly average of 2,300 pesos for the poor, to 7,100 for the middle group, to 10,000 pesos for the upper class. In terms of 1978 pesos, the income levels were: lower class, 6,000 pesos (US$150); middle, 18,000 pesos (US$450); and upper, 25,000 pesos (US$650).

The Cortés Díaz study goes on to discuss the division of households between 60 percent legitimately married couples and 40 percent free unions. Women suitable for marriage with men of status had to seem pure and innocent. This characteristic was shown by lack of enthusiasm for and skill in lovemaking, which in turn led husbands to frequent houses of prostitution or have lower-class concubines and second families. According to Cortés Díaz, these relations were public knowledge and hence in line with public morals, a function of the social structure, quite unlike European experience.[4] Second families or concubinage were due to rigidities in marriage customs, criteria of suitability, and the impossibility of divorce.

The lowest class consisted of domestic servants who earned 1,000 (1978) pesos monthly plus room and board, as well as unskilled workers,

Table 3-2. *Characteristics of Occupied Housing, According to the 1973 Census*

Housing type	Occupants	Occupants per dwelling	House-holds per dwelling	Number of dwellings	Number with piped water	Number with sewerage connection	Electricity
Single family	264,276	7.2	1.1	36,868	27,812	10,083	30,504
Apartment	15,725	5.2	1.1	3,050	2,892	1,885	2,937
Room or rooms	1,186	5.2	1.1	1,043	729	178	754
Rented rooms in outbuildings	4,988	28.7	6.8	174	157	55	162
Shack made of refuse	425	4.3	1.0	100	25	0	25
Dwelling in building for other uses	1,103	5.2	1.1	213	138	75	188
Huts and hovels	7,384	7.1	1.1	1,035	76	25	227
Grottoes and caves	25	1.0	1.0	25	0	0	0
Dwellings under construction	4,377	7.3	1.1	597	422	33	347
Others	200	50.0	7.0	4	4	4	4
Total	303,942	7.1	1.1	43,109	32,225	12,338	35,248
Percentage without service	—	—	—	—	25.2	71.4	18.2

— Not applicable.
Source: 1973 census.

waiters, delivery men, shoe shiners, street sellers, and the like earning 2,000 pesos monthly or less. Free unions were common among them, and Cortés found that only 17 percent in that state were embarrassed about it. In fact, in about half of the entire population, the attitude was favorable (38 percent) or indifferent (9 percent). Completely monogamous males, according to Cortés, were rare, and were gossiped about and considered abnormal by both sexes.[5] Among the poor, a wedding was regarded as a great expense that yielded no benefits. Like concubinage, free unions benefited poor young women by reducing the pressure to become prostitutes, given other social rigidities. Moreover, it prevented the pattern of homeless vagabond children observed in some interior Colombian cities.[6]

Throughout this study one should therefore bear in mind that a household is not a simple and obvious concept, but one that varies from country to country, from city to city within countries, and from class to class within cities. Our definition (and that of the 1973 census) of a household as people who live in the same dwelling and who share at least one meal daily evades these complexities without denying their significance. Fifty-one (17.4 percent) of the sample households received aid in cash from absent people who considered themselves family members. Ten households (3.4 percent) received aid from absent people who were not considered family members, but who might nevertheless be fathers of some of the children. The four households for whom cash aid from nonfamily members was even the primary income averaged only 3,725 pesos (US$96) monthly. This amount compares with 9,751 pesos (US$250) for those depending primarily on wages and salaries and with 7,143 (US$183) for those depending mainly on aid in cash from absent acknowledged family members. The four households lived in dwellings worth only 68,500 pesos (US$1,800), compared with 367,000 pesos and 257,000 pesos for the other two types of households. So the difference in dwelling value was greater than that in incomes. In general, households headed by females lived in dwellings worth only 47 percent as much as those of households headed by males. Related sociological questions could not be pursued in this study, but the work of Cortés fills in much of the gap.

The Housing Deficit in 1973

The 1973 census collected qualitative information about dwellings and can help in assessing the qualitative housing deficit. For example, Table 3-2 shows that the most overcrowded dwellings were 174 "rented rooms

Table 3-3. *Cross-Tabulation of Number of Occupants and Number of Rooms in Occupied Housing, According to the 1973 Census*

Number of occupants	Number of rooms per house					Total rooms	Persons per room	Total dwellings
	1	2	3	4-5	6+			
1-2	1,013	838	725	475	125	7,664	0.70	3,476
3-4	1,413	2,521	2,064	1,938	639	25,531	1.2	8,875
5-6	976	3,102	2,711	2,330	946	31,693	1.8	10,065
7-8	754	2,362	2,036	2,506	613	26,455	2.3	8,271
9+	878	2,753	3,271	3,715	2,405	51,306	2.8	13,022
Total dwellings	5,034	11,576	10,807	10,964	4,728	142,650	2.1	43,109
Percentage of dwellings	11.7	26.9	25.1	25.4	11.0	—	—	—

— Not applicable.
Source: 1973 census.

in outbuildings." Such structures averaged 6.8 households each and were looked on with great disfavor. One hundred dwellings were classified as "shacks made of refuse," and 1,035 were "huts and hovels." Twenty-five dwellings were grottoes and caves—no doubt qualitatively unsatisfactory.

Table 3-2 also shows that 18.2 percent of dwellings were qualitatively deficient in not having electricity, that 25.2 percent lacked piped water, and that 71.4 had no connection to a public sewerage disposal system. A number of finer distinctions are also possible. For example, apartments contributed only 7.1 percent of the housing stock, but 38.2 percent of these lacked a sewerage connection. In discussing all these aspects of the deficit, we have begun to cite facts that might just as well have been left to the chapter on the old housing stock. The difference between the existing stock and its characteristics and the number of households is the housing deficit. A physical needs survey simply surveys the supply in relation to whatever population total is to be served.

According to the 1973 census, the median number of occupants per dwelling was six, and the median size of a dwelling was three rooms. The combination implies that 2.0 persons typically occupied each room. The precise average density of 2.1 persons per room is relatively acceptable; but, as always, concern goes to those on the unfavorable side of the average. Only 7.9 percent of dwellings had one or fewer persons per room, but 47.6 percent had more than two per room. Especially crowded were the 15.7 percent of one- and two-room houses occupied by seven or more people. One-eighth of these (or 878) were one-room shacks with nine or more inhabitants. Altogether 30.2 percent of dwellings were occupied by nine or more people. Most of these dwellings had three or four rooms. Further details can be seen in the cross-tabulation of Table 3-3.

Household Size in 1978

Our sample suggests that the size of households had not changed much by 1978. The mean was 7.03 persons (standard error 0.19). The smallest households were twelve couples, some elderly, not necessarily married, possibly siblings or parent and child. The largest were two households with twelve adults, one with four, and the other with twelve children, living in four and five large rooms. In both households, men were sailors and presumably absent much of the time. Altogether 9.2 percent of households had twelve or more members. Median and modal size was six (18.8 percent). The percentage distribution of occupants per dwelling in 1973 and 1978 is

Occupants per dwelling	1973	1978
1–2	8.1	4.1
3–4	20.6	16.4
5–6	23.3	33.1
7–8	19.2	21.8
9–11	20.0	15.4
12+	10.2	9.2

The richest and poorest districts, Bocagrande (1) and Magdalena-Fredonia (10), had the smallest households with 4.3 and 4.6 members. Largest households were in San Isidro (15) and Boston-Tesca (8), with 9.6 and 8.5 members. The sample for each district was only seven to nine households, and hence the results are not statistically significant. If districts are combined into the six zones defined earlier, statistically significant differences do emerge with smallest households along the high-income coast, largest ones in the long-established North and Lomas, and with the Southeast closest to the Cartagena average.

Zone (district numbers)	Population (thousands of persons)	Household mean size (number of persons)
Coast (1, 2, 3, 6)	75.3	6.00
North (4, 5)	78.7	7.69
Southeast (7, 8, 9, 10)	85.2	7.05
Lomas (13, 14, 15, 16)	88.0	7.88
ICT (12, 17, 18, 19)	74.9	6.37
Outskirts (11, 20, 21, 22)	27.3	6.60

Owner-occupants had larger families (average household size of 7.3) than did tenants (6.0). For both groups, the smallest households were in the best and worst housing categories. The largest family size (10.3) occurred for households with an income of from 8,000 to 16,000 pesos and living in dwellings valued at from 80,000 to 160,000 pesos.

The Need for and Supply of Water

In 1978 much of the population still carried home their water supply in rectangular cans called *latas de manteca* (lard cans). About fifty such cans add up to a cubic meter. The typical family of seven members consumed about 1,000 such cans monthly, or 20 cubic meters.

The price of water varied with the income level of the neighborhood in accordance with seven categories, from 70 centavos per cubic meter to 8 pesos (US$0.205) according to official rates.[7] But in the poor neighborhoods water was resold at rates that ranged from 20 to 50 centavos per can. Where it had to be delivered by donkey, it cost 2 pesos. But even at 20 centavos a can the cubic meter would be worth 10 pesos, that is, more than the price charged to the rich. Some water retailers had paid for their own connections to the water mains to be able to enter that business. They could sell water at ten times the price charged by the city. Entry into this business was limited by lack of capital and by reluctance to live in or close to the poorest quarters of the city. Our interviews indicated that the water sellers earned an additional 3,000 pesos (US$77) monthly from selling 500 cans daily. In the Southeast Zone this typically raised their income from 4,000 to 7,000 pesos (US$103 to US$180).

The government tried to reduce water costs by installing public stand-pipes with varying success. Someone had to guard the installation to make sure that none of the components of the faucet, especially the handle, would be stolen. In some cases the guard became a water seller more or less like any other. Those who did not pay had to get their water at the most inconvenient hours.

According to our sample, as shown in Table 3-4, 71.5 percent of the dwellings had piped water, and of these 20 percent had more than one bathroom. In the high-income Coastal Zone, 60 percent of the dwellings with piped water had more than one bathroom. Only in this zone and that dominated by ICT developments did more than 90 percent of the dwellings have piped water. Worst off was the Southeast Zone where two-thirds of the dwellings lacked water. As already mentioned, this is the zone of the water sellers. Here are 61.5 percent of the water sellers of Cartagena, and they supply 63.5 percent of the households in this zone. Water wagons are found primarily in the Outskirts, and multiple sharing of a faucet is occasionally found in the Northern Zone. The effect of alternative water and sewerage systems on the value of owner-occupied housing is examined in Chapter 5, and Chapter 6 shows how lack of indoor piped water discouraged the process of home improvement.

With loans from the World Bank, however, some of the water problems were to be resolved in the early 1980s. The tank at Nariño below La Popa and another farther west in Carmelo were ready but generated a level of water pressure that was too great for the deteriorating old network of pipes.

The Sewerage System

Only about 35 percent of households had connections to the urban sewerage system in 1978: those in the old walled city; those in the high-income sectors of Bocagrande, Manga, and Pie de la Popa; and those in

Table 3-4. *Percentage Distribution of Water Source and Sanitary Facilities, by Zone, 1978*

Item	All	Zone					
		Coast	North	Southeast	Lomas	ICT	Outskirts
Water							
Piped; more than one bathroom	14.8	59.1	7.3	0	14.0	5.8	10.0
Other piped water	56.7	38.7	59.9	31.8	68.5	88.4	50.0
Neighbor sells water	22.3	0	18.2	63.5	14.0	3.8	25.0
Water wagon, public standpipe, and others	6.2	2.2	14.6	4.7	3.5	2.0	15.0
Total	100.0	100.0	100.0	100.0	100.0	100.0	100.0
Sanitary facilities							
More than one toilet; public sewerage system	10.3	50.0	0	0	8.6	3.8	5.0
Single toilet; public sewerage system	25.0	31.8	5.5	0	19.0	82.7	10.0
Septic tank	30.1	18.2	49.1	27.0	39.7	1.9	60.0
Communal toilets and other	2.7	0	7.3	1.6	5.1	0	0
Latrine	18.2	0	29.1	27.0	20.7	9.6	15.0
None	13.7	0	9.1	44.4	6.9	1.9	10.0
Total	100.0	100.0	100.0	100.0	100.0	100.0	100.0

Source: Cartagena household survey, 1978.

ICT developments. The northern sectors of Torices, Le Maitre, Siete de Agosto, and others had had sewer pipes installed since the 1950s, but this system had never been put into operation. Two pumping stations were under construction in 1980, partly with World Bank loans, and sometime during the decade sewerage is expected to be pumped away to the Cienaga at San Francisco. Together with a 10 percent addition of connected dwellings in the Prado-Amberes section, total coverage will come to 60 percent of the city. Work now underway in the Southeast Zone will eventually raise the total to 70 percent, taking into account the continual inflow of migrants and squatters elsewhere in the city. In 1978 two collectors in the Southeast Zone were planned some blocks away on either side of Avenida Pedro Romero, and pumping stations were about to be installed. Even with massive international support, treatment plants were not part of the plan, and the sewerage was to be pumped 100 or 200 meters into the Cienaga de Tesca o la Virgen. Simple drainage channels were also under construction in 1978—relatively complete in Esperanza; actively in process in the next sector, Boston-Tesca; still less in Olaya Herrera; and merely contemplated for Magdalena-Fredonia. In December 1980 nearly all were finished throughout the zone.

A small sewerage tax was paid by all owners of dwellings, whether they were serviced or not. This charge caused considerable resentment, but dwellings actually serviced were charged an additional much larger amount, equal to half the fee for water.

Septic tanks were the most common form of sewerage disposal in the North, Lomas, and the Outskirts. Human waste was dumped in the Cienaga or nearby creeks by 44.4 percent of households in the Southeast Zone—who were 70 percent of the population of Cartagena who had no sanitary facilities whatsoever. Another 27 percent of Southeast households had latrines. As can be seen in the lower part of Table 3-4, the priority assigned to supplying this sector with a sewerage disposal system is justified.

In Colombia, expanding water, sewerage, and drainage infrastructure for housing is the responsibility of the ICT. In 1972 this agency inventoried slum conditions in sixty-nine cities and set up a credit program for utilities, home improvement, and legalization of tenure.[8] The program was called the Plan for Integrated Servicing of Substandard Urban Areas (PHIZSU), and it included help with community facilities. Operations started in 1976. World Bank support for water supply and sewerage projects in Cartagena began with the Instituto Nacional de Fomento Municipal (INSFOPAL). This agency makes funds available to ICT or municipal authorities.

Next came the $35 million project for the Southeast Zone and Pasacaballos, scheduled for $13.2 million of World Bank support although only $10.1 million in foreign exchange costs were foreseen. The aim was partly to improve urban conditions for 12,000 households living on 355 hectares in the Southeast. One-third of this area was situated a mere 50 to 150 centimeters above sea level, and one-third was lower than that. Filling in began in November 1977. All streets were given curbs and gutters (but no pavement) to serve as storm drains. Six major drainage ditches were replaced with concrete canals, and interlot drains were dug with communal effort. Water mains had to be extended to one-third of the area above 1.5 meters in elevation and everywhere below that. The low area was not provided with a waterborne sewerage disposal system, by contrast with the sections above 1.5 meters. Hooking up was not mandatory but was done only in response to family and neighborhood contributions and commitments.

To make room for streets and community facilities, about 7 percent of households were scheduled for relocation. They were to be given 80-square-meter lots and US$685 loans for construction. The community facilities included primary schools, child welfare centers, health centers, and an employment and productivity unit. ICT was in charge of implementation, including design, bidding, and construction through contractors of all public works. For subprojects, participants were expected to pay 5 percent down and to pledge land or dwellings as collateral.

The project would have a substantial effect on relieving poverty, since 84 percent of households in the Southeast Zone earned less than the Colombian per capita income. A rate of return cannot be estimated easily for such investments, including their intangible benefits. On the assumption that the residential value of land would rise to a level comparable to the rest of Cartagena, a 15 percent rate of return seemed plausible to a group of World Bank appraisers. The project was to be completed in June 1984, but further improvements and loans were expected to follow. Specific aspects of the project will be discussed later in this study.

Conclusion

Housing needs in a physical sense are derived from the number of households and their distribution by size. Most Cartagena surveys, including ours, have reported that the average household contains seven persons. If that is divided into the 1978 population of 428.8 thousand, approximately 61.3 thousand dwellings are needed. The need for vacant units to facilitate stock redistribution and the exact dispersion of households by size explain why that estimate is only approximate. The population is expected to rise to no more than 721 thousand, but will household size remain at seven? If so, upper-income families would have larger families than is now the case, so perhaps it is best to assume that family size will remain constant within broad income ranges. A detailed demographic analysis was not the object of this study, so assumptions will be kept simple. If average household size falls to 6.84 with rising incomes by 1990, then 105,340 dwellings will be needed for occupancy alone—an increase of 72.2 percent.

The distribution of this increase depends partly on how much of the present housing stock is considered adequate and likely to survive in a purely physical sense. The distribution also depends on how much households can afford and are willing to pay for improved housing. This question is complicated by the durability of housing, its stock characteristics, the alternatives in long-term finance, and the possibilities for self-help and upgrading. Broader needs that involve location, transport, neighborhood quality, and public amenities are clearly important, but are not the main focus of this study.

Notes to Chapter 3

1. Lácydes Cortés Diáz, *Familia y Sociedad en Cartagena* (Departamento de Investigación Económica y Social, Universidad de Cartagena, July 1971). In 1978 Cortés was manager of the Northern Bolivar Planning and Development Council.

2. Ibid., pp. 10–11.

3. Humberto Triana y Antorveza, *Cultura del Tugurio en Cartagena* (Bogotá: Impresa en Italgraf for UNICEF, 1974).

4. Cortés Diáz, Familia y Sociedad en Cartagena, pp. 20, 44.

5. Ibid., p. 34.

6. Ibid., p. 45, and Virginia Gutierrez Pineda, *Familia y Cultura en Colombia* (Bogatá: Ediciones Tercer Mundo, 1968).

7. For a detailed analysis of water and sewerage systems in Cartagena and related charges in the early 1970s, see Johannes F. Linn, "Urban Public Finances in Developing Countries: A Case Study of Cartagena, Colombia," Urban and Regional Report no. 77-1 (Washington, D.C.: World Bank, January 1975; processed), pp. 238–76.

8. Instituto de Crédito Territorial, "Inventario de Zonas Subnormales de Vivienda y Proyectos de Desarrollo Progresivo" (Bogotá, 1972; processed).

4

Effective Demand and Housing Finance

EFFECTIVE DEMAND DOES NOT INDICATE the kind of housing that families ought to have, but the kind that they are actually renting, buying, or building at given prices. It is a function of income, wealth, access to land and credit, government subsidies or taxes, and the need for competing goods and services. This need varies with the size of a family, its history, and its life cycle from marriage to retirement. What matters for planning is the expected proportion between income and rent, mortgage payments, or housing value.

Information from our 1978 sample gives the level and distribution of income in Cartagena, its origin by occupation and other sources, and its association with household size and zone of the city. Both tenants and owner-occupants have distinct characteristics. Logit analysis gives the probability of being an owner or a tenant because of factors such as the age of the head of the household or the household size. Regressions and cross-tabulations show how rent and value change with income and family structure, although these effects are partly due to the housing supply conditions discussed in the next two chapters. The cost of land, finance, and the type of taxes change the amount that can be spent on the dwelling structure. For comparison, Appendix I summarizes results of housing budget surveys by others.

Household Income

In our sample, monthly household incomes ranged from zero to 60,000 pesos (US$1,538). Nothing had been earned in the previous month by the family of a secretary who had just lost her job. Her permanent income was obviously higher, but we did not find it practical to identify transitory income components. The highest incomes were received by two technicians who also sold property or had property income. Average income was 9,947 pesos (standard error 502 pesos). The median income was 7,500 pesos (US$192). The distribution of income ranges is shown in Table 4-1. If these ranges are grouped in categories that double (2,001–4,000 pesos, followed by 4,001–8,000 pesos, then, 8,001–16,000 pesos, and so forth), ranges 3 and 4; 5, 6, and 7; and 8 and 9 should be combined. The pattern of percentages that emerges is 1.4, 4.4, 16.4, 36.2, 27.3, 11.6, and 2.7 and fits the widely observed lognormal distribution of household incomes.

The Gini coefficient for this income distribution is 0.419, which is close to the 0.415 found for Barranquilla in 1974 and substantially below the 0.430 for Cali, 0.459 for Medellín, and 0.510 for Bogotá.[1] It may be compared with 0.408 for urban Sri Lanka in 1971 and 0.338 for Lansing, Michigan, in 1970.

The income level may be higher than that observed by other surveys and the census because great care was taken to make respondents think of all sources of income (see Appendixes F, G, and H). Only 29 percent of households received their income from the wage or salary of a single person. More than one-third of households (36.5 percent) had no wage or salary income. The remaining 34.5 percent had at least one source of labor income plus additional income from various other sources. The percentage of households receiving income from different types of sources is shown in Table 4-2. Income for meals received at work was included, but no income was imputed for living in one's own dwelling. In only twenty-five households (8.5 percent) did anyone receive meals on the job. These meals were perceived by the household as a receipt from outsiders, unlike the im-

Table 4-1. *Distribution of the 1978 Housing Sample, by Monthly Income Level*

	Monthly income (pesos)	Number of cases	Percent
1.	0–1,000	4	1.4
2.	1,001–2,000	13	4.4
3.	2,001–3,000	18	6.1
4.	3,001–4,000	30	10.2
5.	4,001–5,000	24	8.2
6.	5,001–6,000	26	8.9
7.	6,001–8,000	56	19.1
8.	8,001–12,000	54	18.4
9.	12,001–16,000	26	8.9
10.	16,001–32,000	34	11.6
11.	32,001+	8	2.7
	Total	293	100.0

Note: 1,000 pesos = US$25.64.
Source: Cartagena household survey, 1978.

Table 4-2. *Sources of Household Income*

Type of income	Percentage of households
Wages and salaries	63.5
Sales or work on one's own account	39.9
Aid in cash from absent family members	17.4
Pensions	13.0
Rent from lodgers on the premises	4.1
Other rent, property income, interest, dividends	5.8
Aid from other than family members	3.4
Other income	0.7

Source: Cartagena household survey, 1978.

puted rent from owner-occupied dwellings. No estimate of the imputed rent was added later because the guesswork involved might easily offset a possible gain in realism. Since 88 percent of the poor (those earning 4,000 pesos per month or less) were not tenants, compared with 79 percent in the 4,001–8,000 peso range and 71 percent of those receiving more than 8,000 pesos, imputing rent would raise incomes of the poor as a group relative to others. It was considered preferable to keep housing purely a dependent variable influenced by other household characteristics, hence we used income without imputed rent.

The greatest variety of income sources was found in the household of an illiterate forty-one-year-old man who sold goods from a wheelbarrow downtown. He shared his 91-square-meter wooden house with another street seller, two domestic servants employed elsewhere, and some lodgers. Besides a grown daughter, who sent money from Venezuela, there were five children. Including the meals eaten by the servants at their jobs, income amounted to 6,000 pesos. The house lacked water and sanitary facilities—even a latrine. Land was acquired by squatting, and one room was built with mutual aid at the time. When the additional relative joined the original couple and their three children, two other rooms were added by self-help. The shack with its cardboard roof was considered to be worth 12,000 pesos. A neighbor sold water at the approximate rate of four lard cans for 1 peso.

One family of three elderly adults received 5,000 pesos monthly from four children in Venezuela, and nearly half of that went for rent. An unskilled, retired construction worker, aged fifty-three, lived with three other adults and twelve children in a five-room house in Boston-Tesca in the Southeast Zone. Their only source of income was 7,000 pesos sent monthly by six married children in Venezuela. One couple had ten close relatives in Venezuela, but with an income of 14,000 pesos did not need their help. More common was the case of a grandmother whose daughter had been in Venezuela for twelve years and who supported the five remaining family members in Cartagena with a monthly remittance of 5,000 pesos, their only income. By contrast, another family of twelve lived on 2,000 pesos earned locally but said that the head of the household was the father who worked as a pilot of a ship in Aruba. He sent no money. A street seller had six children in Venezuela; none sent money.

The rates of pay for specific occupations and activities during the summer of 1978 are given in Table 4-3.

Unemployment

In 293 households we encountered 98 unemployed workers. These are defined as anyone willing to look for work but unable to find an activity that pays at home or elsewhere. They represented 19 percent of the sample labor force. If the unemployed were evenly distributed among households, one out of three households would have one member unemployed. The number of unemployed per household was:

Monthly income (pesos)	Average number of unemployed per household
0–2,000	0.35
2,001–4,000	0.64
4,001–8,000	0.31
8,001–16,000	0.32
16,001–32,000	0.08
32,000+	0

Unemployment was highest in the second-lowest income range where average family size was 5.9. This family size was lower than that of the higher-income households that had unemployed members. Comparison of this table with the classification of occupations in Table 4-3 shows that unskilled workers, messengers, stevedores, and construction workers were most likely to be unemployed. The assumption is that those without jobs were more or less in the same types of activities as relatives with jobs.

Occupations

Table 4-4 shows that in our sample the largest number of principal workers, 84 (19.9 percent), classified themselves as skilled. Owning a store or business and office work came second and third. The kind of store

Table 4-3. *Income Levels for Specific Occupations*

Monthly income (pesos)	Occupation
0–2,000	Domestic servant, carpenter, street seller of lottery tickets, jewelry credit collector, owner of soft drink stand, informal teacher.
2,001–4,000	Street seller of charcoal, hotel bellboy, night watchman, messenger, agricultural worker, mason, stevedore.
4,001–6,000	Telephone operator, policeman, street seller of contraband cigarettes, bus driver, welder, caldron tender, jeweler, maintenance man, mechanic, marine sergeant, warehouse keeper, smuggler, airport office worker.
6,001–8,000	Office workers, newspaper worker, shopkeepers, taxi drivers not owning their vehicles, denture maker, brewery technician, warehouse supervisor, natural science teacher, contractor.
8,001–12,000	Chemical plant workers, boat repairer, marine pilot, public utility electrician, bank clerk, cashier, shopkeepers, contractor.
12,001–16,000	Chief of accounting department, coconut merchant, private school teacher, chemical plant shift foreman, owner of one bus, unlicensed lawyer, other technicians and salesmen.
16,000+	Lawyers, doctors, chemical plant superintendent, wholesale merchants, owners of multiple buses and taxis, auto repairshop owner-operator, owner of family-run jewelry store, administrator of family properties, other store owners.

Source: Cartagena household survey, 1978, subset of eighty-five with only one source of wage, salary, or other currently earned income.

owned by the spouse was usually a little shop in the home. For wives, domestic service and indoor sales were next in importance. The fact that 52 out of 293 heads of households reported no occupation is due to the frequent designation of retired fathers or grandmothers as household heads. Heads of households and third workers were either male or female, but spouses were always wives.

The primary source and amount of household income is given in Table 4-5. The six households for whom property income was the primary source of income had the highest earnings, 16,083 pesos monthly. Self-employed workers or owner-operators were next, followed by households in which the leading source of income was pensions, wages and salaries, aid from absent family members, and aid from others. Only seven households did not receive more than half of income from a single source. Aid or pensions were the main source of income for 18.1 percent of house-

Table 4-4. *Occupations of Principal Workers*

Occupation	Head of household	Spouse	Third worker	Total
Skilled worker	58	9	17	84
Owner of store or business	32	15	3	50
Unskilled worker	25	2	16	43
Office worker	23	5	24	52
Technician, semiprofessional	19	8	17	44
Professional	19	3	2	24
Indoor salesperson	17	10	10	37
Highly skilled worker	13	0	4	17
Personal services	12	3	4	19
Street vendor	9	2	7	18
Foreman	7	0	2	9
Police and military	5	0	0	5
Domestic service	2	11	7	20
Total	241	68	113	422

Source: Cartagena household survey, 1978.

Table 4-5. *Primary Source of Household Income, Income Levels, and Housing Value*

Source of more than half of income	Average income (pesos)	Percentage of households	Average value of dwelling (pesos)
Rent, interest, dividends, or other property income	16,083	2.1	600,000
Sales or work on one's own account	11,555	26.2	495,000
Pensions	10,279	6.6	776,000
Wages and salaries	9,751	53.5	367,000
Aid in cash from family members living away	7,143	10.1	257,000
Aid from others	3,725	1.4	68,500

Note: Seven additional households had incomes for which no single source accounted for more than 50 percent.
Source: Cartagena household survey, 1978.

holds. These families were not especially poor, and pensioners lived in the most valuable housing.

One might expect that a larger number of adults in a household would mean a higher average income, creating both a need and the means for more expensive dwellings. In fact households with a single adult and more than six adults had the highest incomes, and others in between were lower. In half of sample households, two or three adults were present.

Number of adults	Average income (pesos)	Percentage of households
1	13,143	4.8
2	9,830	28.8
3	8,947	21.2
4	10,016	16.8
5	8,261	13.7
6+	11,716	14.7

Household income might be derived from various sources and from different numbers of adults per household without any overwhelming statistical association. What does cluster household income, however, is the neighborhood or part of town in which the household is located, as shown in Table 4-6. The monthly income of 31,400 pesos of Bocagrande families living in the Coast Zone was substantially greater than the 4,600 pesos of those in Olaya Herrera in the Southeast Zone. But even Bocagrande had a few of the poorest living in odd corners, above shops, in boats, or in half-finished and abandoned mansions. They did not turn up in our sample. Nor did Rocky Valdez, a world boxing champion, and his mansion in his old neighborhood of Olaya Herrera.

The last column of Table 4-6 shows that a zone did not have to be newly settled or long established to attain its income characteristics. The least mobility was in the North and Southeast Zones. Average income outside of the Southeast Zone was 11,168 pesos, that is, 103.5 percent higher than

Table 4-6. *Household Income, Age of Dwellings, and Duration of Occupation by Present Owner, by Zone*

Zone	Average income (pesos)	Percentage of dwellings ten years old or less	Percentage of owners ten years or less at a site
Coast	20,923	18.8	72.1
ICT	9,673	73.4	80.5
Lomas	9,201	54.0	62.7
North	8,521	29.1	54.7
Outskirts	6,685	78.5	90.0
Southeast	5,488	68.3	64.5

Source: Cartagena household survey, 1978.

that zone's 5,488 pesos. Newest dwellings and most recent occupants were in the low-income Outskirts and average-income ICT developments. In the Coastal Zone, 44 percent of dwellings were more than twenty years old, but only 12 percent of households had lived there that long. Fifty-four percent had been at their present site five years or less. Only the Outskirts and ICT Zones had higher mobility than that.

One reason for the high mobility among upper-income households was that it was more difficult for them to get loans to buy dwellings, and thus they were more likely to be tenants. High-income families were more likely to be tenants because they were not as likely to be squatters and self-help builders as the poor and because subsidized ICT credit was not directed at them—although quite a few nevertheless managed to obtain some. One-third of the Bocagrande sample were tenants, compared with 22 percent for the city as a whole.

Payments and Willingness to Pay

Although households moved often, this frequency cannot be attributed to a feeling among most that the current house was a poor value for money. Only 6.4 percent gave a desire to pay less as the main reason for having moved. The median amount of monthly payments that households thought their dwellings were worth, 1,992 pesos, is close to 1 percent of the 200,000-peso estimated median value, a conventional rule-of-thumb proportion. The mean of 3,072 pesos (standard error 271 pesos) that they were willing to pay is only 0.7 percent of the mean value of dwellings, 418,000 pesos.

But how does willingness to pay compare with actual payments among tenants and mortgagors? Among mortgagors it depends on the extent that the payments lagged behind the rate of inflation, the annual rise in payments, or system of indexing. This change in payments, in turn, depends on the following sources of finance, which will be described later.

	Percent
Sources of mortgage finance	*(N = 86)*
Instituto de Crédito Territorial (ICT)	55.8
Banco Central Hipotecario (BCH)	15.1
Employers	15.1
Corporación de Ahorro y Vivienda or other banks	2.3
Relatives	2.3
Other	9.3

Among the fifty respondents whose mortgage had not yet been paid off, monthly payments ranged from 43 to 6,000 pesos, with a median of 781 pesos and a mean of 880 pesos (standard error 133 pesos). The median monthly payment that mortgagors said they were willing to make was 1,859 pesos or 2.4 times as much as the actual payments. As a share of income, they would have gone (by implication) from 8.8 to 21.0 percent. One cannot say that they felt overburdened by housing costs.

More surprising is that tenants felt the same way. Median rent was 1,206 pesos, but the median amount they were willing to pay was 1,992 pesos monthly. The actual average amount was 1,957 pesos, but the average amount that they were willing to pay for the identical premises, if necessary, was 3,072 pesos. If the ratios of acceptable to actual payments are estimated for each household and then averaged, the median would rise by 50 percent and the average by 66.4 percent (standard error 11.1 percent). At such rentals, the share of monthly income would rise from 18 to 27 percent. The ratio of the median amount owners were willing to pay to their median income was also 27 percent.

Although many households were considering moves to better housing or were improving their existing premises, none said that they were dissatisfied with what they had to pay. On the contrary, one may infer that they were eager to acquire more housing because the services received thereby were a relatively good value compared with competing commodities and services. Among other factors, construction prices for workers' housing rose only 71 percent as much as the workers' cost of living index from 1969 through 1977. The competitiveness of housing helps to explain the large proportion of households living in surprisingly good dwellings.

Income and Tenure

The income of tenants averaged 12,814 pesos or 35.7 percent above the 9,446-peso income of owners without mortgages. If the two groups were identical except for housing payments, one could assume that the difference is the imputed income from being an owner-occupant. The implication would be that the owner-occupants are really devoting 26.3 percent of their income for housing. Rent of tenants was only 18.0 percent of their income (standard error 2.1 percent).

Upper-income groups were, in fact, more likely to be tenants than the poor. Below monthly incomes of 4,000, 12.3 percent of occupants were renters. In the 4,001–8,000 peso range, 20.8 percent of occupants were tenants and above 8,000 pesos, 28.7 percent were tenants.

Income of the fifty-three owner-occupants with mortgages was slightly above (1.6 percent) that of those with clear title, 9,595 pesos (standard error 879 or 9.2 percent) and not statistically significant. Their amortization payments were only 8.8 percent of income (standard error 1.0 percent). Mean income of the twenty-one households who freely occupied the premises of others averaged 5,638 pesos.

Tenants

Twenty-two percent of households were tenants in dwellings presumably subject to rent control. Rents could be raised only for new tenants, but landlords had ways of evicting families, such as claiming to need the dwelling for themselves. As a result, we found that 84.1 percent of tenants had been in their premises five years or less, compared with only 41.8 percent of all others in the survey.

Rental payments ranged from 100 to 8,000 pesos monthly and averaged 1,957 pesos (standard error 223). Median rent was 1,206 pesos. The distribution of rental payments was:

Monthly rent (pesos)	Percentage of tenant households
0–500	16.9
501–1,000	29.2
1,001–2,000	20.1
2,001–4,000	21.6
4,001+	12.3

By zone, monthly rent was twice as high in the richer coastal districts as the Cartagena average and only half as high in the poor Southeast (Table 4-7). The rental share of income rose from less than 17 percent in three poorer districts to more than 20 percent in richer ones. Highest was Bocagrande with 27.4 percent. The implication is that the income elasticity

Table 4-7. *Average Rent and Share in Income, by Zone*

Zone	Mean rent (pesos)	Income share (percent)
Coast	3,959	20.5
North	1,031	16.6
Southeast	856	13.6
Lomas	1,491	16.6
ICT	2,417	21.8
Outskirts	1,340	20.9
Weighted average	1,957	18.0

Source: Cartagena household survey, 1978.

of demand for housing by tenants exceeded unity; but that was not, in fact, the case. Whoever lived in better districts, regardless of income, had to pay higher rent, or rather, for given income levels, rent would be higher. By income category, the share of rent tended to fall slightly, in accordance with an income elasticity of 0.786 as shown below (see Table 4-18, line 11).

Monthly income (pesos)	Share of rent in income (percent)
2,001–4,000	19.5
4,001–8,000	14.9
8,001–16,000	17.8
16,001–32,000	17.8
32,001+	9.1
Mean 12,814	18.0

The pattern can be seen in more detail in the cross-tabulation of Table 4-8, called a stock-user matrix. Users are shown in rows of income categories, and the stock is shown in columns of rental ranges. The six household categories are F0, F1 ... F5, each with twice the income of the next lower category. The housing ranges similarly are H0, H1 ... H5, each with doubled rental value.

On the matrix diagonal (underlined numbers) were one-third of households, 33.9 percent. Sixty percent were in cells below the diagonal, and

Table 4-8. *Stock-User Matrix for Tenants*
(percentage in each cell; N = 65)

Household income (pesos per month)	H0 (0–500)	H1 (501– 1,000)	H2 (1,001– 2,000)	H3 (2,001– 4,000)	H4/5 (4,001+)	Σ_F (sum of row)	Index
F0 (0–2,000)	1.5					1.5	(100)
F1 (2,001–4,000)	4.6	6.2				10.8	79
F2 (4,001–8,000)	10.8	12.3	7.7	3.1		33.8	67
F3 (8,001–16,000)		9.2	10.8	10.8	3.1	33.8	73
F4 (16,001–32,000)		1.5		3.1	7.7	12.3	68
F5 (32,001+)			1.5	4.6	1.5	7.7	
Σ_H (sum of column)	16.9	29.2	20.0	21.5	12.3	100.0	71

Note: Household-dwelling combinations on the diagonal are assigned an index of 100; those one cell to the left, 50, and so forth.
Source: Cartagena household survey, 1978.

only 6.2 percent were above. Since the tenant sample is very small ($N =$ 65), little significance can be attributed to any individual cell. What is significant is that one-third of tenants were in cells to the left of the diagonal. The most frequent combination (12.3 percent) was F2 families living in H1 housing. By contrast, among owner-occupants, the most frequent combination was F2 families living in H3 housing, a cell to the right of the diagonal (see Table 4-19). Evidence will suggest that these families had upgraded their housing.

An alternative explanation for so many tenants being on the left of the diagonal might be that tenants use less housing because their families are smaller—6.0 members compared with 7.3 for owner-occupants. But as can be seen in line 12 of Table 4-18, the regression coefficient for family size is not significant and is even slightly negative among tenants. Average household size among tenants rises from 5.5 for those living in H0 housing to 7.3 for those in H2 housing, and then falls off to 4.4 for those in H4 housing. More significant is the number of adults. The greater the number of adults who lived in a dwelling the less the rent was likely to be in absolute terms, and that smaller amount was also a smaller share of income.

Number of adults (excluding servants)	Average rent (pesos)	Rent as percentage of income
1	1,833	16.6
2	2,179	20.3
3	2,069	19.9
4	2,022	17.0
5	1,217	12.9
6+	980	13.1

Owner-Occupied Housing

Value of housing could be discussed in Chapter 5, which covers supply as a characteristic of the stock, or in Chapter 7, which covers the interaction between supply and demand, since only that determines value. But effective demand and finance, the subject of this chapter, cannot be discussed without mentioning housing values, so the subject has to be introduced here.

Values reported in our sample for nonrental housing ranged from 10,000 pesos for a shack to 5 million pesos for a mansion. Average value was 418,000 pesos (US$10,700, standard error 44,000 pesos), and median value was 200,000 pesos.

Still under amortization were 26 percent of owner-occupied dwellings. Their value averaged 309,000 pesos compared with 479,000 pesos for those without mortgages. Those in free use averaged only 169,000 pesos. Mortgage payments averaged 9 percent of income (standard error 1.0 percent). None was higher than 35.6 percent, but some old, non–price-indexed loans were a negligible 0.4 percent.

Values for housing ($N = 231$) and amortization-income ratios for those with mortgages were:

Zone	Average value (pesos)	Amortization-income ratio (percent)
Coast	1,510,000	15.2
Outskirts	448,000	(too few observations)
Lomas	361,000	11.0
ICT	261,000	9.4
North	204,000	3.4
Southeast	113,000	7.2

More than half of the housing in Cartagena was built without the assistance of financial institutions but not mainly informally by unpaid workers. Communal and self-help building, some of it by squatters, was about 40 percent of self-financed construction. The remaining 60 percent paid cash, and built one-third of the dwellings. Credit was used in building some 45 percent of all housing occupied in 1978, which compares with about 40 percent found in the census of 1973 (Table 4-12). Moreover, before deciding to buy or build, 34.2 percent of owner-occupants in our sample had received some kind of special income, such as an inheritance or a retirement benefit.

The way that owner-occupied buildings were built suggests which income group was most likely to own, as shown in Table 4-9. The first four

Table 4-9. Housing, by Type of Builder
($N = 207$)

Type of builder	Percentage of owner-occupants
1. Mutual aid or communal effort	1.9
2. Self-help by the family	14.5
3. Workers paid directly by the family head	22.7
4. Designed and built by ICT	17.9
5. Private developer on speculation	4.8
6. Private developer's plan chosen by the family	3.4
7. Family works with an architect and a contractor	5.3
8. Unknown (house was acquired from previous occupants)	29.0
9. Other	0.5

Source: Cartagena household survey, 1978.

categories account for 57 percent of the total and are the main way that middle- and low-income families become proprietors. Categories 5, 6, and 7 are the building methods used by high-income families if they are going to acquire something new. They come to only 13.5 percent of dwelling origins. The remaining 29 percent of owner-occupants live in old housing. All income groups use this type of housing, but the majority are from the high-income group. Finance is not as readily available for such housing, so the poor will make such a purchase only if they have suddenly come into an inheritance or received a substantial sum from Venezuela. In general, since the poor have more alternative ways of becoming owners, they are less likely to be tenants, and, therefore, the average income of tenants will be higher than that of owners, as we have found.

With logit analysis we found that the probability of owning is only 24.8 percent for a childless couple with a household head aged twenty-five, living in a dwelling with water. For a household of nine with a head aged forty-five, the probability rises to 71.5 percent. Owning is thus positively associated with age and family size. If the dwelling has no water, the probability goes up to 85.6 percent, since owning is negatively associated with access to piped water (and income). Rather than build and own a waterless shack on land reclaimed from a marsh, the well-off will rent a house or apartment with plumbing. They also have less access to subsidized housing finance for building or buying a dwelling they consider acceptable. The logit coefficients are given in Table 4-10.

Family Size and Housing Value

Although family size (number of adults) was negatively correlated with the share of income spent on amortization, no corresponding association was shown by value. This contrast may be due to the fact that mortgages are usually granted in proportion to the earnings of the head of the household only. The presence of other adults, some working, brings down the amortization–income ratio.

Number of adults (excluding servants)	Amortization– income ratio (percent; N = 54)	Average value (pesos; N = 231)
1	14.6	563,000
2	10.8	364,000
3	10.9	410,000
4	6.1	374,000
5	6.2	298,000
6+	5.9	606,000

Table 4-10. *Estimators for Owning or Renting: Logit Analysis*
(N = 251)

Constant and independent variables	Coefficient	t ratio
Constant	−1.859	−2.622
Indoor piped water	−0.867	−1.994
Public sewerage system	0.704	1.904
Relatives working in Venezuela	0.400	1.043
Household size	0.137	2.277
Age of household head	0.054	4.073
Income mainly from sales or property	−0.184	−0.528

Note: The dependent variable is $\ln(P_o/P_r)$. P_o is the probability that a dwelling is owned; P_r is the probability that it is rented. Lowest t ratios apply to the proxies for transitory income: relatives working in Venezuela and property or sales as sources of income. Indoor piped water is negatively associated, as explained in the text.
Source: Cartagena household survey, 1978.

Table 4-11 is a stock-user matrix showing average household size (including servants and children) for various income-dwelling combinations. For nontenants the largest family-size (8.4) was in the entire F3 income range, 8,001 to 16,000 pesos monthly. Richest and poorest families were smallest. Similarly, occupants of H2 housing had the largest households with 8.3 members, and those in best and worst housing had the smallest families. As one might suspect, the eleven F3 households occupying H2 housing had the most members (10.4). Households in the extreme corners of the stock-user matrix had the smallest families. The richest and best housed and the poorest and worst housed had a family of four. Since income and value of housing were highly correlated, one can see that family size is correlated with neither. If anything, the association was slightly negative (Table 4-18, column 3).

Housing Finance

Income and the size and age structure of a family are not enough to determine effective demand for dwellings. Access to land and finance are important contributing factors. Since dwellings are expensive but durable and can serve as collateral, the use of long-term finance for their acquisition is natural and was common, as shown in Table 4-12. By controlling the loan terms for different income groups, governments can easily add elements of penalty and subsidy that either reinforce or offset the effects of taxes and charges for public utilities. For many owner-occupants, housing demand is expressed mainly through this medium of long-term finance, mingling the desire for housing with that for an investment and a capital gain. Some studies have arbitrarily divided monthly payments into equal parts for housing and investment. To the monthly payments should be added the opportunity cost of any down payments. Whether the unit prices of housing services are constant, so that a larger expenditure implies a greater purchase, is a complicating issue that will come up later in this chapter. At this point, however, it seems appropriate to discuss first the two principal institutions of housing finance in Cartagena before analyzing income-value elasticities.

In purchasing housing with credit, down payments were required except for some evacuees from Chambacú. The down payments averaged 19.1 percent (standard error 2.6 percent). On the average, these down payments did not cover the share of the serviced lot in total value, or 41.6 percent. For ICT minimal housing, the share of the lot was about 37 percent, for basic housing 27 percent, and for the intermediate 13.7 percent, according to 1977–78 information provided by the agency. The 1973 census reported that 25.2 percent of Cartagena housing had been financed by the ICT and BCH (Banco Central Hipotecario), and our sample found 20.8 percent.

Source of loan	Mean monthly income of household (pesos)	Mean value of dwelling (pesos)	Value-income ratio	Number of cases
ICT	8,059	285,000	35.4	48
BCH	12,808	790,000	61.7	13

BCH loans went to higher-income families who could afford larger down payments and price-indexed repayment rates. ICT loans were supposed to go to lower-income families, but not all income was declared, and some households experienced an increase in income soon afterward.

Territorial Credit Institute (ICT)

In our sample thirty-nine dwellings had current ICT mortgages, meaning 18.8 percent of all those occupied by owners. Five years earlier the census had reported a 15.8 percent share, but ICT had financed a lot of building since then: El Socorro, Las Gaviotas, Nuevo Bosque, Los Calamares, and others. With its continual experiments in design, finance, and organization, ICT ranks easily among the most creative housing institutions in the world.[2]

Since 1977 the work of ICT has been organized in four programs. The first program calls for "progressive development of subnormal districts."

Table 4-11. Household Size Matrix for Income-Dwelling Combinations, for Tenants and Others

Household income (pesos per month)	Dwelling value (pesos)						
	H0 (0–40,000)	H1 (40,001–80,000)	H2 (80,001–160,000)	H3 (160,001–320,000)	H4 (320,001–640,000)	H5 (640,001+)	Σ_F
F0 (0–2,000)	4.1	7.4	4.5				5.6
F1 (2,001–4,000)	6.7 (5.0)	6.5 (6.5)	5.1	5.1	4.3		5.8 (5.9)
F2 (4,001–8,000)	7.9 (5.6)	7.7 (7.6)	9.1 (8.0)	7.5 (2.5)	7.6	5.7	7.8 (6.6)
F3 (8,001–16,000)		10.3 (5.3)	10.4 (5.6)	7.6 (6.9)	7.4 (4.0)	8.7	8.4 (5.8)
F4 (16,001–32,000)				4.5 (7.0)	8.5 (4.2)	6.6	6.7 (5.1)
F5 (32,000+)				(3.7)		4.0	4.7
Σ_H	6.3 (5.5)	7.5 (6.6)	8.3 (7.3)	7.1 (5.6)	7.3 (4.4)	6.9	7.3 (6.0)

Note: Average household sizes for tenants are in parentheses. Housing categories for tenants are as in Table 4-14. Single observations in some cells (4 tenants, 1 other) are omitted.
Source: Cartagena household survey, 1978.

Table 4-12. *Sources of Finance for Owner-Occupied Housing, 1973*
(number of units)

Source of finance	All owner-occupied dwellings	Paid-up dwellings	Dwellings with debts
Instituto de Crédito Territorial (ICT)	5,292	902	4,390
Banco Central Hipotecario (BCH)	1,722	308	1,414
Other loans from government institutions	534	258	276
Loans from private entities	2,261	1,616	645
Owner's funds	14,881	13,931	950
Others	1,956	1,652	304
No information	1,182	956	226
Total	27,828	19,623	8,205

Source: DANE, *La Vivienda en Colombia 1973*, advance sample of the fourteenth national census (Bogotá, 1978; processed).

This program helps to legalize land tenure, supply basic public utilities to squatter settlements, and provide schools, playgrounds, neighborhood centers, and other facilities. Loans can be made for rebuilding and expanding the worst dwellings. The limit of loans, as in other ICT programs, is some multiple of the legal daily minimum wage in Bogotá. For example, to acquire a lot the limit is 650 daily wages. Terms are for fifteen years at 13.8 percent interest and insurance. In most ICT programs, monthly payments rise by 5 percent per year, not an inflationary adjustment, but a way of starting low and then accelerating repayment. Loans for housing improvements have similar terms with a limit of 970 daily wages.

In Cartagena 500 home improvement loans with a limit of 60,000 pesos (US$1,540) were authorized in December 1977 for settlements north of La Popa, for others along the bay in district 16, and for some in the eastern Outskirts. To qualify, a family head must earn at least 2,500 pesos monthly, which disqualifies about half the households in these areas. Loans less than 25,000 pesos are not considered worth administering. ICT usually sends out an engineer to make sure that proposed changes are structurally sound. For each district one type of improvement is given priority, such as providing electricity or septic tanks. Loans are made until the budget for that district is exhausted, and then a different district with a different priority gets a turn. This program has a high rate of default, perhaps because of inadequate collateral.

The second ICT program is for "progressive housing construction." Everything from serviced lots to luxury housing is included in this pro-

Table 4-13. *Characteristics of Some ICT Dwellings under Construction from 1977 to 1978*

		Location and type of house			
			Las Gaviotas		
Characteristic	Nuevo Bosque, minimal	Minimal	Sulfur, minimal	Basic	La Gavia, intermediate
1. Floor space (square meters)	31	34	36	57	83
2. Number of rooms	2	2	2	3	4
3. Cost of construction without ICT overhead or the site (pesos per square meter)[a]	2,155 (56.7)	1,922 (50.6)	1,593 (41.9)	2,455 (64.6)	3,168 (83.4)
4. Total cost of construction (1. × 3.) (pesos)	66,800	65,300	57,300	139,900	262,900
5. Housing type	one-family, one-story, front plastered	one-family, one-story, exposed blocks	one-family, one-story, sulfur over blocks	one-family, two-story, plaster floor	two-family, two-story, completely finished
6. Size of lot (square meters)	98	81	126	126	150
7. Cost of lot (pesos per square meter)	75.5	60.9	60.9	60.8	93.9
8. Cost of improving lot (pesos per square meter)	502.2	385.8	382.4	402.9	361.9
9. Total cost of lot (pesos)	56,600	36,200	55,900	58,400	68,400
10. Cost of lot and construction (pesos)	123,400	101,500	113,200	198,300	331,300
11. Share of lot in 10. (percent)	45.9	35.7	49.4	29.5	20.6
12. ICT markup (pesos)	4,300	23,500	26,800	21,700	167,300
13. ICT markup (percent)	3.4	23.2	23.7	10.9	50.5
14. Sales price (pesos)[a]	127,700 (3,360)	125,500 (3,300)	140,000 (3,680)	220,000 (5,790)	498,600 (13,120)
15. Number of units	210	200	39	222	24

gram, but naturally the upper limits in terms of MDW (minimum daily legal wages) and the terms of financing vary. The limit for a lot is 400 MDW; for a lot with a plumbing core, 650 MDW; for a minimal house, 1,290 MDW; for a basic house, 1,935 MDW; for an intermediate dwelling, 3,225 MDW; and for maximal dwellings, 6,456 MDW.[3] Except for dwellings that ICT builds jointly with other agencies, the maximum floor space is 100 square meters. One such exception was to be the 115-square-meter design for 1.15- million-peso apartments planned for Chambacú before that terrain of 9 hectares had to be sold to the BCH. Owners of lots can receive 1,290 MDW to help them organize construction. In other cases, ICT will hire the contractors and supervise the construction of several hundred units of a type.

Financial terms are more rigorous for the more expensive dwelling types. Amortization periods range from a dozen years for minimal houses to fifteen years for basic and better houses. Minimal (130,000 pesos of 1978) houses have only 10 percent down payment required, basic dwellings (225,000 pesos of 1978) call for 15 percent, and others 20 percent. Interest and insurance are 14 percent for the minimal, 16 to 19.5 percent for the basic, and 7 percent on the outstanding but price-indexed balance for more expensive housing. Intermediate dwellings are indexed at only 65 percent of the UPAC (units of constant purchasing power) rate, and maximal dwellings at 75, 85, and 100 percent as their value rises. The progressive aspect of these dwellings, however, is not only the different rate of financing, but also their design which facilitates improvements and expansion. The smaller the house is, the more likely it is to be delivered unplastered, unpainted, and with rudimentary doors, windows, and floors. All have electricity, kitchens, water, and toilets connected to sewerage systems.

In Table 4-13, the first three columns give information about minimal houses in Cartagena. Even more minimal 20-square-meter dwellings were begun in Los Calamares in 1980. The 34-square-meter, two-room house for Gaviotas required 6,300 pesos for a down payment and 1,392 pesos in monthly payments. This amount was 30 percent of the 4,640-peso minimum family income needed to qualify.

For a Gaviotas basic house, the down payment was 44,000 pesos, and the initial level of monthly payments was 1,855 pesos. Households with incomes below 8,250 pesos did not qualify. Those at the minimum level paid 22.5 percent of their incomes on the mortgage. To afford this type of house the family had to be in the upper half of the Cartagena income distribution. Indeed, housing finance was in such short supply and these financial terms with their mere 5 percent annual increase in payments on a nonindexed balance were so favorable that buyers had to be chosen by lottery.

The gain to ICT depended not only on the financial terms, however, but also on the markup. For the Nuevo Bosque minimal house, the markup was only 3.4 percent, but for the La Gavia intermediate dwellings it was 50.5 percent. Nevertheless, accelerating inflation decapitalized ICT. After national subsidies to ICT were curtailed for macroeconomic, anti-inflationary reasons during 1977–80, most ICT residential construction had to be delayed, and for a while nothing was built.

The third ICT program helps to finance public and commercial installations, and the fourth program promotes community improvements through cooperatives and training. Some of these are prerequisites for upgrading of housing but will not be described further.

There are several restrictions on ICT loans. They must not go to any family that has assets more than ten times the value of the loan, that owns dwellings or lots, or that has lived less than a minimum number of years in a city (for Cartagena the minimum is four years). An upper limit to incomes is not specified, but social workers can decide that a family drawn by lot is not really suitable for a neighborhood for a given income class. Families may take three months to improve and add to the dwelling before moving in, and this practice is widespread. After five years of occupancy, the dwelling may be sold to ICT and the equity recovered. Alternatively the entire debt may be paid off and the dwelling sold to another directly, a transaction that is likely to be far more lucrative, given inflation. Inspections exist to make sure that first buyers occupy their premises and do not become landlords who go off to Venezuela for a job. Some ICT policies have been influenced by the Caja de Vivienda Popular of Bogotá, which is described in Appendix J.

Banco Central Hipotecario (BCH)

The BCH deals only with private employees. After three years of employment, workers can obtain a loan twenty-seven times the monthly earnings (salaries plus fringe benefits). Public employees have a similar system administered through the Caja de Previsión Social. Alternatively, one can borrow 90 percent of the value of the house, whichever is less. The house must be less than one year old. The employers must pay to the BCH all the amount including interest that would have gone into *cesantías*, the retirement fund. This interest includes a price-indexed amount. If the pay increase has been very large, then an arrangement can be made whereby only 85 percent of the *cesantías* (plus all the interest) is paid to the BCH. The maximum amortization period is fifteen years. A house worth 200,000 to be paid for in fifteen years by an employee with only three years of employment requires a job that pays 7,400 pesos monthly.

For dwellings in the 200,001–400,000 peso range, BCH lent 80 percent or twenty-seven monthly earning equivalents, whichever was less. In the first year, monthly payments had to be 12 percent of the previous year's income of the head of the household from all sources. In the second year payments were stable at a rate 8 percent above the first year's payments. Through the fifteenth year payments would thus rise at 8 percent compounded: $0.12\ Y\ (1.08)^n$. Of course, the loan may be paid off earlier at the owner's discretion.

Older houses less than fifteen years old are financed by a different scheme. Any amount will be lent, but the outstanding balance is due in terms of units of constant purchasing power (UPAC). Thus amortization and interest are indexed in a complex manner that originally kept up with, but now lags behind, the rate of inflation. Since the ancient walled historical center of Cartagena is a special case, loans can be acquired for rebuilding old dwellings, but each structure is investigated individually for its merits.

Real Estate Taxes

Real estate taxes are part of housing costs to the family, yet they divert spending from shelter itself. The system of taxes in Cartagena makes it difficult to assess their effect, but they do not seem important. Dwellings financed by a public institution such as ICT or BCH were charged no taxes at all for ten years on the grounds that government institutions are tax exempt. Since this exemption applied to dwellings worth less than 120,000 pesos, inflation had eroded its significance. Inflation also made it impossible to know the rate of taxation, nominally 1.4 percent, because the time of assessment had been changed from every two years to every four years. Since construction costs had tripled in four years, the initial percentage fell rapidly.

Land was assessed separately from structures, and in the best commercial zones and tourist sectors—La Matuna and El Laguito—land prices rose faster than building costs, from 1,500 to 5,000 pesos per square meter during 1976–78. A few choice spots were sold for double or triple the latter value. The Oficina Nacional del Catastro de Bolivar had maps of isobars of land values of Cartagena, but these were confidential.

A typical case concerned a 158-square-meter house built in 1955 on 334 square meters of land near Bazurto. In 1966 the house was worth six times as much as the land. Five years later the site value had risen so much that the house was worth only 2.6 times as much. When the city market moved to a location a few blocks away, the site value moved within 8 percent of structural value.

	Site value (pesos)	Structural value (pesos)	Total (pesos)
1966	8,800	53,500	62,300
1971	24,400	62,800	87,200
1978	152,600	165,200	317,800

Most important, however, is that in Cartagena only a limited attempt is made to collect real estate taxes regularly. Those who wish to pay can do so and have the amount added to their regular charges for water, light, sewerage, garbage collection, police protection, and other services. Since 1976 such collections have been computerized. But those who do not wish to pay need not do so. Taxes in arrears are collected whenever a property becomes involved in a legal transaction, a sale, or an inheritance.

At the time of our survey, a description of the system in 1975 still appeared valid:

> The assessment procedures are biased towards lower than market value assessments, occur too infrequently, and do not appear to concentrate on the high value and rapid growth areas, when partial assessments are required. Complex and poorly designed rate structures, collection problems, and lags in the application of reassessed property values for tax purposes cause further difficulties.[4]

Property was assessed by the National Geographic Institute "Agustin Codazzi" in a system that involved much self-assessment by realtors and owners. Tax and service charge rates were set by various levels of government, and Empresas Publicas Municipales (EPM) did the collecting. Water and sewerage service charges, like the taxes, were in proportion to property values. These values were the sum of separate assessments of land and improvements. Land value assessment began by estimating several hundred "key sites" on the basis of recent sales and then interpolating contours of equal value throughout the city. Size and specific characteristics would then modify the value of each site from that suggested by the contours. Improvements were assessed separately on the basis of a point system for materials, finish, state of conservation, and age. The points were multiplied by a price index from construction surveys in an area. Adjustments were then made for the dimensions of the structure and other features to get the final value.

The average assessment of property values along the Coast (Zone 1) was 3.5 times that in Lomas (Zone 4) in 1972, which compares with a 4.2 ratio according to the estimates of sample owner-occupants in 1978. The average Lomas property, in turn, had 3.5 times the value of a Southeast sector (Zone 3) property according to the 1972 assessment, compared with 3.2 times in our survey. Coastal rents in 1978 were 2.7 times those of Lomas, which were 1.7 times those of the Southeast. In 1972 pesos, the average values were: Zone 1, 360,000 pesos; Zone 4, 100,000 pesos; and Zone 3, 30,000 pesos. The changes in relative values from 1973 to 1978 seem plausible, given such factors as the tourist boom in Bocagrande. In addition, income in 1978 on the Coast was 2.3 times that of Lomas, which in turn was 1.7 times that of the Southeast. Differences in housing values were greater than the differences in the owners' incomes.

Tax and service charge collections grew at a slower rate over time than property values during 1961–72, although perhaps at the same rate as per capita income.[5] This trend continued during the rest of the 1970s. None of the families surveyed said they did or did not move, buy, build, or expand because of taxes.

The Demand for Land and Location

Dwellings come linked to public utilities, land, a neighborhood, and distances to employment centers and other urban activities. For many years the amount and cost of space and the distance of journeys to work were considered the key determinants of residential choice in theories about different income groups in developed countries. Lately this emphasis has faded, and maintenance and improvement of structures in preferred neighborhoods regardless of density or distance has seemed more plausible.[6] In a medium-size city such as Cartagena, density and distance were definitely of secondary importance compared with neighborhood and access to utilities.

The average Cartagenian travels fifteen minutes or 2 or 3 kilometers to work, but this need is not especially associated with incomes or density of settlement. Size of a lot correlates significantly with income and the number of adults in a household but not with the distance that principal workers must travel daily. Indeed, the sign is wrong, and those with the longer commutes have smaller lots. Around a mean lot size of 251 square meters the standard deviation is 185 square meters, and income accounts for only 3.2 percent of the variation. Qualities other than size or distance explain why the rich picked their 333-square-meter lots compared with the 200-square-meter lots of the poor, as shown below.

Monthly income (pesos)	Average lot size (square meters; N = 285)	Average distance from work (kilometers; total for two principal workers)
0–4,000	199	4.6
4,001–8,000	241	4.5
8,001–16,000	263	6.0
16,001+	333	3.9
Weighted average	251	4.8

Bringing in the number of adults in a household raises the R^2 from 0.032 to 0.097.

What mattered was not the size or distance of the lot but whether it had water and public sewerage service and whether it was located in a prestigious district. In the highest income range, lot size was even negatively (and significantly) associated with income. The best land in Bocagrande and the Centro was scarce, expensive, and subdivided into small parcels.

Of course, occupants realized that conversion to commercial use could affect their property values. This effect was most marked among the five dwellings that turned up in the Pie de la Popa district near the intersection of Zones 1, 3, and 4. Pie de la Popa was the principal crossroads of Cartagena. Much traffic had to pass by here below the steep promontory of La Popa and the lagoon Caño Bazurto. Some of it went along the north-south route from Torices to Manga, but more went between the Centro and Bocagrande on the east to the numerous poorer quarters to the west. Transfer of the municipal market from Getsemaní, near the center, to Bazurto further raised the commercial value of sites in this sector.

Owners of dwellings were well aware of the way economic and population growth had raised the value of their assets. Elsewhere in the city we usually found that multiplication of the purchase price of a house by the construction cost index, with some allowance for improvements, came astonishingly close to the price people thought they could sell their house for. But in Pie de la Popa, three respondents out of five believed that they could charge about double the price-index-corrected amount; and one believed he could charge more than ten times as much. This last family owned 1,350 square meters on the Avenida Don Pedro de Heredia, the principal highway. They had bought the site in 1946 and built their present house in 1948. As an exception, the owner of a four-room house in a little dead-end alley thought his value had only tripled when the price index would have suggested a quintupling.

Moves and Location

According to a 1976 survey of migrants to Cartagena, 81 percent had remained more than four years in the first residential area occupied after arrival. The proportion was the same whether the migrants settled in established housing, slums, squatter settlements, or nearby communities. Whether mobility was not sought or was too costly is not clear. They did move within their areas, however, and only a few had remained in one dwelling. A substantial number of those with long periods of residence had become owners.

The same study found that half the employers were natives of Cartagena, but that they all had lived two or more years in larger Colombian cities or abroad. Second-level managers came primarily from the interior. According to the employers, office workers and laborers came mainly from the Department of Bolivar (including Cartagena) or from the rest of the coast.

One employer made revealing comments about housing as an obstacle to recruiting technicians from the interior who, in turn, could raise local productivity through better supervision:

> The cost of living is very high and Cartagenian society is very polarized … as can be confirmed by a simple look at the city. Rent for a house or a comfortable apartment is very high, partly due to the competition of tourists … It differs from cities like Bogotá, Manizales, Bucaramanga, and others where one can live comfortably in intermediate neighborhoods. Although we pay technicians from elsewhere good salaries, it's hard for them to live as well here as they did in Bogotá, for example; and, therefore, after one or two trial years, they prefer to go back.[7]

The relation between type of tenure and mobility in 1978 is shown in Table 4-14.

More than two-thirds of Cartagenians had lived ten years or less at their present site, and more than half five years or less. At the time of our interviews, 13.6 percent of households—one in seven—was thinking of moving again. Table 4-15 compares the reasons for moving the previous time with those for moving again.

Becoming an owner had been the primary reason the previous time and would again be a motive for those new households, tenants, free users, and prospective migrants who were not yet part of the population.

Table 4-14. *Relation between Mobility and Type of Tenure*

Number of years at present site	Total sample	Tenants	Others	Southeast zone	ICT zone
1–5	51.0	84.1	41.8	50.0	60.8
6–10	17.0	11.1	18.7	14.5	19.6
11–15	11.5	3.2	13.8	11.3	13.7
16–20	9.0	0.0	11.6	9.7	5.9
21–30	5.9	1.6	7.1	9.7	0.0
31+	5.6	0.0	7.1	4.8	0.0

Source: Cartagena household survey, 1978.

Table 4-15. *Reasons for Moving to Another Dwelling*
(percent)

Reason	Previous time	Next time
Become an owner	56.2	13.2
Be in better neighborhood	6.4	13.2
Pay less	6.4	0
Have a bigger house	3.5	5.3
Be closer to work	3.5	0
Be closer to relatives	3.2	0
Have better quality dwelling	2.1	26.3
Have better public utilities	2.1	13.2
Have a shop, store, or office	1.1	0
Move away from relatives	1.1	2.6
Other	14.5	26.3

Source: Cartagena household survey, 1978.

Hence this reason would not fall as much in importance as the table suggests. Improved quality of dwelling, better neighborhood, and better public utilities would otherwise be the principal motives. Compared with alternative reasons, these reasons reflected higher income levels and higher aspirations.

In 64.5 percent of the ninety-three dwellings that had had previous occupants, the present owners felt that their predecessors had been approximately as well off as their own family. Some 14.0 percent thought the previous occupants had been somewhat richer, and 16.1 percent said somewhat poorer. Only 5.4 percent thought that substantial upward or downward filtering had occurred. By the same token, 76.4 percent thought that they were about as well-off as their neighbors, and only 1.1 percent thought there was much of a difference in economic status. If anything, the neighbors were richer.

At the time of moving the average family size had been 6.3 (standard error 0.2), which was not much below the current average family size of 7.0. Perhaps these households were about to grow from somewhat below to substantially above average, whereas some others formed new small households.

Travel time to a job was not a very important criterion of housing choice. More than half the family heads and principal second workers traveled by bus, as shown in Table 4-16.

After moving, average travel time had not changed dramatically for family heads, meaning an increase of 20.6 percent (standard error 9.7 percent). For the spouse or other second worker, time had risen by a sta-

Table 4-16. *Modes of Transport Used to Get to Work*
(percent)

Mode of transport	Head of household	Spouse or other second worker
Public bus	50.9	57.1
None, works at home	13.6	25.6
Transport provided by employer	13.2	3.0
Car	11.8	4.5
Walk	8.6	8.3
Bicycle	0.9	0
Other	0.9	1.5

Source: Cartagena household survey, 1978.

tistically insignificant 7.4 percent (standard error 14.2 percent). The implied change in distance was less than a kilometer.

Average one-way travel time to work for owner-occupants and free users was 26.8 minutes (Table 4-17). This figure is the combined time for the two principal workers of the household: the head and spouse or the head and one other. The breakdown by income range or dwelling value shows no particular association of either with travel time. The combined time for the two workers varied from 19 to 32 minutes without any particular pattern. The only exception was the 48.3-minute time for the 32,001+ peso group. These richest workers had to drive up the long Bo-

Table 4-17. *Combined Travel Time to Work of Household Head and Spouse or Other Second Worker, by Income and Dwelling Value, for Nontenants*
(N = 220)

Monthly income (pesos)	Travel time (minutes)	Dwelling value (thousands of pesos)	Travel time (minutes)
0–2,000	19.4	0–40	27.3
2,001–4,000	29.6	40.1–80	31.6
4,001–8,000	26.1	80.1–160	28.7
8,001–16,000	28.6	160.1–320	24.2
16,001–32,000	22.7	320.1–640	28.9
32,001+	48.3	641+	23.1
Weighted average	26.8	Weighted average	26.8

Source: Cartagena household survey, 1978.

cagrande peninsula to the bottleneck of the Centro and continue from there to hospitals or factories if they did not have an office in La Matuna. Some were moving to Turbaco.

More detailed analysis did not appear worthwhile. Travel time for households on the stock-user matrix diagonal was 30.2 minutes. Those below the diagonal took 28.5 minutes and those above 23.9 minutes—a saving of 6.3 minutes for two workers or 21 percent of travel time.

Demand Elasticities

The relative unimportance of distance and sheer space or density as determinants of value in Cartagena means that higher expenditures on housing went for bigger and better physical structures and utilities. These are highly correlated with other aspects of neighborhood quality.

The prices that occupants were willing to pay for each installed square meter of bedroom, window, faucet, and so forth, cannot be separated; only the total expenditure for the dwelling on its site was available. In comparing the physical structure of one dwelling with another, if one assumes that doubled expenditures produce twice as much in housing services one thereby assumes that the unit price for each component of given quality is the same for both dwellings and that one building has twice as many components as the other. That additional components may yield diminishing marginal utility to the buyer is a different matter altogether. If, however, unit prices vary from one dwelling to another or from one part of a city to another, it cannot be determined whether richer families spend more because of their higher income or because of shopping in a more expensive market or both. The effects of unknown price variations must be disentangled from income variations to analyze the housing market. In Cartagena it appeared that the assumption of constant unit prices was reasonable, given the size of the city in 1978, its tendency to expand toward areas less confined by lagoons and bays (described in Chapter 2), and the ready availability of construction materials and skills to all.[8]

If housing values can be related to income without unbundling the complex package of expected services, it is much easier to assess imperfections in the housing market and to project future demand. Demand and spending move together. An estimate of the income elasticity of demand will suggest how much more housing will be sought in the future when incomes have risen by some percentage. If incomes double, demand for housing will rise by 50 percent if the elasticity is 0.5; by 100 percent if the elasticity is 1.0; and by 150 percent if the elasticity is 1.5.

Of course, these percentages have to be translated into space, materials, finishes, and components by suppliers. The way in which the demand is met—by adding to and transforming the housing stock—is the topic of coming chapters.

Housing markets are subject to imperfections, especially barriers to the flow of capital under inflationary conditions. Families may have no opportunity to devote a fifth or so of their income to amortizing a fifteen-year mortgage at a realistic rate of interest, one that reflects the scarcity of savings. Until they expand their dwelling, they may be "out of equilibrium": living in premises that are too small and otherwise inferior. Under some circumstances, the shortage of housing may have raised the price of the inadequate dwelling together with the rest of the housing stock, and the household will pay its expected share for housing without receiving the expected utility. In an imperfect market, housing that is actually occupied and prices that are actually paid are an uncertain guide to future demand.

If the income elasticity of demand has been estimated accurately by observing behavior and comparing willingness to pay with actual payments, including improvements, the extent to which households are in desired housing "on their demand function" can be determined. It is entirely possible that because of reductions in family size with age or imperfections in housing and other markets, some households will be in better housing than might have been expected. The tendency to invest transitory income in the best available outlet may also lead to this situation. If, however, high-income households appear to live in surprisingly good housing, the income elasticity of demand may simply have been underestimated.

Only if the income elasticity of demand has been properly assessed will the diagonal of the stock-user matrix have normative implications: as many households should be above as below. Typically F2 households will live in H2 dwellings, F3 households in H3 dwellings, and so forth. If the elasticity of demand is 1.5, a doubling in the range of housing values in the columns of the cross-tabulation goes with a two-thirds rise in the level of household income for the rows. A normative implication of the matrix is that moving any out-of-equilibrium household from one cell below the diagonal to the diagonal is as good as moving any other. It represents an equal percentage improvement. For a given amount of resources, more poor than rich households can be moved to the diagonal to an extent that outweighs any downward transfers from the rich to the poor or "filtering."[9]

The overall housing-income elasticity for owners was estimated with regression analysis to be 1.18 and thus higher than that of 0.87 for mort-

Table 4-18. *Logarithmic Regressions of Values, Rents, and Mortgage Payments against Incomes, Household Size, and the Proportion of Adults*

Sample	Constant	Income[a]	Household size[a]	Ratio of adults to household[a]	Adjusted R^2	F ratio
1. All owners (N = 205)	1.764	1.178[b] (0.083)	—	—	0.498	203.41[b]
2. All owners (N = 205)	1.898	1.238[b] (0.085)	−0.355 (0.138)	—	0.512	107.83[b]
3. All owners (N = 205)	1.455	1.150[b] (0.081)	—	0.974[b] (0.278)	0.524	113.51[b]
4. All owners (N = 205)	1.575	1.185[b] (0.086)	−0.182 (0.151)	0.812[b] (0.308)	0.526	76.32[b]
5. Southeast Zone (N = 47)	2.818	0.983[b] (0.202)	—	—	0.330	23.67[b]
6. Southeast Zone (N = 47)	2.048	1.123[b] (0.258)	−0.296 (0.326)	0.258 (0.705)	0.322	8.29[b]
7. Income 0–4,000 (N = 50)	7.135	0.287 (0.372)	−0.376 (0.386)	1.760[b] (0.639)	0.120	3.22[c]
8. Income 4,001 to 8,000 (N = 70)	5.141	0.853 (0.527)	−0.391 (0.268)	0.577 (0.574)	0.051	2.24

9. Income 8,001 to 16,000 ($N = 55$)	−2.377	1.615[b] (0.556)	−0.171 (0.247)	0.434 (0.565)	0.108	3.22[c]
10. Income 16,001+ ($N = 29$)	6.792	0.635 (0.571)	0.261 (0.507)	0.369 (0.824)	0.058	0.48
11. All tenants ($N = 65$)	−0.024	0.786[b] (0.110)	—	—	0.440	51.25[b]
12. All tenants ($N = 65$)	0.515	0.777[b] (0.111)	−0.258 (0.233)	−0.311 (0.424)	0.437	17.53[b]
13. All mortgagors ($N = 50$)	−0.619	0.873 (0.275)	—	—	0.156	10.08[b]
14. All mortgagors ($N = 50$)	−1.319	0.940 (0.258)	−1.215 (0.418)	0.918 (0.884)	0.267	6.95[b]

Note: The dependent variable for the first ten equations is the logarithm of the estimated value of the dwelling. For the last four it is the logarithm of monthly rent or mortgage payment. Substituting actual values for the logarithms of income and household size did not significantly change results. Adults were defined as aged 18 and more. Household size in line 14 is the log of the number of adults.

— Not applicable.
a. Standard error is given in parentheses.
b. Significance = 0.01.
c. Significance = 0.05.
Source: Cartagena household survey, 1978.

Table 4-19. *Stock-User Matrix for Owner-Occupants and Rent-Free Tenants*
(percentage in each cell; N = 220)

Household income (pesos per month)	Dwelling value (pesos)						Σ_F	Index
	H0 (0–40,000)	H1 (40,001–80,000)	H2 (80,001–160,000)	H3 (160,001–320,000)	H4 (320,001–640,000)	H5 (640,001+)		
F0 (0–2,000)	3.2	3.2	0.9				7.3	(181)
F1 (2,001–4,000)	4.5	5.0	4.1	3.2	1.4		18.2	217
F2 (4,001–8,000)	3.2	3.2	6.8	14.1	6.4	1.4	35.0	212
F3 (8,001–16,000)		1.8	5.0	10.5	5.0	4.1	26.4	151
F4 (16,001–32,000)				0.9	1.8	9.1	11.8	173
F5 (32,001+)				0.5		0.9	1.4	73
Σ_H	10.9	13.2	16.8	29.1	14.5	15.5	100.0	189

Source: Cartagena household survey, 1978.

70

gagors only or the 0.79 that has already been reported for tenants. Incorporating household size or the share of adults in the household (as a life-cycle proxy) changed these elasticities only slightly. Household size adds little to explaining the variance, but the life-cycle proxy raises the adjusted R^2 from 0.498 to 0.524, and like income is highly significant (Table 4-18).

Except for the ICT sector, the income elasticity was also close to unity and highly significant within zones: Coast, 0.801; North, 0.896; Southeast, 0.983; Lomas, 0.734; and Outskirts, 1.102. For the ICT Zone it is 0.111 and not significant. ICT dwellings were administratively allocated. The regression constant for the ICT sector was correspondingly high, 11.5, or four times that for the Southeast's 2.8. The intercepts for Zones 1, 2, and 4 were 6.1, 4.1, and 6.0, respectively, and may reflect an upward shift because of upgrading. In the new Outskirts that had not yet occurred, as may be expected, and the intercept was 2.7.

Elasticities were also not high within all income ranges for the entire city. For incomes of 0–4,000 pesos monthly and 4,001–8,000 pesos, the elasticities were 0.287 and 0.853, respectively. For 8,001–16,000 pesos, the elasticity doubled to 1.615; and for 16,001 pesos and above it fell back to 0.635. Only the high elasticity for 8,001–16,000 pesos is statistically significant. If the regressions are run, not against value, but against the monthly payments a respondent would be willing to make for the occupied dwelling, the elasticities for ranges become significant: 0.658, 1.047, 1.621, respectively, and 1.484 (not significant) for those above 16,000 pesos monthly. The overall willingness-to-pay elasticity is 0.973.

An elasticity of 1.0 thus seems most plausible and was used to set up the stock-user matrix of Table 4-19. The population is generally distributed along and above the matrix diagonal from northwest to southeast, as a unitary overall elasticity would suggest. The northeast and southwest corners are empty. But within each row, a substantial dispersion nevertheless exists: by investing windfall income—from inheritances, Venezuelan remittances, and even smuggling—in new housing or improvements, households had put themselves above the diagonal and had brought the overall index of housing to 189. The overall index would be 120 if positions above the diagonal were weighted at a diminishing rate of increase: 150, 175, and 187.5. At an index of 100 everyone would be on the diagonal.

The index of housing for tenants was only 71 (Table 4-9). (If cells above the diagonal were weighted as 150, not 200, the index would be 66.) Tenants were hardly likely to invest in their landlord's property if they had a windfall of income. Rather, the very lack of windfall income to cover a down payment may explain their tenant status. In any case, tenants were mainly below the diagonal.

Closest to the diagonal were the households with incomes of 8,001–16,000 pesos and with the high elasticity of 1.615. Forty percent of these were on the diagonal, 26 percent were below, and 34 percent were above. Why this group of skilled technicians and fairly young managers should behave somewhat differently than others is not clear. In this income range, improvement may have ceased on upgraded H2 housing at the low end, and a large effort to acquire something close to H4 housing may have been made at the high end. Physical characteristics of these housing types are described in the next chapter, suggesting a discontinuity between the two extremes. Neighborhood effects have already been mentioned. Perhaps these households are also too rich to accept windfall remittances from family migrants in Venezuela and too poor to get the sort of windfall gains associated with managing property.

The significant finding from all this is more general: the overall income elasticity of demand for housing appears close to unity—somewhat higher for owners and somewhat lower for tenants. Provided there was access to indoor piped water, owners would expand their dwellings so that about half would live above the matrix diagonal in housing twice as good as might otherwise be expected. Tenants lived below the diagonal with about half in housing that is half as good as might otherwise be expected from the level of income.

Summary

Median monthly income in Cartagena in the summer of 1978 was 7,500 pesos per household, and average income was 9,900 pesos. Per capita average annual income was 17,000 pesos (US$440), and per capita product may have been 20 percent higher than that. Thirteen percent of households received pensions, and 21 percent received interpersonal remittances, especially from Venezuela. For 17 percent of households, these were the primary sources of income and were large enough to leave them close to the median level.

Residential mobility was high among households, with one-half of the households having been at their present site for five years or less, and with less than one-third having been there for more than ten years. Mobility was especially high among tenants. Roughly one-third of owner-occupants had bought used dwellings, one-third had bought formally constructed new houses, and one-third had built their own. The measured income elasticity of demand was 0.8 for tenants and 1.2 for owner-occupants with variations within income ranges. Corrections for market imperfections might bring both of these estimates closer to unity. Investment of temporary income in housing expansion on lots with water had put nearly half of owner-occupants in better housing than would otherwise be expected. Household size and stage in the life cycle, as measured here, did not greatly affect housing demand apart from income effects. Other unimportant factors were density of settlement, lot size, distance from work, and real estate taxes.

Notes to Chapter 4

1. Marta Izabel Gutiérrez de Gómez, "Política Tarifaria y Distribución de Ingresos" (Bogotá: National Planning Department, 1975; processed), cited by Johannes Linn, *Policies for Cities in the Developing World: Their Equitable and Efficient Growth* (New York: Oxford University Press, 1982), p. 283.

2. Its history will not be recounted here, but a good account in English is Rafael Stevenson, "Housing Programs and Policies in Bogota: A Historical and Descriptive Analysis," Urban and Regional Report no. 79-8 (Washington, D.C.: World Bank, June 1978; processed).

3. These categories are described in Chapter 5.

4. Johannes F. Linn, "Urban Public Finances in Developing Countries: A Case Study of Cartagena, Colombia," The World Bank, Urban and Regional Report no. 77-1 (Washington, D.C.; January 1975; processed), vol. 1, p. 4.

5. Ibid.

6. William C. Wheaton, "Monocentric Models of Urban Land Use: Contributions and Criticisms," and John Quigley, "What Have We Learned about Urban Housing Markets?" in *Current Issues in Urban Economics*, ed. Peter Mieszkowski and Mahlon Straszheim (Baltimore, Md.: Johns Hopkins University Press, 1979), pp. 107–29, 391–429.

7. Ministerio de Desarrollo Económico, "Zona Franca Industrial y Comercial de Cartagena: Area de Población y Medio Ambiente: Informe Final," vol. 1 (Bogotá, December 1976; processed).

8. Gregory K. Ingram has applied an ingenious way of representing intrametropolitan price variations to Bogotá in "Housing Demand in the Developing Metropolis," paper presented at the Econometric Society Meetings, Atlanta, Georgia, December 1979. He segmented the housing market according to the location of the work place of the household head among renters. Income elasticities ranged from 0.5 to 0.8, and price elasticities clustered around −0.8.

9. A semilogarithmic utility function for housing services is assumed. See W. Paul Strassmann, "Housing Priorities in Developing Countries: A Planning Model," *Land Economics* (August 1977), pp. 310–27.

5

The Housing Stock
and New Construction

THE PROCESS OF EXPANDING, UPGRADING, AND TRANSFORMING HOUSING cannot be discussed without knowing what kinds of old housing exist and what it would cost to build completely new housing. Some of the characteristics of the old housing stock have already been given in Chapter 3. The sections in this chapter on new construction discuss the type of housing, rate of cost increases, employment effects, and innovations.

In 1978 the occupied Cartagena housing stock—not counting barracks, hospitals, and hotels—was worth 16,641 million pesos or 2.2 times the aggregate annual household income. This estimate assumes that housing and incomes of the 61,200 households were distributed in the same way as in our sample (Table 5-1).

In this chapter the distribution of the housing stock is disaggregated into six categories: temporary, substandard, minimal, basic, intermediate, and excellent. The value of each housing type is half that of the next higher

Table 5-1. *Distribution of Housing, by Income*

Income (pesos per month)	Percentage of households	Average value of dwelling (pesos)
F0 (0–2,000)	6.2	52,200
F1 (2,001–4,000)	16.8	117,600
F2 (4,001–8,000)	35.2	213,600
F3 (8,001–16,000)	27.8	300,000
F4 (16,001–32,000)	11.2	691,200
F5 (32,001+)	2.7	440,000
Mean/total 9,900	100.0	271,900 (weighted average)

Source: Cartagena household survey, 1978.

type. The cross-tabulation (stock-user matrix) of Table 5-2 shows what type of housing is occupied by households in the six income ranges. Thus, of the 3,800 households that receive less than 2,000 pesos monthly, 1,800 live in some of the 8,000 dwellings that are classified as temporary. As explained in the previous chapter, the income ranges were selected to fit the income elasticity of demand, so that the average household will be in equilibrium when in a cell on the diagonal: as many households should be above the average as are below it. Since the distribution is the result of interaction between supply and demand, much of the analysis is deferred until Chapter 7.

Characteristics of the Housing Stock

As is well known, housing has many components and features that range from neighborhood amenities, public services, and access to transport to security, durability, space, and aesthetic design. The value of a house reflects the combination of all these factors, and with hedonic analysis the relative contribution of each component to the total can be determined. Except for space, better housing characteristics are highly correlated with one another, and only minor tradeoffs occur at the margin. That space can contradict this pattern can be shown by comparing remote, waterless Boston-Tesca (district 8) with the fashionable Laguito section of Bocagrande (district 1). The three Laguito apartments in our sample had an average value of 1.4 million pesos (US$36,000) and an average size of 41 square meters. Six Boston-Tesca houses were worth an average of only 98,000 pesos (US$2,500), but their floor space was 76 square meters. The poor had 85 percent more space, but its value was only 1,300 pesos per square meter, compared with 34,000 pesos in Laguito—twenty-six times as much.

Three-quarters of the dwellings were made of concrete blocks, and 60 percent had asbestos cement sheet roofs. Most of the 18.5 percent of dwellings made of wood or adobe were considered inferior and were partly roofed with metal sheets or cardboard. Only 9 percent of dwellings were made of the preferred wall materials (bricks or reinforced concrete), but 29 percent had tile or reinforced concrete roofs, as shown in Table 5-3.

Ninety percent of the households sampled lived in single-family housing, and, of these, 94 percent were in single-story dwellings. Twelve families or 4.1 percent of the total were in low-rise apartments or buildings with five or fewer stories. A mere four households (1.4 percent) were in high-rise apartments. Thirteen families (4.4 percent) had rooms in outbuildings (*piezas accesorias* or *inquilinatos*).

Table 5-2. Distribution of the Occupied Housing Stock

(thousands of household-dwelling combinations; percentages of the total in parentheses)

Household income (pesos per month)	Dwelling type						Σ_F	Index
	H0 (temporary)	H1 (substandard)	H2 (minimal)	H3 (basic)	H4 (intermediate)	H5 (excellent)		
F0 (0–2,000)	1.8 (3.0)	1.5 (2.5)	0.4 (0.7)				3.8 (6.2)	174
F1 (2,001–4,000)	2.9 (4.8)	3.2 (5.3)	2.0 (3.2)	1.4 (2.3)	0.7 (1.2)		10.3 (16.8)	196
F2 (4,001–8,000)	3.2 (5.2)	3.2 (5.3)	4.4 (7.2)	6.7 (11.0)	3.4 (5.6)	0.6 (0.9)	21.6 (35.2)	178
F3 (8,001–16,000)		2.1 (3.5)	4.0 (6.5)	6.1 (10.0)	3.2 (5.2)	1.6 (2.6)	17.0 (27.8)	125
F4 (16,001–32,000)		0.2 (0.4)		0.8 (1.3)	2.2 (3.6)	3.6 (5.9)	6.9 (11.2)	144
F5 (32,001+)			0.2 (0.4)	0.8 (1.3)	0.2 (0.4)	0.4 (0.6)	1.7 (2.7)	44
Σ_H	8.0 (13.0)	10.4 (17.0)	11.0 (18.0)	15.9 (26.0)	9.8 (16.0)	6.1 (10.0)	61.2 (100)	157

Note: The overall index is computed only for those households that can afford more than a temporary dwelling, F1 to F5. If dwellings above the diagonal are weighted as 150, 175, and 187.5 (not 200, 400, and 800), the overall index falls from 157 to 115. The justification would be diminishing marginal utility of additional housing sufficient to match the 50, 25, 12.5 sequence of values to the left of the diagonal.

Source: Cartagena household survey, 1978.

Table 5-3. *Wall and Roofing Materials Used in Dwellings*
(percent)

Wall materials		Roofing materials	
Concrete blocks	74.3	Asbestos cement sheets	60.4
Wood	16.8	Clay tiles	22.2
Reinforced concrete	4.5	Reinforced concrete	6.5
Bricks	2.4	Metal sheets	6.5
Adobe	1.7	Concrete blocks	3.4
Other	0.3	Wood or cardboard	1.0
Total	100.0	Total	100.0

Source: Cartagena household survey, 1978.

Among the characteristics of Cartagena housing in 1973, reported in Chapter 3, was the number of rooms (Table 3-3). About 11.7 percent had one room, 26.9 percent had two rooms, 25.1 percent had three, 25.4 percent had four or five, and 11 percent had more. Table 3-2 showed that according to the census only 18.2 percent lacked electricity, and 25.2 percent lacked piped water, but 71.4 percent had no connection with a sewerage system. The northern parts of the city, Torices and LeMaitre, had had sewerage pipes installed since the 1950s, but the system had never been completed with pumping stations and the like, as previously described. If such dwellings had access to piped water, they could make a septic tank function.

Further details on the distribution of plumbing facilities appear in Table 5-4. Some of the inhabitants in dwellings that had piped water combined with latrines may have disconnected their toilets because they

Table 5-4. *Type of Plumbing Facilities in Housing, 1973 and 1978*

Type of housing	Type of plumbing facility	Percent	
		1973	1978
H3–5	Piped water and sewerage connection	27.9	34.8
H2–4	Septic tanks	32.9	35.3
H1–2	Latrines and piped water	12.9	6.1
H0–1	Latrines but no piped water	7.3	10.2
H0–1	No sanitary facilities, but piped water	5.9	1.0
H0	No sanitary facilities and no water	13.1	12.6
Total		100.0	100.0

Source: DANE and Cartagena household survey, 1978.

could be flushed only a few hours each day, that is, when the city allowed water to flow that way. Dwellings with water but no sanitary facilities are often in areas so close to sea level that latrines cannot be dug. Some of the owners may have paid extra to get the water connection to become water retailers to the neighborhood, as previously described. On the average their extra income seems to have been around 3,000 pesos (US$77) monthly in 1978.

Six Types of Housing

The Cartagena housing stock can be divided into six categories, based on plumbing, number of rooms, materials, and a few other features: temporary, substandard, minimal, basic, intermediate, and luxury. The number of rooms overlaps more categories (as many as three), than do other characteristics, since space was the main characteristic that some households traded off against other improvements. Plumbing facilities are usually the best indicator of value, but in Cartagena their presence or absence was mainly due to the wavering priorities of government. For the construction of new housing, other than those of ICT and other official developments, more prosperous families would bid for and acquire sites in neighborhoods equipped with piped water and sewerage systems. Poorer families would acquire unequipped lots, and the poorest would take sites that were so remote or so close to sea level that they were unlikely to be serviced soon. The importance of public utilities is shown by the first question that potential buyers asked in Cartagena when they saw a "For sale" sign outside a house. It was not "How many rooms does it have?," but "During what hours does it get water?" In this climate the late-afternoon shower is a must and an unflushed toilet a calamity. Once a dwelling had access to piped water, it would be upgraded rapidly, as shown in the next chapter. With a slight lag, therefore, better plumbing and higher value will go together.

Materials are another good indicator of value. Temporary (H0) housing may be temporary in name only and have earth floors, cardboard roofs, and walls made of scrap lumber. Some lack windows. Fences are made of bamboo. Substandard (H1) housing will not only be somewhat larger, but have unplastered concrete block walls and metal or asbestos cement corrugated roofs.

Minimal (H2) housing will never have metal roofs or earth floors. Foundations will allow for expansion without loss of stability, and the front wall will often be plastered, as in ICT houses of this category in Las Gaviotas and Nuevo Bosque. Basic (H3) housing resembles low-cost housing projects throughout the world (the least that most governments can bring themselves to finance) and is out of the price range of perhaps two-thirds of households. Compared with H2 it will be completely plastered, have tile floors, glass windows, and a rudimentary terrace by the front door.

Intermediate (H4) and luxury (H5) housing was completely finished and had high-quality fixtures. Carved balconies and decorative railings around terraces were popular in Cartagena. The rich also preferred clay bricks and tiles over concrete blocks. Two or more bathrooms was the rule.

This comparative inventory of characteristics is summarized in Table 5-5. Also shown are typical 1978 values and their tendency to double from one category to another. The same applies to the typical income of occupants with normal access to finance, given the unitary demand elasticity derived in Chapter 4. The table also shows the percentage distribution of housing among these categories according to the 1973 census and our 1978 sample. Minimal (H2) housing was most common in 1973, and 71 percent of the stock was in the substandard to basic (H1 to H3) categories.

Determinants of Value

The way construction was organized determined the general kind of dwelling that resulted (Table 5-6). Self-help efforts, whether communal or only by the family, resulted in no more than temporary, substandard, or minimal dwellings. Most likely, such dwellings began as temporary and were eventually upgraded to the minimal level. Any household that was wealthy enough (with an income of about US$100–200 monthly) to afford ICT housing was likely to see the alternative as a standard dwelling constructed by workers, perhaps in stages, under the direct pay and supervision of the owner. Such housing would typically be improved from basic to intermediate over time. Housing that was otherwise built by commercial contractors and developers was either intermediate or excellent in specification.

An added room doubled the value of a dwelling, up to four rooms (Table 5-7). One-room dwellings were typically temporary (H0) shacks, and two rooms went with substandard (H1) dwellings. Three rooms were generally of basic (H3) quality, and four to six rooms were typical in intermediate level (H4) dwellings. The fifth and sixth rooms were associated with 30 percent increases in value. The seventh room brought dwellings into the excellent (H5) range. This progression is statistically highly significant ($F = 11.6$); nevertheless, each value range is likely to include two or three room numbers.

Table 5-5. *Characteristics of Housing Categories*

Characteristic	H0(temporary)	H1(substandard)	H2 (minimal)	H3 (basic)	H4 (intermediate)	H5 (excellent)
				Type of housing		
Number of rooms	1–3	2–4	2–4	3–5	4–6	5+
Building materials	Wood, sticks, refuse, card-board	Wood, concrete blocks, un-plastered	Concrete blocks, asbestos-cement sheet roofs	Concrete blocks, asbestos-cement sheet roofs	Concrete blocks or clay bricks, concrete or tile roofs	Concrete blocks or clay bricks, concrete or tile roofs
Plumbing	No sanitary facil-ities, no water	Many without water or latrines	Piped water, septic tank	Some sewerage connections, some septic tanks	Piped water and sewerage con-nection	Piped water and sewerage con-nection, several bathrooms
Value in 1978 (pesos)	30,000	60,000	120,000	240,000	480,000	1,000,000
Upper boundary (pesos)	40,000	80,000	160,000	320,000	640,000	None
Income range of typical occupants (pesos)	0–2,000	2,001–4,000	4,001–8,000	8,001–16,000	16,001–32,000	32,001+
Percentage of dwellings, 1973	16	23	28	20	9	4
Percentage of dwellings, 1978	13	17	18	26	16	10

Source: Cartagena household survey, 1978.

Table 5-6. *Value of Owner-Occupied Dwellings, by Type of Builder*
(*N* = 220)

Type of builder	Value (pesos)	Percent	Type
Mutual aid or communal effort	69,500	1.9	H0–1
Self-help by the family	81,900	14.5	H1–2
Workers paid directly by the family head	303,000	22.7	H3–4
ICT	270,000	17.9	H3–4
Family chose contractor's plan	385,000	3.4	H4
House acquired from previous occupants	642,000	29.0	H4–5
Architect-designed, contractor-built	710,000	5.3	H4–5
Private developer on speculation	927,000	4.8	H5
Other	100,000	0.5	—
Total	417,000	100.0	H0–H5

— Few observations.
Source: Cartagena household survey, 1978.

Lack of piped water and sanitary facilities consisting of a latrine or nothing clearly put a dwelling in one of the lowest value categories, H0 or H1 (Table 5-8). The basic (H3) or intermediate (H4) categories generally had a sewer-connected toilet or a septic tank and a rudimentary or complete bathroom with piped water. Multiple bathrooms and toilets would usually be found in dwellings worth more than 1 million pesos (US$25,600).

Table 5-7. *Number of Rooms and Value of Owner-Occupied Housing*
(*N* = 220)

Number of rooms	Average value (pesos)	Percentage of total	Change in value	Percentage change
1	36,000	2.7	—	—
2	73,000	5.9	37,000	103
3	182,000	27.7	109,000	149
4	364,000	29.1	182,000	100
5	473,000	14.5	109,000	30
6	616,000	11.4	143,000	30
6+	1,350,000	8.6	—	—
Total/average	417,000	100.0	—	95

— Not applicable.
Source: Cartagena household survey, 1978.

Table 5-8. *Source of Water, Sanitary Facilities,*
and Value of Owner-Occupied Housing, 1978
(N = 219)

Item	Percentage of total	Value of housing (pesos)
Source of water		
Neighbor sells	24.7	80,900
Faucet without shower	11.0	179,000
Shower only	20.5	275,000
Complete bathroom	22.8	403,000
Multiple bathrooms	15.5	1,450,000
Other	5.5	97,000
Sanitary facilities		
None	15.1	49,000
Latrine	17.4	132,000
Septic tank	29.2	410,000
Connected toilet	26.5	361,000
Multiple connected	9.6	1,700,000
Other	2.3	123,000

Note: Five households shared a faucet with another family; four used a public standpipe; and three received water from a water wagon. Two families shared a toilet with others. F = 27.6 for water sources, and F = 28.1 for sanitary alternatives.
Source: Cartagena household survey, 1978.

The association of various characteristics with value can be seen in more detail in Table 5-9. Row 3 shows that 95.8 percent of owners in dwellings worth 40,000 pesos or less bought water from a neighbor and that this percentage gradually diminished to 0 in dwellings worth over 640,000 pesos—all of which had piped water. Nearly 80 percent of lowest-value, owned housing had no toilet or latrine and was made of wood or impermanent, inferior materials. It is not that H0 housing turned out to be like this, but, rather, that these are the characteristics that define H0 housing: worst water and sanitary conditions, worst materials, and fewest kitchens. The 40,001 to 80,000 peso range is called substandard (H1) because in this range there were latrines, many more kitchens, and substantially better materials. Beyond 80,000 pesos, piped water and septic tanks predominated, inferior materials were phased out, and dwellings had reached the minimal level. At the basic level of more than 160,000 pesos, piped water was common, public sewer system connections predominated, and inferior materials were rare. Septic tanks were the only shortcoming of a substantial number of dwellings in the highest two categories, but if the sewerage lines had not come through, most owners could do nothing about that.

The coincidence of value ranges with physical characteristics occurred because site value did not seem to vary independently, as already discussed in Chapter 4. The main exception was the Pie de la Popa–Bazurto area because of the new municipal market and expanded transport

Table 5-9. *Percentage of Dwellings with Various Characteristics in Different Value Categories*

Characteristic	Value category					
	H0	H1	H2	H3	H4	H5
Value (pesos)	0–40,000	40,001–80,000	80,001–160,000	160,001–320,000	320,001–640,000	640,001+
Monthly rent (pesos)	0–500	501–1,000	1,001–2,000	2,001–4,000	4,001+	—
Water bought from or shared with neighbors	95.8 (80.0)	69.0 (31.6)	30.6 (0)	12.5 (0)	3.1 (0)	0 —
Have piped water	0 (20.0)	2.7 (68.4)	66.7 (100.0)	87.5 (100.0)	96.9 (100.0)	100.0 —
No toilet	79.2 (36.4)	31.0 (5.3)	11.1 (0)	1.6 (0)	0 (0)	0 —
Latrine	16.7 (36.4)	44.8 (47.4)	22.2 (0)	18.8 (0)	3.1 (0)	0 —
Septic tank	4.2 (9.1)	13.8 (31.6)	47.2 (76.9)	26.6 (28.6)	46.9 (0)	29.4 —
Connected to public sewer system	0 (0)	10.3 (10.5)	13.9 (23.1)	53.01 (71.5)	43.17 (100.0)	67.6 —
Have own kitchen	33.3 (45.5)	69.0 (84.2)	83.8 (92.3)	92.2 (92.9)	96.9 (100.0)	97.1 —
Walls made of wood, metal sheets, or impermanent materials	79.2 (54.5)	37.9 (22.2)	13.5 (0)	4.7 (0)	0 (0)	0 —
Roof made of wood, metal sheets, or impermanent materials	25.2 (36.4)	13.8 (21.1)	5.4 (0)	3.1 (0)	0 (0)	0 —

— Not applicable.

Note: For owner-occupied dwellings $N = 219$; for rental dwellings $N = 65$. Percentages for rental housing are given in parentheses.

Source: Cartagena household survey, 1978.

routes. About 1,000 households lived in this section, a part of the Manga district, which in turn was part of the Coastal Zone. It represented less than 2 percent of the Cartagena population.

Amount and Value of Space

The typical dwelling in Cartagena had 100 square meters of space divided into four rooms plus kitchen and washroom. As can be seen in Tables 5-10 and 5-11, three-quarters of smaller dwellings had at least 50 square meters of space and were divided into three rooms. Around 11 percent of the stock consisted of one- and two-room dwellings with less than 50 square meters. At the other end of the scale, less than a quarter of the housing stock had a floor space of more than 200 square meters or more than five rooms.

As the tables show, these distributions varied with the type of tenure. Owner-occupied houses without mortgages were the largest in size, with 27 percent of these having areas of 200 square meters or more, and 25 percent having six or more rooms. Nearly half of mortgaged dwellings were in the 50 to 99 square-meter range, reflecting primarily the sort of structure that ICT was selling. By the time the mortgage would be paid off, many of these dwellings would be considerably larger.

Rental units were typically somewhat larger than owner-occupied housing that was new enough to be still under amortization. Only 30.7 percent of rental dwellings were less than 100 square meters, compared

Table 5-10. *Amount of Floor Space, by Type of Tenure*
(percent)

Floor space (square meters)	Owner-occupied		Rented (N = 62)	Other (N = 20)	All (N = 284)
	With mortgage (N = 52)	No mortgage (N = 150)			
1–49	13.5	10.7	11.3	15.0	11.6
50–99	46.2	34.7	19.4	40.0	33.8
100–149	11.5	16.0	27.4	10.0	17.3
150–199	15.4	11.3	17.7	10.0	13.4
200–299	11.5	14.0	16.1	10.0	13.7
300+	1.9	13.3	8.1	15.0	10.2
Total	100.0	100.0	100.0	100.0	100.0

Source: Cartagena household survey, 1978.

Table 5-11. *Number of Rooms, by Type of Tenure*
(percent)

Number of rooms	With mortgage (N = 53)	No mortgage (N = 154)	Rented (N = 65)	Other (N = 21)	All (N = 293)
1	0	3.9	1.5	4.8	2.7
2	9.4	4.5	16.9	9.5	8.5
3	32.1	24.7	26.2	33.3	27.0
4	32.1	27.9	30.8	33.3	29.7
5	17.0	13.6	9.2	14.3	13.3
6	5.7	14.3	7.7	4.8	10.6
6+	3.8	11.0	7.7	0	8.2
Total	100.0	100.0	100.0	100.0	100.0

Source: Cartagena household survey, 1978.

with 48.6 percent for all others. Only 8.1 percent reached 300 square meters, however, compared with 15.3 percent for the owner-occupied dwellings without a mortgage. Only 24.6 percent of rental dwellings had five or more rooms compared with 34.2 percent for all others.

Not only did the amount of space matter, but also its quality or value per square meter. Type of plumbing, location, and a large number of other factors helped to determine this value. The average value per square meter of owner-occupied housing was 3,491 pesos (standard error 418 pesos). New ICT housing sold for about 3,900 pesos per square meter if it was minimal or basic and for 6,000 if it was intermediate. Value of the 1978 housing stock per square meter, by income group, was

Monthly income (pesos)	Value per square meter (pesos)
0– 2,000	986
2,001– 4,000	1,462
4,001– 8,000	2,089
8,001–16,000	3,573
16,001–32,000	9,653
32,000+	17,333

Hedonic Analysis

A hedonic price index was estimated to determine how much indoor piped water and other elements contributed to value of owner-occupied housing (Table 5-12).[1] The thirteen explanatory variables were often correlated with one another but most of all with water. More than any other variable, water was correlated with floor space, number of rooms, a kitchen, sanitary facilities, adequate roofing, and superior walls. Insofar as a line of causation from one variable to others existed, it was from water to better materials and fixtures. One did not install these and then hope for the water authorities to follow through. On the contrary, one

Table 5-12. *Determinants of Dwelling Value:*
Hedonic Regression Coefficients

	Coefficients	
Variable	*Value (pesos)*	*Log value*
Age of dwelling	4,771	−0.00023
	(4,174)	(0.0055)
Neighborhood desirability	147,300	0.430[b]
	(160,500)	(0.210)
Area of the lot	1,183	0.00045
	(339)	(0.00044)
Floor space	−1,216	0.00069
	(627)	(0.00082)
Number of rooms (logs)	453,000[a]	0.768[a]
	(152,000)	(0.198)
Kitchen	15,500	0.153
	(133,000)	(0.173)
Permanent roofing	−119,900	−0.304
	(228,000)	(0.298)
Good wall materials	−54,900	0.521[b]
	(177,000)	(0.232)
Latrine	−79,300	0.428[b]
	(149,000)	(0.195)
Septic tank	6,880	0.581[b]
	(188,000)	(0.246)
Sewerage system, one toilet	140,900	0.755[a]
	(192,000)	(0.251)
Sewerage system, multiple toilets	1,032,000[a]	1.543[a]
	(239,000)	(0.313)
Indoor piped water	104,000	0.689[a]
	(154,000)	(0.207)
Constant	−527,700[b]	9.179[a]
	(253,000)	(0.332)
Adjusted R^2	0.448	0.692
F statistic	10.74	28.01
Number of observations	157	157

Note: The standard errors are given in parentheses. $1.00 = 39$ pesos.
a. Statistical significance of 0.01.
b. Statistical significance of 0.05.
Source: Cartagena household survey, 1978.

might have installed one's own well and then discouraged the coming of public utilities and extra charges.

The coefficient for indoor piped water in column 1 of the table suggests that it always added 104,000 pesos to the value of a house, but this figure lacks statistical significance. The coefficient based on a logarithmic regression in column 2 becomes highly significant, however, and implies that water nearly doubled the value of a dwelling, say, from 80,000 to 159,000 pesos or from 160,000 to 319,000 pesos. Alternatively, it seems plausible that a million-peso dwelling would lose nearly half its value if the occupants had to carry water in lard cans.

If a 160,000-peso (US$4,100) dwelling switched from a latrine to a septic tank, its value rose by 16.5 percent to 186,400 pesos. Connection to a public sewerage system and installation of one toilet would raise the value by a further 19.0 percent to 220,000 pesos. But if the neighborhood was undesirable (that is, settled by families with lower incomes), then value would be 35 percent less. Inferior wall materials would cost a dwelling 41 percent of its value. Important as they are, these factors did not matter as much as piped water. The stock-user matrixes of Appendix C present more detail on housing characteristics and their association with value and the income of occupants.

Housing Eradication

In the early 1960s social housing had to meet rather extravagant standards despite economic realities. The typical Blas de Lezo house had three large rooms besides the kitchen and bathroom, making a total floor space of 120 square meters. A cost of 40,000 pesos in 1963 made them equivalent to an intermediate (H4) 360,000-peso (US$9,200) house in 1978.

In those years the way to convert and to upgrade a slum was to eradicate all the huts and to start over. The case of Chambacú has been mentioned several times in this study. Over several decades 4,000 squatter households had made their own land during the dry season by filling in the lagoon between the Fortress of San Felipe and the business district of La Matuna. In 1965 the first squatters were removed to create space for the broad Avenida Don Pedro de Heredia. They were paid a mere 500 pesos (worth 3,600 in 1978, or US$92) for their lost improvements. No equivalent housing could be obtained for less than twenty times that compensation.

As the idea of removing the entire eyesore caught on, opposition became vehement, as might be expected in a democracy. Compensation for squatters was raised to the value of a serviced site at an alternative location plus a 1.0 percent, twenty-year ICT loan with no down payment for a minimal house. Owners were given 42-square-meter houses with bathrooms in Chiquinquirá or La Republica de Venezuela or an indemnity of 20,000 pesos (1978 US$2,200). A survey of 1,509 households remaining in Chambacú was made to determine who needed what and who could afford what. But incomes were unpredictable, and some households lost their new dwellings when they failed to keep up payments.

The reluctance to move was great; but after several false starts, the eradication process went smoothly during 1970–73. Band music accompanied the demolition. Holdouts were allowed to stay in huts here and there, but trucks moved in and dumped vast amounts of fill to be shoved around by bulldozers. The holdouts therefore found themselves in disagreeable, possibly unsafe holes. The Chambacú eradication, although nonviolent, was nevertheless so traumatic and costly that it was not repeated. On the contrary, ICT is in charge of redeveloping the Southeast Zone without extensive demolitions. As fear of being evicted faded throughout the city, poor access to water remained the principal inhibition to self-help improvement. According to present regulations, eviction of squatters is difficult after a month of occupancy. During 1978–80 more squatters appeared on the back of La Popa, in the Lomas (Nuevo Bosque) Zone, in the Outskirts at La Ternera and at Policarpa Zalabrieta on the road to Pasacaballos, behind the ICT development of El Socorro, in the Southeast Zone, and at the former country club where they were evicted.

From time to time, eviction and demolition nevertheless remain necessary as space is reallocated from one use to another in the public interest. As one of his last official acts, on July 24, 1978, President López Michelsen laid the cornerstone for the International Convention Center on the site of the former Public Market of Getsemaní. Everything had been cleared except for La Carbonera, eighteen squatter shacks of former charcoal sellers, built partly on the quays of Playa del Arsenal and partly on posts in the bay. These families refused to move.

In February 1978, the Department of Municipal Public Works informed the families that their shacks would be demolished after June 30. In July all of them were still there. They were told that on Sunday morning, August 13, bulldozers and troops would clear them out.

When we arrived on the site shortly before 8:00 AM that day, the process of clearing was under way. Some fifty troops with clubs and white arm bands loitered in the shade of buildings on one side of the street, and a bulldozer was knocking down a shack on the other, raising a cloud of dust. The heat was like midday.

Down the street men and boys were dismantling metal and asbestos cement sheets from roofs. Supporting lumber, aluminum pans, and other household goods were being loaded on small trucks. Occasionally a trooper crossed the street and exchanged a few words with some head of a family. Everything went slowly in the heat but without trouble. The most pitiful, windowless shacks of some old couples were passed by. Dogs slept in the dust, chickens scratched for food in clumps of weeds, and children played as if nothing were happening. Perhaps it was like that at Chambacú.

Housing Construction by ICT

The most reliable figures on new construction costs come from ICT, although these include the contractor's profits. Data from DANE (the national census department) and CAMACOL (the national chamber of the construction industry) are sometimes contradictory. A reconciled series on costs is published by a National Center for Construction Studies (CENAC). Some of the data from all these sources are presented here.

Minimal (H2), basic (H3), and intermediate (H4) ICT houses were within the ranges of values just given for those categories (Table 4-13). Unfinished two-room minimal houses were sold for around 125,000 pesos (US$3,200). Some had an extra room or extra land that raised their value by 20 percent. Basic units were sold for about 200,000 pesos (US$5,100), and intermediate ones for 500,000 (US$12,800). The luxury units planned for Chambacú were to be sold for twice that, adjusted for inflation. But these sales prices included ICT markups that ranged from 3 to 50 percent, which the buyer was willing to pay to get the financing and a variety of locational advantages. Construction cost and value are not the same thing.

For building a minimal house, contractors in 1977–78 charged ICT around 2,000 pesos (US$51) per square meter. When construction resumed in 1980 after a two-year financial crisis caused by the decapitalization of ICT because of inflation, costs had nearly doubled. A basic house cost 2,500 pesos (US$65) in 1978, and an intermediate one 3,200 pesos (US$83) per square meter. Floor space increased from 34 to 57 to 83 square meters for the three types. Lot sizes increased from 70 to 150 square meters from minimal to intermediate, and their square-meter cost went from 60 to 95 pesos. The site improvement cost of 380 to 500 pesos per square meter had to be added, but that cost depended more on the type of terrain than on the type of structure to be built. Altogether the lot cost ranged from 35,000 to 70,000 pesos in 1977–78. For minimal houses this amounted to around 40 percent of the total cost, for the basic units 30 percent, and for the intermediate units 20 percent.

The layout of minimal ICT houses can be shown with some cases from Las Gaviotas and El Bosque. In the fourth stage of Las Gaviotas, 202 40-square-meter units with three rooms were built on 81-square-meter lots. Lots were 9 meters wide, and houses had three equal rooms side by side along the front, with one set back a little to allow for a terrace. Behind the middle room were the kitchen and bathroom, back to back. Behind the other two rooms, occupants could build expansions.

Since buyers complained about back-to-back kitchens and toilets, given the irregularity of water and possibility of a stench, some later ICT houses such as Nuevo Bosque type A avoided this arrangement. A 5.7-square-meter room was on one side of the lot, and an 11-square-meter room was on the other, but set back substantially. The bathroom was behind the forward room, and the kitchen was behind the other. Additions could be made behind the bathroom or in front of the large set-back room. Details of this unit are given in Table 4-14.

Since water is expected to flow regularly everywhere when worn-out pipes have been replaced and connected to the new reservoirs, back-to-back kitchen and toilets should cease to be objectionable. For the Los Calamares development, ICT planned minimal houses that consisted of such a combination on the side of a single 11.7-square-meter room. The total was a 20-square-meter dwelling that could have one 7.7-square-meter room added in back and another in front. Without the ICT markup, cost of the initial units would have been around 78,000 (1978) pesos (US$2,000), including the lot (72-square-meters at 32,000 pesos). Only the poorest quarter of households, those receiving less than 4,000 pesos monthly, would have been unable to afford this unit. By the time ground was finally broken for these units in November 1980, costs had doubled, but ICT planned to quadruple prices as an inflation hedge.

What large families with varied cultural backgrounds will accept and expand cannot, however, be easily foreseen. For example, communal washing and sanitary facilities in the middle of a cluster of half a dozen small houses was unacceptable in Cartagena. Houses could be designed to allow friendly interaction with neighbors on the street side, but privacy was demanded for backyard patios, no matter how small. ICT officials in Cartagena felt that their effectiveness rose substantially after 1974 when they were given more control over housing design.

Housing Construction by Other Developers

Apart from ICT, which controlled approximately one-quarter of the licensed residential construction, both licensed and unlicensed developers were active in Cartagena. The unlicensed ranged from squatters to builders in unapproved subdivisions. They did not generate statistics as readily as the municipal license bureau. Table 5-13 shows the breakdown of licensed housing construction in Cartagena in 1976 and 1977.

Table 5-13. *Licensed Housing Construction in Cartagena, 1976 and 1977*

Variable	1976	1977
Number of licenses, by square meters of floor space (Value, in thousands of pesos, in parentheses)		
0–75	38	45
	(6,180)	(14,922)
76–150	70	59
	(12,912)	(13,863)
151–225	24	34
	(7,115)	(13,942)
226–300	10	18
	(4,184)	(10,486)
301–500	25	25
	(15,854)	(20,919)
501–1,000	16	17
	(19,132)	(29,590)
1,000+	16	26
	(91,433)	(190,209)
Area of site (square meters)	138,917	195,357
Floor space built (square meters)		
Total	100,239	125,025
One-story	23,666	27,913
Two-story	39,534	60,148
Three-story	12,718	13,500
Four or more stories	24,316	23,464
Type of construction licenses		
New	130	160
Expansion	63	42
Remodeling	6	22
Total budget (millions of pesos)	156.8	293.9
Public loans: ICT, BCH, and so forth	14.5	78.3
Commercial banks or institutos financieros	31.8	74.4
Private loans	1.1	15.2
Nonprofit loans	3.8	.3
Owners' investment	109.2	125.7

Note: In 1978 1 peso of Cartagena construction equalled 0.7179 of a 1977 peso and 0.5685 of a 1976 peso.

Source: DANE unpublished, preliminary figures.

Table 5-14. *Price Inflators for Housing Construction
and Annual Increases in Construction Costs,
Cartagena, 1971 to 1977, and Barranquilla, 1954 to 1972*

Year	Price inflator	Annual increase in construction cost (percent)
1977	1.393	39.3
1976	1.759	26.3
1975	2.380	35.3
1974	3.030	27.3
1973	3.730	23.1
1972	4.249	13.9
1971	4.712	10.1(10.9)
1970	5.094	8.1
1969	5.394	5.9
1968	5.691	5.5
1967	6.072	6.7
1966	6.685	10.1
1965	7.260	8.6
1964	8.139	12.1
1963	8.953	10.0
1962	10.842	21.1
1961	11.752	8.4
1960	12.575	7.0
1959	13.304	5.8
1958	14.581	9.6
1957	15.354	5.3
1956	17.642	14.9
1955	17.183	−2.6
1954	17.338	.9

Sources: For 1972–77, Centro Nacional de Estudios de la Construcción (CENAC), *La Construcción en Cifras* (Bogotá, January 1977, October 1977, February 1978, and May 1978; processed). The April–June 1978 price rise was estimated to be equal to that of October 1977–March 1978. CENAC cost estimates are a reconciliation of those of DANE, the national statistical institute, and CAMACOL, the chamber of construction. For 1954–72 the DANE cost series for worker's housing in Barranquilla was used. Costs in these two Caribbean ports did not always move in proportion, but the rates are probably close enough. In 1971–72 costs in Cartagena rose by 10.1 percent and costs in Barranquilla by 10.9 percent. In 1954–71 the cost of workers' housing rose by 268.2 percent and that of employees' housing by 270.9 percent, or 1 percent faster. Afterward employee housing costs rose faster by 12.4 percent (a growth rate one-eighth higher), probably because of the introduction of the UPAC indexing system of finance for this group. The DANE statistics appear in *Indice de Precios* (Bogotá, 1977).

Owners were the most important source of investment funds and provided 69.6 percent in 1976 and 42.8 percent in 1977. Two-story houses were the most important category (accounting for 48 percent of the total floor space). Apartments with four and more stories (18.8 percent) were almost as important as single-story houses (22.3 percent). In both 1976 and 1977 the most licenses were given for dwellings between 76 and 150 square meters, but more was spent on apartment buildings, mostly in Bocagrande, with over 1,000 square meters allocated among separate units.

Apart from the large number of small contractors and individual laborers working on their own account, all this construction was carried out by seventy-three construction firms that in 1976 employed an average of thirty-three workers. In the leaner years of 1975, 1977, and 1978 about half the workers were laid off.

Housing construction costs rose after 1976, and the average compound cost increase for 1973–78 was 30.1 percent annually, as may be seen in Table 5-14. During the preceding five years, the average increase was only 8.8 percent. Throughout this period construction prices lagged behind costs in other economic sectors.

Inflation and Relative Price Changes

During the 1970s construction costs rose at a much lower rate than the general rate of inflation—a pattern that had begun in the 1950s. With 1954–55 as the base, by December 1969 the national housing cost index for workers was 394.0 compared with a general level of 437.1. By June 1977 the workers' housing cost index was 1,188, and the general workers' cost of living index was 1,843. On the Atlantic coast the difference was even more pronounced. Here the general index had reached 1,886 for Barranquilla, or double that of housing with 945. The pattern will not be analyzed in detail here. An important factor is that construction was a competitive labor-intensive activity, which used local materials that were also made by labor-intensive activity.

In Cartagena, housing costs reached an index level of about 370 (1970 = 100) in mid-1978, much less than the (Barranquilla) workers' cost of living index of 655. The index for construction labor reached only 363, as may be seen in Table 5-15. The concrete blocks used in workers' housing rose only to 348, but the clay bricks used for better middle-class housing rose to 605. A relative shortage of bricks had been created by the shift in finance to the price-indexed Corporaciones de Ahorro y Vivienda.[2] Plumbing, finishes, electrical fixtures, and cement (including asbestos ce-

Table 5-15. *Index of Housing Construction Costs for Three Basic Housing Types, May 1978*
(January–December 1971 = 100)

Cost category	Commercial, 162 square meters, three baths	Intermediate, 75 square meters, one bath	Basic, 48 square meters, one bath
Materials	401.9	374.7	360.0
Aggregate	242.0	242.6	242.2
Cement	401.6	401.6	401.6
Electrical fixtures and wiring	367.3	382.9	381.2
Bricks or concrete blocks	604.8	347.6	347.6
Wood products	360.6	477.1	360.6
Plumbing	378.1	378.1	378.1
Roofing	344.0	379.0	404.6
Bathroom fixtures	283.6	285.6	274.0
Finishes	475.1	475.1	475.1
Labor	363.4	363.4	363.4
Foreman or master	330.8	330.8	330.8
Skilled worker	335.2	335.2	335.2
Unskilled worker	396.0	396.0	396.0

Source: DANE, unpublished data, 1978.

ment roofing) also rose faster than construction wages. Cement aggregates, wood products (doors), and bathroom fixtures rose at a lower rate. According to DANE, the incomes of less-skilled workers rose faster than those of more-skilled workers. Since the materials index for minimal houses was about the same level as the construction workers' wage index, this type of housing did not become relatively more costly for those who built them.

Construction and Employment

Little is known about the effects of construction on employment because the contractors do not keep records of the number of people employed. Large builders may hire as many as 60 percent of their workers because they are big enough for vertical integration, but the small builders in residential construction hire only 30 percent of the workers needed. The rest are hired by a series of subcontractors who bid for some component of each structure. Needless to say, that proportion varies from week to week and from project to project, and the contractors do not themselves know what the proportion is.[3]

Special surveys and analyses are needed to estimate employment in construction. Employment generation in low-cost housing in Medellín and in Lima, Peru, was studied by Norma L. Botero and the author in 1979 and 1980. Results are discussed below. Another study of construction costs and employment was made by the National Planning Department in 1971. Comparisons were made of costs of 90-square-meter housing with given intermediate-level specifications but different densities: single-family, four- to five-story apartments, and thirty-story high-rises. The results are given in Table 5-16.

According to this study, single-family housing generated only 62 percent as much employment per square meter as four- to five-story apartments and 46 percent as much as high-rises. But per peso of construction cost, which is what really matters, single-family housing generated 12 percent more than the four- to five-story apartments and 21 percent morethan the high-rises. Since apartments cost from 50 to 100 percent more than single-family dwellings but generate less employment, they can be justified only by a great need to conserve land through higher densities, a need that will be expressed in high land prices. Low-rise apartments become preferable when the price of land rises above 45 percent of combined lot-and-house costs, and land prices must nearly quadruple before high-rise use is competitive.

The share of labor costs in selected dwelling components can be seen in Table 5-17. The greatest increases in labor intensity in single-family, compared with multifamily, housing were in the foundations, the roof,

Table 5-16. *Residential Construction Costs and Employment*

Item	Single family	Four to five stories	Thirty stories	Core house, 19.5 square meters
Construction cost per square meter (1978 pesos)	4,200	6,100	8,500	5,060
Labor costs per square meter (1978 pesos)	1,205	1,568	2,023	1,361
Labor costs as a percentage of construction costs	28.7	25.7	23.8	26.9
Man-hours per square meter	18	29	39	45

Source: Departamento Nacional de Planeación, *Posibilidades de Reducción de Costos de Edificación*, vol. 2 (Bogotá, November 1972), pp. 202–11 and Table 5-18, below.

Table 5-17. *Share of Labor Costs in Costs of Selected Components of Dwellings, Colombia, 1971*
(percent)

Component	Single family		Multifamily		
	1 story	2 stories	4–5 stories	12 stories	30 stories
Foundations	30	35	30	10	15
Structural framework	—	28	25	20	20
Masonry	35	35	35	35	40
Roof	25	20	20	15	—
Floors and closets	25	25	25	20	19
Plumbing	20	25	25	25	25
Carpentry and fixtures	15	12	12	10	10
Total cost	31.5	31.4	29.7	26.8	25.8

— Not applicable.
Source: Departamento Nacional de Planeación, *Posibilidades de Reducción de Costos de Edificación,* vol 2 (Bogotá, November 1972), table 6.6.

and carpentry. In addition, walls could be built of labor-intensive, load-bearing masonry, not a capital-intensive, steel-reinforced framework.

The 1977 study by the Colombian Chamber of Construction found that the share of labor in direct costs was 22 percent for single-family housing and 23 percent in multifamily housing. Per 1,000 square meters of construction, an isolated house generated nineteen man-years of construction labor, that is, 1.5 years for an 80-square-meter dwelling. The same 1,000 square meters would yield only seven man-years in multi-unit developments, about 0.56 of a man-year per apartment. Per 1,000 square meters, projects of less than 200 square meters generated thirty man-years, and larger ones thirteen man-years. One out of eleven construction workers would be off the site in an administrative job. For every three workers in construction, the chamber estimated that two others would be employed making materials.

This proportion is about the same as that found elsewhere. Materials had a labor intensity of about one-fifth if the labor content of inputs into the materials was added. In Mexico the labor share of materials costs was stable, at around 22 percent. Since materials make up a larger share of more expensive and multifamily, multistory dwellings, more indirect labor is also required for such buildings. In single-family basic housing it was 12.1 percent of structural cost, and in luxury housing it was 15.5 percent. In low-cost four- to five-story apartments, it was 12.8 percent; and in high-rise luxury apartments, 17 percent.[4] In Peru, Rufino Cebrecos Revilla found that indirect employment was 28 percent of total employment in low-cost single-story housing and 35 percent in good housing or in ten-story apartments. Nevertheless, total employment for a given expenditure would be 18 percent less in high-rise buildings.[5] In Rio de Janeiro the author found indirect employment equal to 18 percent of employment in minimal 33-square-meter housing, and equal to 21 percent in eight-story apartments. Once more the apartments failed to generate more employment.[6] No doubt the pattern was similar in Colombia.

Among the on-site workers, 48.4 percent were reported as unskilled workers. Among the skilled workers 43.4 percent were *oficiales*, and 8.2 percent were highly skilled workers and supervisors (*maestros* and *capaces*). Eighty percent were masons.[7]

In connection with later research in Medellín, a building firm was asked to estimate the cost and employment implied by one of the Expandable Core House plans proposed by ict for the Calamares development in Cartagena. The results are shown in Table 5-18. The dwelling had exterior dimensions of 6 by 3.25 meters or 19.5 square meters. It was built with concrete blocks on a slab, had a reinforced concrete collar beam, and a slanted roof of corrugated asbestos cement sheets. Two-thirds of the floor space consisted of a multiple-use room with a door to the street and another toward the back. The rest of the space was divided between a kitchen and a bathroom with toilet and shower. There was a washbasin outside the bathroom, a sink in the kitchen, and a laundry tub outside the kitchen window. The four windows had open concrete work, not glass. Plans showed how two rooms can be added at ground level to double the floor space.

A contractor estimated that this dwelling would cost 106,300 pesos in 1979 (US$2,530) if 100 units were built (this amounts to about US$2,000 at 1978 prices and exchange rates). If only one unit were built, cost would be 12 percent higher, and 7 percent more jobs would be created. There would be fourteen more workdays per unit in labor-intensive site preparation for one unit than for 100, but other components would require eight extra workdays per unit for the larger volume, a total of 109. The main findings were that labor costs made up one-quarter of the total (including the builder's off-site costs), that the shell cost 57 percent, and that it provided two-thirds of the employment (see Table 5-18). At the unskilled wage rate of about 168 pesos (US$4) daily, it would be economical to mechanize site clearing but not excavation and trenching for 100 units. The wage difference of from 66 to 200 percent for skills in Medellín was very high; nevertheless, apart from excavation, only about one unskilled man (or less) was used with each skilled one in all other activities.

Table 5-18. Employment and Cost to Build a 19.5-Square-Meter Expandable House, by Component

Component	Cost (U.S. dollars)	Percentage distribution of cost	Share of labor in costs	Ratio of skilled to unskilled wages	Unskilled employed per skilled worker	Employment (workdays)
Site preparation	89 (88)	3.5 (3.1)	0.135 (0.750)	3.0 (2.174)	1.0 (0.20)	1.5 (15.1)
Excavation and trenching	40 (42)	1.6 (1.5)	0.594 (0.538)	1.666	15.0	5.7 (5.4)
Shell	1,455 (1,628)	57.5 (57.4)	0.324 (0.273)	2.735	1.230	66.3 (62.5)
Carpentry	458 (537)	18.1 (18.9)	0.135 (0.109)	2.608	1.00	8.6 (8.1)
Painting	96 (104)	3.8 (3.7)	0.475 (0.417)	2.608	.20	7.4 (7.1)
Plumbing	251 (282)	9.9 (10.0)	0.298 (0.250)	1.856	.60	12.1 (11.5)
Electrical	140 (157)	5.5 (5.5)	0.295 (0.250)	1.790	1.00	7.4 (7.0)
Total	2,530 (2,838)	100.0 (100.0)	0.269 (0.263)	2.438 (2.432)	1.112 (1.406)	109.0 (116.7)

Note: Estimates are per unit at a volume of 100 units. Estimates for single units are in parentheses if different.
Source: The floor plan and specifications for this dwelling were provided by the ICT office of Cartagena. The plan was to be used in the Calamares development. Cost estimates were made by a construction firm in Medellín and were collected by Norma Botero. The extent to which the estimates apply to Cartagena is uncertain.

The more detailed unpublished study of costs in Lima, Peru, by the author and Norma Botero in 1980 showed how costs and employment per square meter rose from 45-square-meter minimal H2 housing to 75-square-meter basic H3 housing and more. Costs rose from US$56 to US$71 per square meter. On-site employment rose from 3.6 to 4.2 work-days per square meter. In H5 luxury housing costs reached US$100 per square meter and generated 5.5 workdays for each. The proportions in Cartagena did not appear much different: US$51 and US$77 per square meter for minimal and intermediate housing, respectively. Without a survey of contractors, employment estimates could not be made.

Total employment in Cartagena construction could double or fall by half, and when times were bad workers tended to move to the interior and to Venezuela. Shortages were noticeable only during the beginning of construction booms, before the word got around. The national apprenticeship service (SENA) had three or four instructors in construction skills in Cartagena, but officials felt that the sector was too unstable and that rises in productivity merely benefited the contractor because wages would not rise as a result. The best newly trained workers would be enticed away by Venezuelan recruiting agencies and would not benefit the local economy directly. SENA preferred training people for more stable and lucrative careers. They found that construction workers and unskilled labor made up 15 percent of employed workers in Esperanza (district 7) and earned only 1,800 pesos monthly, which was the lowest wage except for domestic servants.

In our sample, 6.8 percent of household heads were in construction, which is close to the 6.5 percent reported for 1975 (Table 2-1). In this mini-sample of twenty, the least skilled earned less than 2,000 pesos and made ends meet only with aid from some absent family members and with money from street peddling and petty trade by other family members. Skilled and relatively fully employed masons and painters earned from 3,400 to 4,500 pesos monthly. Two small contractors earned 7,000 and 8,500 pesos monthly. These incomes should be compared with the 11,000 earned by skilled electricians with nonconstruction firms. Construction was indeed a low-paid sector, and no doubt that feature helped keep it labor-intensive and lagging behind other sectors in cost inflation.

That the labor-intensity of construction cannot be taken for granted may be illustrated by the experience of Peru. In that country militant unions were effective in gaining benefits and having them enforced. During 1955–67, daily earnings rose 14.6 percent a year compared with 8.7 percent for both construction materials and the consumer price index, or 9.1 percent for the GNP deflator. By 1967 unskilled construction workers received 40 percent more than unskilled workers in manufacturing. But skilled construction workers legally received only 7 percent more than the unskilled by the late 1970s by law, but perhaps 30 percent more in reality. A comparatively high degree of mechanization and substitution of skilled for unskilled workers held back employment. Because of labor-saving changes during 1955–67, construction costs rose only 9.3 percent, not 11.3 percent.[8] In a detailed analysis of cost estimates for building two types of identical 24.9-square-meter core houses in six developing countries in 1979, the author found that doubling wages eventually lowered employment by nearly half.[9] The pattern applied to the structure as a whole and to all principal components (such as the roof, plumbing, and so forth) separately. Elasticities of labor-nonlabor substitution were between 0.5 and 1.0.

Innovations in Building Materials

In Cartagena, as elsewhere in Colombia, the houses of the rich were likely to be built out of hollow clay bricks, or, in the case of apartments, reinforced concrete. Cost-oriented innovations were more likely to involve the concrete blocks used in houses for the poor.

Concrete blocks when properly mixed and cured should have a strength of 350 pounds per square inch. The price of a 4-inch block in Cartagena was slightly above 5 pesos in 1978, and there was some resistance to paying more. Consequently architects noted a tendency to adulterate the mixture with an excessive amount of sand, so that a strength of 80 pounds per square inch was more typical of blocks made on a small scale with aluminum forms and manual pressure. Blocks from a new factory, founded by a company based in Medellín, were more dependable and not more expensive considering the reduction in waste from more regular blocks.

For emergency use, some twenty-seven dwellings were built out of asbestos sheets in the village of Zambrano in 1972 when the Magdalena flooded; but, though cheap and quickly built, these "Colombit" houses were not likely to find wider use in the tropical climate, according to architects. In effect, they competed with refuse and bamboo. Light concrete panels have also been tried without spectacular effects in the district República de Chile and at Las Gaviotas.

More significant have been the houses that glue concrete blocks together by painting them with a mixture of sulfur, talc, glass or asbestos fiber, and dicyclopentadine, a process developed by the Southwest Research Institute of San Antonio, Texas, and sponsored by AID.

ICT first built forty such houses in the República de Chile section and then another thirty-nine in Las Gaviotas during June 1976 to December

1977. The strength of the sulfur mixture meant that architects had to be less concerned about possible losses in stability when people changed walls in rearranging their dwellings. After the earthquake of 1975 only the sulfur houses were without cracks in República de Chile. Cracks had appeared in some Gaviotas houses, but apparently these were primarily in the poor-quality blocks. A special advantage of the sulfur design is that blocks can be joined easily to make ceiling beams that otherwise would cost as much as 20 percent of the structure.

When blocks are merely laid one on the other without mortar, irregularities may occasionally call for small wedges. Architects who have supervised the two projects estimated that the cost of a structure could be reduced by one-quarter by painting the mortarless block walls with sulfur. In addition, the resulting structure is more stable and waterproof. Nevertheless, the process will depend on the continued availability at competitive prices of the key ingredients, especially fuel. Moreover, requirements for the proper 150-degree-centigrade temperature call for better supervision. A cooler temperature may mean a less spreadable mixture, and higher heat may make the material too sticky, possibly impairing structural quality. Working with the heat and unpleasant odors is disagreeable but not dangerous and had led to no organized opposition among workers. The real problem was that the skills involved are somewhat unusual and therefore such workers were more likely to be lured to Venezuela.

It is still too early to assess the potential of the sulfur bonding as a replacement for mortar and reinforced ceiling beams. Perhaps projects of several hundred dwellings will need to be built. Use on a small scale by home improvers depends on the development of a marketing network for the ingredients and the spread of skills, especially willingness to use a thermometer. Perhaps it will be most attractive to areas that are more seismic than Colombia's north coast. Of course, the sulfur technology also has other uses, such as making concrete sewer pipes more resistant to corrosion and possibly cheaper than the alternative of clay or asbestos pipes.

The best assessment of the potential of sulfur houses at this point can be made by referring back to Table 4-10, which contains data on two minimal two-bedroom dwellings in Las Gaviotas. The sulfur house cost 113.2 thousand pesos, 11.5 percent more than the conventional block dwelling. With 36 square meters of floor space, however, it was 6 percent larger; and its 126-square-meter lot was 56 percent larger. Construction cost as a whole was 12.3 percent less or 17.1 percent less per square meter. Further experiments with sulfur bonding appear warranted.

Notes to Chapter 5

1. The coefficients of Table 5-12 or "hedonic prices" are neither supply nor demand curves, but are the result of the interaction between them. They are the most that different households will pay for the various components (given the presence of all the others) and the least that different suppliers will accept for producing them. In technical terms, they are the upper envelope of the bid-rent functions of households and the lower envelope of the offer functions of different suppliers. They equate marginal utility for the households and profits at the short-run margin for the suppliers and are therefore based on the usual competitive equilibrium assumptions. Being a joint determination, the coefficients do not reveal anything about supply and demand characteristics separately. See John M. Quigley, "What Have We Learned about Housing Demand," in Peter Mieszkowski and Mahlon Straszheim, *Current Issues in Urban Economics* (Baltimore, Md.: Johns Hopkins University Press, 1979), p. 402; and Sherwin Rosen, "Hedonic Prices and Implicit Markets: Product Differentiation in Pure Competition," *Journal of Political Economy* (January 1974), pp. 34–55.

2. Throughout Colombia during the mid-1970s the demand for upper-middle-class brick housing rose in accordance with the theories and policies of Lauchlin Currie, the economic advisor to President Misael Pastrana.

3. CAMACOL, *Empleo Generado por la Construcción en Colombia* (Bogotá, October 1977), p. 5.

4. Christian Araud, Gerard Boon, Victor Urquidi, and Paul Strassmann, *Studies on Employment in the Mexican Housing Industry*, Development Center Studies, Employment Series no. 10 (Paris: OECD, 1973), pp. 80, 163.

5. Rufino Cebrecos Revilla, "Construcción de Vivienda y Empleo" (Lima: Departamento de Economia, Pontificia Universidad Catolica del Peru, April 1978; processed), p. 39.

6. W. Paul Strassmann, "Employment Generation through Residential Construction in Rio de Janeiro," report for the U.S. Agency for International Development (Washington, D.C., October 1975; processed).

7. CAMACOL, *Empleo Generado*, 1977.

8. David Greene and W. Paul Strassmann, "Peruvian Construction Statistics and Productivity Changes," *Journal of Development Studies* (January 1971), pp. 189–95; and W. Paul Strassmann, "Innovation and Employment in Building: The Experience of Peru," *Oxford Economic Papers* (July 1970), pp. 243–59.

9. W. Paul Strassmann, "Employment in Core House Building: A Comparison of Estimates from Six Cities in Six Countries" (East Lansing: Housing-in-Development Unit, Michigan State University, 1980; processed). The cities studied were Medellín, Tunis, Nairobi, Lusaka, Rawalpindi, and Colombo.

6

Transformation of the Old Housing Stock

MAINTENANCE, SUBDIVISION, CONVERSION, AND IMPROVEMENT of the old housing stock give jobs to the poor and better housing to all income groups. People are expanding and improving all types of urban housing on a vast scale in developing countries, using both commercial and informal organization. Within the constraints of income and time, this enables households to get better shelter more cheaply than by moving to newly built dwellings. Since the process is largely informal, poorly documented, and little understood, it has received meager support from public agencies and financial institutions in many countries. Indeed, officials often hinder the process. This tendency may now be reversed, however, as suitable financial mechanisms are developed and as governments limit themselves merely to preventing what is unsafe. Such programs have a high potential for raising urban welfare if they are designed, not in a paternalistic or utopian manner, but in terms of the priorities and capabilities of different types of occupants. The prerequisites are security of tenure and access to piped water and subsequent drainage.

In describing the upgrading behavior of owner-occupants of Cartagena, distinctions are made between the rich, the poor, and those at the intermediate or ICT level (earning between 4,001 and 12,000 pesos monthly, averaging 8,900 pesos). How much and what types of improvement are likely to be carried out by each type of household in various kinds of dwellings in the short and long run? With data on the distribution of incomes and dwellings, the rate of improvement of that part of the housing stock can be projected. The amount of employment generated depends on the labor intensity of both the building activity and the types of materials used. Unfortunately informal building is characterized by lack of records and poor data.

Better records are kept by landlords who must keep track of rent payments and who presumably compare a given investment with other possibilities. Whether the landlord operates through a rental agency or handles his affairs personally, whether houses are leased to families or rooms to lodgers, and whether the landlord is a profit-seeking individual or a branch of government, all affect maintenance and upgrading decisions. In our sample 22 percent of dwellings were rented quarters. As mentioned before, in the census of 1973 the rental share was 30.4 percent. The decline since that year has been due partly to the disincentive of strictly enforced rent controls during inflation and partly to illusion, because nonrented shacks were undercounted by the census, according to local experts.

This chapter also discusses actual and potential government and financial policies toward housing improvements. In Cartagena access to public water and sewerage disposal systems was the critical factor that made households think their dwellings were worthy of continual transformation. This assertion is supported by several econometric tests.

Housing Analysis

The analysis of housing markets and policies in Colombia, as anywhere else, is complicated by the relatively high cost, durability, heterogeneity, and fixed location of dwelling units. The rent or mortgage payment that a household is willing to make depends partly on the bundle of services provided by the structure—space, security, convenience, comfort, beauty—and partly on that provided by the site—access to work, public goods, and neighborhood amenities. If there were only three levels of quality for the structure and three for the site, and if the best, medium, and worst of each were always associated with that of the other, only three combinations of dwelling and site would exist. In fact, however, many more options and combinations exist with complex and poorly understood tradeoffs.

Entrepreneurs—either developers, owner-occupants, or landlords—should respond to existing prices and vacancy rates with new construction or transformation of old units at locations where the rate of return appears highest, thus again altering prices and vacancy rates. As equilibrium is approached, the volume of new building and conversion should fall, as should each household's desire to move, until it reaches a new income level or stage in the life cycle.

In principle these elements applied in Cartagena. Specific results, however, reflected great variations in the characteristics of households, the general spatial configuration, the public utilities network, and the actual opportunities for combining factors of production. Within a budget and credit constraint, households will seek the best yield from the combination of site and structure, and a few may even quantify their decision in monetary terms and seek maximum profits with given risk preferences.

Any housing survey should cover both the locational and structural aspects of housing choices. In exploring specific analytical points, however, one may concentrate on either the structural or the locational aspect and hold the other constant. For example, as in many early models, one may examine only which household locates where (distances and densities) without stressing what they occupy at that spot. Alternatively one can focus on what is built, expanded, or subdivided and assume that one location is more or less like another. One can begin either way and then see if the results are plausible and robust enough to withstand complications with other elements. In any case it must not be forgotten that simplifications involve omissions. Beyond the dual problems of investment yields and consumption streams with respect to site and structure, are those involving the general competition for space and other resources in an urban economy. (See Appendix D for a more rigorous statement of some of these issues.)

Improvements by Owner-Occupants

An analysis of housing transformation can begin by simply recording the number and types of changes made—description first, explanation later. Our interviewers probed for the number of improvements in various ways. One way was to investigate improvements only by category, regardless of their extent or cost. Any owner-occupant who had improved a kitchen in any way was thus in the category of kitchen improver. After the trial interviews, thirteen improvement categories and one for "other" were set up, as shown in Table 6-1.

Most of the owner-occupants (88 percent) had made some kind of improvement, with an average of 2.9 types of changes. The remaining 12 percent had made no changes because they considered that their dwelling was finished and that nothing else was needed. The average number for changers and nonchangers combined was 2.7. All the changes mentioned in the table were planned by the owners when they acquired the dwelling. No one said that they had not planned to make any changes although some were needed.

Much improvement in the Southeast Zone consisted of better materials. Improvement in roofs progressed from cardboard (stage A) to corrugated metal (stage B) and to tile or asbestos cement sheets (stage C). According to the 1976 census of the Boston sector of the Southeast Zone conducted for ICT, only 5 percent of owner-occupied dwellings were still in stage A, and 8 percent were in stage B, whereas 87 percent had gone to stage C in roughly equal proportions between the two materials. Because they provide comfort and security, roofs have high priority.

Table 6-1. *Owners Making Specific Changes,*
by Years of Occupancy
(percent)

	Years of occupancy				
Type of improvement	1–2	3–5	6–10	10+	Total
Sample size (N)	36	42	32	74	184
Add room(s)	25.0	42.9	45.0	50.0	39.7
Plaster or paint	30.6	52.4	45.0	43.8	35.9
Improve kitchen	13.9	19.0	35.0	34.4	26.6
Improve toilet	11.1	19.0	25.0	25.0	25.0
Improve windows or doors	13.9	31.0	35.0	37.5	23.9
Improve basic wall materials	16.7	23.8	27.5	31.3	23.4
Improve flooring	11.1	26.2	27.5	28.1	19.6
Improve roofing materials	11.1	16.7	15.0	15.6	18.5
Add earth fill to site	8.3	9.5	5.0	3.1	9.2
Add more convenient water connection	0.0	19.0	7.5	9.4	4.9
Totally reconstruct the house	2.8	0.0	2.5	3.1	3.8
Add terrace and railing	5.6	2.4	2.5	3.1	2.7
Finish inside ceiling	0.0	4.8	2.5	3.1	1.6
Other	16.7	21.4	20.0	18.8	19.6
Average number of changes	1.9	2.8	3.0	2.9	2.7

Source: Cartagena household survey, 1978.

With respect to floors, 45 percent of the households had only an earth floor (stage A), another 46 percent had stopped with uncovered cement floors (B), and only 7 percent had gone to ceramic tiles (C).

Only 19 percent had gone to stage C in walls, plastered concrete blocks. Unplastered concrete blocks (B) characterized 5 percent, and 76 percent had wooden walls of various quality levels (A). The census showed that four of the 1,064 dwellings were thought to be between forty and forty-nine years old, and four were between fifty and fifty-nine years old, that is, built around 1920.

Additional Rooms

Additional rooms or more space was the most popular change that owners could accomplish on their own. Access to water (if lacking) was even more desirable, but changing that was not within the capability of many households. The average household that had lived three or more years in a dwelling had added 0.83 rooms (standard error 0.09). For every five families that had added one room, one family seemed to have added nothing, but since some families had added two or three rooms, and one as many as six, the proportion of those adding rooms was actually only 39.7 percent of households. The average cost of an added room was 58,800 pesos (US$1,500). Since the average value of housing per square meter was 3,450 pesos, a reasonable guess is that the average addition was less than 17 square meters.

Occupants with mortgaged dwellings were very likely to make additions because their dwellings were smaller than the average. Floor space was below 100 square meters for 59.7 percent of mortgage payers, compared with 41.4 percent for others. Dwellings with three rooms or less were 41.5 percent of those mortgaged, but were only 33.1 percent of those fully owned. Since households made additions within a few years of occupancy, much of the difference was in the newest dwellings. From 1973 to 1978 the average number of rooms per dwelling rose from 3.3 to 4.1, according to the census and our sample. The increase of 0.8 rooms between the two surveys matched the increases reported per house in the second survey. The rise was not due to the larger size of new dwellings, because these continued to be mainly one- to two-room shacks and two- to three-room ICT or similar houses; it was due to expansion. The distribution of dwellings by number of rooms had changed from 1973 to 1978:

	Percentage share of dwellings	
Number of rooms per dwelling	1973 (N = 43,109)	1978 (N = 293)
1	11.7	2.7
2	26.9	8.5
3	25.1	27.0
4–5	25.4	43.0
6+	11.0	18.8

Addition of a room is not the same thing as adding floor space. The percentage increase of floor space with more adults is only half as much as the percentage change in the number of rooms (Table 6-2). Extra rooms were smaller, and some were created by subdividing existing rooms. As a function of income, the floor space elasticities were also lower, and for incomes greater than 16,000 pesos it became significantly negative. This phenomenon among the well-to-do of giving up space, both indoors and outdoors, to be in a more elegant coastal neighborhood has already been discussed in previous chapters.

To offset this lack of space, the wealthier families disproportionately raised the value per square meter, or perhaps the causation went in the other direction. Either high density was made tolerable by more elegant

Table 6-2. *Logarithmic Regressions of Rooms, Floor Space, Value per Square Meter, Added Rooms, and Improvements against Income and the Number of Adults per Household*

Dependent variable	Constant	Slope coefficients		Adjusted R^2	F ratio
		Income	Number of adults		
Number of rooms, all owners	−4.148	0.929[b] (0.115)	n.a.	0.182	65.8[b]
Number of rooms, all owners	−4.082	0.803[b] (0.114)	0.770[b] (0.196)	0.235	45.9[b]
Number of rooms, 4,001–8,000 pesos	−10.352	1.493[a] (0.630)	0.966[b] (0.267)	0.134	9.1[b]
Number of rooms, 8,001–16,000 pesos	−8.883	1.274 (0.900)	1.032[b] (0.328)	0.101	5.5[b]
Number of rooms, Southeast Zone	−5.531	0.935[b] (0.290)	0.790[a] (0.318)	0.295	14.0[b]
Floor space, all owners	1.617	0.297[b] (0.048)	0.368[b] (0.078)	0.206	37.8[b]
Floor space, 4,001–8,000 pesos	−0.849	0.566 (0.321)	0.498[b] (0.140)	0.121	8.0[b]
Floor space, 8,001–16,000 pesos	−5.320	1.023[b] (0.361)	0.483[b] (0.131)	0.180	9.6[b]
Floor space, 16,001+ pesos	13.316	−0.819[a] (0.321)	n.a.	0.120	6.3[a]
Floor space, Southeast Zone	0.464	0.431[b] (0.131)	0.218 (0.145)	0.237	10.1[b]
Value per square meter, all owners	−0.242	0.924[b] (0.092)	−0.357[b] (0.137)	0.333	50.7[b]
Value per square meter, 16,001+ pesos	−8.918	1.762[a] (0.684)	−0.725 (0.487)	0.151	3.4[a]

(*Table continues on the following page.*)

Table 6-2. *(continued)*

Dependent variable	Constant	Slope coefficients		Adjusted R^2	F ratio
		Income	Number of adults		
Value per square meter, Southeast Zone	2.292	0.562[a] (0.223)	−0.280 (0.243)	0.094	3.3[a]
Rooms added, all owners	0.371	0.002 (0.108)	0.288 (0.162)	0.008	1.8
Number of types of improvements, all owners	0.223	0.214 (0.213)	0.111 (0.318)	−0.002	0.8
Improvement cost, all improvers (thousands of pesos)	−160.8	26.0 (15.2)	−8.6 (2.3)	0.008	1.5

Note: Regressions that are not significant at the 5 percent level for subsamples are omitted for rooms, floor space, and value per square meter. In the last two regressions the dependent variable is not expressed in logarithmic terms. Standard errors are in parentheses.

n.a. Not applicable

a. Significance = 0.05.

b. Significance = 0.01.

Source: Cartagena household survey, 1978.

fittings, or the cost of elegant fittings limited the floor space that could be afforded. The value per square meter—income elasticity of 1.8 of those receiving over 16,000 pesos monthly—was about double that of the average owner, 0.9. Everywhere value per square meter was negatively associated with the number of adults; quality had been traded off for space and rooms.

In the poor Southeast Zone, the elasticities for number of rooms were like those for the entire city (0.9 and 0.8, respectively), but those for floor space were less than half as high (0.4 and 0.2, respectively). Both of these were physical elasticities. The Southeast elasticity for value per square meter, however, was somewhat less with respect to income: 0.6, compared with 0.9 for the city. Self-help labor produces space more readily than quality and can do little to offset lack of public utilities and low neighborhood prestige. Indeed, in the Southeast self-help was discouraged by the lack of water and other infrastructure.

The principal reason for building additional rooms was the addition of people to the household. Children provided the need for more space about twice as often as did other relatives. Together these two reasons accounted for 50.5 percent of additions. Other reasons, such as space for lodgers, pure investment, need for a workshop, or space as an end in itself explained less than 10 percent of additions. Nearly two-thirds of rooms had been added within the past five years, and the average age of added rooms was 5.2 years. Only 9 percent of rooms were known to have been added more than ten years ago. Of course, the 29 percent of households that had acquired their dwellings from previous owners were unaware of additions that might have been made previously. Tenants also had little knowledge of the history of their current premises.

The total number of rooms that a household occupied was highly correlated with income and the number of adults, but that correlation did not apply to the number of rooms added or to spending on improvements (mostly for added rooms) as shown in Table 6-2. The total rooms-income elasticity fell from 0.9 to 0.8 with allowance for the number of adults. If the poorest and richest families (below 4,000 pesos and above 16,000 pesos monthly) were excluded, the rooms-adults elasticity was 1.0, meaning the number of rooms doubled when the number of adults doubled. The income elasticity was higher, but far from the same 0.01 percent level of significance. But added rooms were only slightly associated with the number of adults and not at all with income. The R^2 for both was a mere 0.008. Cartagena families seemed to move fairly often, and when they encountered a house that was too small, or when the family grew, rooms were added until the size of the house was appropriate for the income and size of the family. If the family had no savings, the room was added by self-help or with money from temporary incomes, as will be discussed later.

Eighty-five percent of households lived in single-family single-story housing, and, therefore, it was physically easy to add on at the ground level. Consequently the share of added rooms on the ground level was 77.8 percent. Of these, about one-fifth combined adding a room with subdividing an existing room. For example, part of a wall might be removed, with the added room consisting of both new and existing space. A new panel or other division made an existing room smaller. In only 18.9 percent of cases did the added room come only through subdividing existing space. Adding rooms above ground level and other forms of addition came to only 3.3 percent of added rooms.

Improved Kitchens

In the discussion of rooms, kitchens were not included. Among both tenants and others, 83 percent had indoor kitchens. An additional 12 percent of tenants and 11 percent of others cooked indoors but had no separate kitchen. Five and 6 percent of tenants and others, respectively, cooked outside. The most common fuel was kerosene, followed by bottled gas. The rare use of charcoal explains the depressed state of the charcoal sellers who had to be evicted from La Carbonera. The percentage distribution of cooking fuel used in Cartagena in 1978 by 293 households was

Fuel	All occupants	Tenants	Others
Kerosene or gasoline	48.1	44.6	49.1
Bottled gas	38.9	43.1	37.7
Electricity	8.5	7.7	8.8
Charcoal or coal	3.1	1.5	3.5
Wood	1.0	3.1	0.4
Other	0.3	—	0.4

One-quarter of the owners had installed a better kitchen in their dwelling at an average cost of 19,500 pesos. With a standard error of 3,100, the significance of that average cost is rather low.

Improved Plumbing

One-quarter of all owner-occupants tried to improve their sanitary facilities, but only 5 percent tried make better use of what water they had, since that was more difficult. Eleven percent of those with only one or two years at a site had already tried to improve their sanitary facilities; and of those who had lived more than ten years in their house, 35 percent had made such improvements (see Table 6-1). Installing a septic tank at an average cost of 21,000 (1978) pesos was the most common improvement, closely followed by digging and setting up a latrine for 5,000 pesos. Changes involving flush toilets were more expensive, with an average cost of 30,000 pesos. The average plumbing improvement cost was 17,700 pesos (standard error 6,500 pesos).

No household with less than three years at a site had improved water facilities. Nineteen percent had brought in water or added an extra bathroom if they had lived three to five years at a site. Of those with six or more years in a dwelling, only 7 percent had made such changes. Average cost was 24,000 pesos. Improved water installation depended on the availability of public services more than other changes. In our sample,

6.8 percent of septic tanks and 7.0 percent of sewer-connected toilets did not work because the water system had not been extended or was not functioning as expected.

The average monthly expenditure on public utilities was 626 pesos (standard error 46 pesos). By income range it was

Monthly income (pesos)	Monthly utility expenditures (pesos)
0– 2,000	234
2,001– 4,000	301
4,001– 8,000	406
8,001–16,000	531
16,001–32,000	1,736
32,001+	1,225

The income share spent on utilities falls from 10 percent below 4,000 pesos to 4.4 percent in the 8,001 to 16,000 pesos range and then rises to 7.2 percent above 16,000 pesos. The relation is V-shaped. The highest income range with merely eight observations is ignored.

Overall Improvement

Only two respondents thought their dwellings were in "much worse" shape now than at the time of acquisition, and only seven thought they were "worse, but not much worse." By contrast, 77.6 percent thought their dwellings were now in better shape, including 35.8 percent who believed them to be "much better." For those with incomes above 16,000 pesos, this last opinion was that of the majority, 54.2 percent. As can be seen in Table 6-3, dwelling condition was strongly correlated with income. By the same token, those households who wanted to make

Table 6-3. *Dwelling Condition in 1978 Compared with That at the Time of Acquisition, by Income Level*

Monthly income (pesos)	Percentage in row					
	Much better	Somewhat better	Same	Worse	Much worse	Percentage of row
0–4,000	25.6	46.2	20.5	5.1	2.6	23.6
4,001–8,000	31.1	39.3	23.0	4.9	1.6	37.0
8,001–16,000	41.5	43.9	9.8	4.9	0	24.8
16,001+	54.2	37.2	8.3	0	0	14.5
Total	35.8	41.8	17.0	4.2	1.2	100.0

Source: Cartagena household survey, 1978.

changes but had not yet made them gave lack of money as the reason in 88.6 percent of cases. Hardly any respondents attributed failure to improve to lack of space, time, or adverse regulations.

Of interest is the rapidity with which changes are made. Table 6-1 shows that occupants with three or more years in a dwelling typically made about three types of changes. But two types of changes are likely to have been made during the first year. The early changes could also be repeated by these households in future years. If a room had already been added, they could add another. Indeed, 25 percent added a room within the first two years, and 31 percent added plaster and paint. Installing better windows and doors was especially important for those with from three to ten years in a dwelling. More than one-third of households with more than five years at a site had installed a better kitchen.

By income category, all types of households earning more than 2,000 pesos monthly had made an average of 2.5 changes to their dwellings, provided they had lived there three or more years. Those earning 2,000 pesos and less had made only 1.4 changes, showing that such poverty impairs self-help. Households in the 4,001–8,000 pesos income range (F2) had made more than 3.5 different types of changes if they lived in intermediate (H4) or luxurious (H5) housing, that is, far above the stock-user matrix diagonal. Upgrading brought them there.

The two poorest and the best housing types, H0, H1, and H5, had experienced the fewest types of changes, two or less. The middle categories had experienced the most improvement, with H4 housing typically undergoing 3.3 types of changes. These changes are what brought much of this housing to the H4 level.

Age and Value

If dwellings are steadily improved by their occupants, dwelling value would be expected to rise with age, as is shown in Table 6-4. It appears that the typical dwelling began at the basic (H3) level and became intermediate (H4) after some ten years. Both older and newer housing had an average of three types of improvement, but the difference came from the number of times each improvement was repeated.

Since there were more new than old dwellings, old dwellings might have been more likely to survive and be owner-occupied if they were of high quality and high value. At Cartagena's rate of population growth of 4.4 percent, the population doubled in 16 years; thus only half the housing stock would be expected to be less than sixteen years old. In fact, 72 percent of the owner-occupied housing stock was fifteen years old or less. Much older housing has either been demolished or converted to ren-

Table 6-4. *Age and Average Value of Owner-Occupied Housing*
(*N* = 179)

Age of housing (years)	Average value (pesos)	Percentage
1–5	231,000	38.0
6–10	310,000	19.0
11–15	504,000	14.5
16–20	544,000	10.6
21–30	606,000	9.5
31+	690,000	8.4

Note: Differences between groups are significant at the 5 percent level. Bias may be due to inability of occupants of older dwellings to assess value or recall original prices. The construction price index could also overstate or understate appreciation. Site value may account for a larger share of total value in older dwellings in some areas such as Pie de la Popa.
Source: Cartagena household survey, 1978.

tal units or other use. Nevertheless, it seems reasonable to suppose that improvements have had much to do with the higher values of older housing shown in Table 6-4.

Sources of Finance for Improvements

Table 6.5 shows the many ways that improvements were financed. In 73.5 percent of households, it was done with family resources. Those earning less than 8,000 pesos monthly primarily supplied labor themselves, and those earning more than 8,000 pesos preferred to use savings to hire labor. Among the "other" sources were loans from employers. In general, however, home improvements were carried out very intensively without much outside financial support. That statement applies most strongly to the richest 13 percent of the households. The rest would probably have borrowed more if loans had been available without frightening demands for collateral. How much they would have borrowed is uncertain.

Did transitory income stimulate upgrading? Having relatives working in Venezuela had an effect on improvements. Exactly one-third of owners had such relatives, and most of these relatives sent remittances back in widely irregular patterns. The extremes were the streetseller with six children working in Venezuela, none of whom sent back anything, and a couple whose six children in Venezuela sent about 7,000 pesos (US$180) monthly, the couple's only income.

To what extent did such flows seem to raise the probability of adding a room or of making more than the average three types of improvements? Coefficients of two logit estimating equations are given in Table 6-6, and probabilities for households with seven members and a forty-year-old head of household are given in Table 6-7. Relatives in Venezuela raised the chance of adding a room from 25.4 to 30.8 percent for dwellings without water, and from 31.3 to 39.3 percent for dwellings with water. This rise is comparatively low and of doubtful statistical significance since the t ratio is only 0.81.

For making at least three types of improvements, the significance of relatives in Venezuela was much higher ($t = 2.21$). The probability of improving dwellings without water rose from 47.2 to 66.9 percent and for those with water from 59.0 to 75.3 percent. The departure of relatives, usually adults, for work abroad made additional space less needed or less desirable than improved quality.

Although these improvements raised the value of housing, they did not bring it to above-average levels, since households with relatives in Venezuela generally had worse or smaller housing to begin with. Forty-

Table 6-5. *Most Important Source of Finance for Home Improvements, by Income Level*
(percent, $N = 200$)

	Monthly income (pesos)				
Source of finance	0–4,000	4,001–8,000	8,001–16,000	16,001+	Total
Self-help labor, cash for materials	10.5	14.0	8.5	1.5	34.5
Self-help labor, loan for materials	1.5	1.0	1.0	0.5	4.0
Labor and materials purchased with savings or a loan from relatives	6.5	13.5	9.5	9.5	39.0
Labor and materials purchased with retirement funds	0	2.5	1.0	1.0	4.5
Labor and materials paid for with ICT, BCH, or CAV loan	1.0	1.0	0	0	2.0
Other	5.5	7.0	3.0	.5	16.0
Total	25.0	39.0	23.0	13.0	100.0

Source: Cartagena household survey, 1978.

Table 6-6. *Estimators for Adding Rooms or Making Improvements: Logit Analysis*

Constant and independent variables	Coefficients (and t ratios) for dependent variables	
	Added room(s), all owners N = 189 ln (P_A/P_N) (1)	Three or more types of improvements after 1.5 years at site, N = 163 ln (P_3/P_L) (2)
Constant	−1.902 (−3.75)	0.2058 (2.31)
Indoor piped water	0.3724 (1.01)	0.4777 (0.99)
Public sewerage system	—	0.0191 (−0.03)
Household size	0.1180 (2.46)	−0.0703 (−1.29)
Age of household head	—	−0.0203 (−1.46)
Relatives working in Venezuela	0.2685 (.81)	0.8167 (2.21)
Income mainly from sales or property	—	−0.1906 (−0.48)
ICT-financed dwelling	1.024 (2.74)	0.7569 (1.74)

Note: P_A is the probability that one or more rooms will be added; P_N is the probability that they will not. P_3 is the probability that three or more different types of improvements will be made. P_L is the probability that fewer than three will be made. Due to their low level of significance, type of income, age of household head, and the access to the public sewerage system were not included in estimating the coefficients in column 1. For column 2 the assumption is that owners have been at least 1.5 years at the site although some types of improvement may have been made during the first 1.5 years and are counted.

Source: Cartagena household survey, 1978.

four percent lived in housing below the diagonal. The average value was 190,000 pesos (US$4,900) compared with 590,000 pesos (US$15,100) for those without a need to export workers. Even households receiving less than 4,000 pesos monthly with relatives in Venezuela lived in dwellings worth 24 percent less than those in that income range without workers abroad. As shown in Table 6-8, being in that category had little effect on the income elasticity of demand of 1.1, but it shifted the intercept down significantly.

Transitory income was also associated with the receipt of sales, own-account, or property income, rather than wages, salaries, or pensions. If so, positive and negative deviations must have offset one another in Cartagena because type of income had no noticeable effect on intercept or slope. The receipt by 34.2 percent of one-time special income through inheritance, cashing in retirement funds, smuggling windfalls, and the like was associated with a slight downward shift of the intercept. Normally, one-time income might be expected to go into housing investment and thereby to shift the intercept upward.

Water

Lack of title to land has often been identified as a barrier to self-help improvement in squatter settlements. These discussions ignore the fact that land without public utilities is seldom worth much. Of these utilities,

Table 6-7. *Probabilities of Adding Rooms or Making Three or More Types of Improvements, for Different Occupant-Dwelling Combinations*

	Probability	
Characteristics of the occupant-dwelling set	*Added one or more rooms, all owners, N = 189* (1)	*Made three or more types of improvements owners with 1.5+ years in dwelling, N = 163* (2)
1. Owners without indoor piped water, no relatives working in Venezuela or ICT financing	0.254	0.472
2. Same as 1., but with indoor piped water	0.313	0.590
3. Same as 1., but with relatives working in Venezuela	0.308	0.669
4. Owners with both indoor piped water and relatives working in Venezuela, but no ICT financing	0.393	0.753
5. Owners in ICT developments (all have indoor piped water), but without relatives working in Venezuela	0.579	0.752
6. Owners in ICT developments with relatives working in Venezuela	0.643	0.873

Note: If owners with less than 1.5 years are excluded from the estimates for added rooms, the t ratios for the logit coefficients fall, but the probabilities rise slightly in column 1. For row 1, it goes to 0.338, row 4 to 0.446, and row 6 to 0.658. The assumed household size is seven. If it were only four, the probability in row 1 would fall to 0.193 and in row 6 to 0.558. Additional assumptions for the probabilities in column 2 are that the age of the household head is 40 and that income does not mainly come from sales or property. Age and income source were not critical variables and were omitted for the estimates in column 1.

Source: Cartagena household survey, 1978.

Table 6-8. *Income Elasticity Regressions for Tenants, Mortgagors, and All Owners*

Sample	Income (log)	Second independent variable	Third independent variable	Fourth independent variable	Constant	F ratio
Tenants N = 65	0.786[b] (0.110)	n.a.	n.a.	n.a.	−0.024 (1.010)	51.25
Mortgagors N = 50	0.873[b] (0.275)	n.a.	n.a.	n.a.	-1.619 (2.484)	10.08
All owners N = 205	1.178[b] (0.083)	n.a.	n.a.	n.a.	1.764 (0.737)	203.4
N = 205	1.185[b] (0.086)	Household size (log) −0.182 (0.151)	Adults/children 0.812[b] (0.308)	n.a.	1.575 (0.729)	76.32
N = 175	1.140[b] (0.090)	Relatives working in Venezuela (dummy) −0.362[a] (0.144)	Mainly sales or property income (dummy) −0.018 (0.050)	One-time special income (dummy) −0.261 (0.144)	2.339 (0.817)	45.6
N = 175	1.137[b] (0.091)	−0.412[b] (0.141)	n.a.	n.a.	2.289 (0.820)	88.8
N = 201	0.782[b] (0.084)	Indoor piped water (dummy) 1.109[b] (0.142)	Public sewerage system (dummy) 0.217 (0.129)		4.410 (0.708)	119.1

Note: The dependent variable for tenants is rent; for mortgagors, monthly payments; and for all owners, value of the dwelling. The sample of all owners includes the mortgagors. Standard errors are in parentheses.
n.a. Not applicable.
a. Significance = 0.05.
b. Significance = 0.01.

the most important is water. Most households will not be deeply attached to sites that mean four daily hikes (of several hundred meters) with five-gallon cans of water. Once water mains had arrived in Cartagena neighborhoods, the cost of making an individual connection and adding minimal fixtures was estimated as only about 9,800 pesos (US$250), mainly in materials. Installing a complete bathroom cost 30,000 pesos (US$770), and a septic tank was 21,000 pesos (US$540).

Stimulant to Home Improvements

As much as tenure, access to water rouses owner-occupants toward making other expansions and improvement. For the Cartagena household specified in Table 6-7, water connections increased the probability of adding a room from 25.4 to 57.9 percent if the dwelling had ICT financing. The probability of having made three or more types of improvements rose from 47.2 to 59.0 percent without or to 75.2 percent with ICT financing. Since ICT houses were smaller (30 to 85 square meters) and were left partly unplastered and unpainted, they were expected to spur improvements; and they did.

Access to water was more important than access to the public sewerage system, since latrines and septic tanks were relatively acceptable methods for waste disposal. Dwellings lacking water connections had an average value of only 82,000 pesos (US$2,100) compared with 250,000 pesos (US$6,400) for those lacking sewerage connections. The average dwelling with water was worth seven times as much as one without, whereas the average dwelling with a sewerage connection was worth only three times as much as one without. If access to water and the public sewerage system are added as dummy variables to income elasticity regressions, water shifts the intercept up more and is statistically highly significant ($t = 7.79$), whereas a sewerage system connection is marginal ($t = 1.69$, see Table 6-8). Recall that the hedonic estimates (Table 5-12) also suggested that, other things equal, indoor piped water doubled the value of a dwelling.

In some future year we may expect water pipes to have reached most of the city, while the sewerage system will still be far from complete. At that time a sewerage system connection is likely to be a better predictor of variations in home improvement. At least, this seems to be the case in Lima, Peru, where the author organized a similar survey in 1980. Even in the squatter settlements around Lima, 61 percent of dwellings had piped water but only 36 percent were connected to the sewerage system.[1]

As can be noted from Turbaco, uncertainty about water was as discouraging to the rich as to the poor. After 1978 it became apparent that the municipality would not soon extend water lines to the proposed luxury settlement and that electricity was too undependable to keep the pumps of private wells going. As a result, development practically ceased, although streets and lights were already in place. Land values fell in real terms.

Access to water and the resulting faith in improvements showed up in statistics for different parts of the city as an upward shift in the intercept of the demand function for housing. The income elasticities of demand fell somewhat but remain close to unity, as already reported in Chapter 4. For the largely unserviced Southeast Zone and the Outskirts of town, the intercepts were 2.8 and 2.7, and the elasticities were 0.98 and 1.10. In the northern quarters with water, but septic tanks instead of a sewerage connection, the intercept rose to 4.1, and the elasticity remained 0.90. In the fully serviced western or coastal parts of the city (Zone 1), the intercept rose to 6.0, and the elasticity was 0.80. All these coefficients are statistically significant at the 0.01 level.

No Proxy for Neighborhood Quality

The possibility arises that indoor piped water is merely a proxy for neighborhood quality in general. To check that, a regression was run with dummy variables for each of the six major zones of the city. As shown in Table 6-9 the coefficient for water was 1.105. The coefficient for access to the public sewerage system ceased to be statistically significant and was slightly negative at that. Since the most expensive housing existed along the Coast and the eastern Outskirts, the coefficients were highest for these two areas. Lowest were those for the North and the Southeast—the zones with the cheapest housing. But only the Coast and the Southeast had strong (over 0.500) positive or negative correlations with water. The ICT sector was intermediate with 0.257. Regardless of the general quality of settlement in a sector, a dwelling without water would probably lose far more value than the simple cost of that installation, and it would remain small and unimproved.

Inclusion of the dummies for urban zones did not change the apparent effect of water on value. For given income levels, housing values would be higher in the better districts, yet lack of water could more than offset this effect within a district. A household with a 10,000-peso (US$256) income was likely to have a 394,000-peso (US$10,000) house if it lived in Lomas, and one worth only 217,000 pesos (US$5,560) if it lived in the Southeast Zone, provided both had water. But if the Lomas site lacked water, that household would have no more than a 130,000-peso (US$3,340) dwelling. Reluctance to make improvements on a poor site is a reasonable explanation.

Table 6-9. *Value-Income Elasticities for Housing,*
with Dummies for Public Utilities and Location

Independent variable	Regression coefficient	Standard error	Significance	F ratio
Log of income	0.527	0.084	0.000	39.7
Dummies				
Indoor piped water	1.105	0.137	0.000	65.4
Public sewerage system	−0.118	0.158	0.455	0.6
Zonal dummies (average income; correlation with water)				
North	0.172	0.163	0.295	1.1
(8,521; -0.011)				
ICT	0.396	0.197	0.045	4.1
(9,673; -0.257)				
Lomas	0.596	0.162	0.000	13.5
(9,201; 0.152)				
Outskirts	0.676	0.206	0.001	10.8
(6,685; 0.103)				
Coast	1.542	0.238	0.000	42.1
(20,923; 0.523)				
Constant	6.328	0.698	0.000	82.1

Note: The sample consists of 201 owner-occupants. The dependent variable was the log of the declared value. Average monthly incomes per household are given in parentheses and apply to all residents in a zone. Correlation coefficients are those for indoor piped water with residence in a zone. The Southeast Zone values are implied when all other zonal dummies are zero: average monthly income was 5,488 pesos in July 1978; correlation with residence and indoor piped water was −0.504. The overall F ratio for the regression was 64.4, which is significant at the 0.01 level. The adjusted R^2 was 0.717.
Source: Cartagena household survey, 1978.

In terms of averages, incomes in the Southeast were 49.1 percent as high as in the rest of the city, but housing was worth only 22.5 percent as much. Given the demand elasticity, the value was below a level explicable by poverty alone. What was lacking were the conditions for inspiring upgrading with the hope of resale to others. In the Southeast 24.2 percent of households had lived more than fifteen years at a site, compared with only 19.5 percent for the rest of the city and with 18.6 percent for the western Coastal Zone, the oldest part of the city. Incomes in the western and coastal quarter were 2.1 times as high as those of the city as a whole, but the average value of housing was 3.6 times as high. If the poor did less improving than others, it may have been largely due to the physical conditions of the part of the city where they lived since, as reported above, upgrading was not generally associated with income.

Because of the upgrading the Gini coefficient of 0.305 for housing shows that shelter was more equitably distributed than income with 0.419. Where sites were serviced, households could distribute this product to themselves.

ICT Financing

The ICT has gradually moved toward support for upgrading and is still experimenting with policies and physical designs. Since it has been one of the world's pioneers in creative social housing policies, no doubt its experiments will continue to be instructive.

Loan Conditions and Policies

A program of loans for upgrading older housing was initiated by ICT in October 1977 as part of an integral plan for improving subnormal urban zones. First priority went to legalizing tenure. After that came installation of water, sewerage connections, improved roads, and electricity, preferably in that order, although sewerage systems are the most complex and costly and often, in fact, lagged. The occupants had to use loans to make kitchens and bathrooms adequate, followed by improvement of the existing walls and roof. Only then were expansions allowed.

Recipients of loans had to be family heads with adequate incomes and collateral or a cosigner for the loan. No more than 57,000 pesos could be lent for obtaining tenure in 1978, meaning the equivalent of 650 daily minimum wages for Bogotá. No more than 84,000 pesos or 970 minimum wages could be lent for subsequent home improvements. Loans had to be repaid in fifteen years with payments that rose 5 percent annually and a rate of interest and insurance of 14 percent—given the rate of inflation, a negative rate.

Loans for upgrading were not to be used to pay for the labor of the owner-occupants themselves. Funds for materials were to be disbursed as work progressed, as verified by a supervising ICT architect. Materials from ICT warehouses and ICT-associated enterprises were to be used whenever possible, and prefabricated plumbing and structural units were recommended. No loans were to be made to owners with lodgers or tenant families on the premises. ICT did not still object to tenants per se, but it did not see its role as financier of landlords, even if small and probably temporary. To qualify for loans, landlords first had to sell those parts of their premises to the occupants.

In December 1977 the Cartagena branch of the ICT was authorized to lend 30 million pesos (US$770,000) for home improvement. In poor neighborhoods along the bay in the southern parts of District 16, Bosque, 540 loans of up to 50,000 pesos were made as a result. An educational program had to first persuade squatters of the advantages of legalizing tenure and committing part of their future incomes. Many were afraid that agreeing to relocate on better-sited lots was a step toward eradication. Others doubted that the proposed improvements were worth the financial commitments. Without a sewerage system only septic tanks were possible in that sector, and even they depended on promised water connections. After the arrival of water, ICT promised further 10,000-peso loans for making the connection. To qualify for all this, the head of the family had to earn at least 2,500 pesos monthly, a requirement that eliminated nearly one-third of households in Albornoz and nearly one-half in La Cartagenita. Improvement loans were not granted to shacks that engineers designated as too dilapidated to be safe.

Without collateral or mortgaged dwellings at stake, recipients of loans soon lagged behind in payments. Collection costs were so high that the program was considered a financial failure by 1980. Families with uncertain income were reluctant to gamble with their only asset, the house. To keep lending institutions solvent without foreclosing on mortgagors with temporary inability to pay, a more comprehensive insurance system is needed. In Bogotá such a system in the form of the Corporación Distrital de Garantías has already been set up with initial funding of 4 million pesos. Subscribers are a number of official and private financial institutions. Operations are in part delegated to ICT, the Caja de Vivienda Popular, and the Corporación Financiera Popular. For an effective lending program for home improvement, Cartagena may need something similar. The simplest system, however, would be to sell materials at a large discount to qualified households that have accumulated a target amount of prior savings, similar to the system that the Banco de Materiales introduced in Peru in the fall of 1980.

Minimal Improvable Housing

An ICT program of the late 1960s that was not tried on a large scale in Cartagena was organized mutual aid. Elsewhere in Colombia ICT found that this program was expensive to administer, slow in execution, tied up much capital, and that prospective owners subcontracted as much of their own labor obligation as they could afford, up to 90 percent. Professional contractors could build more efficiently, so a policy of minimal semifinished housing was introduced. In Chapter 4 this type of housing was described as consisting of two rooms and about 33 square meters of floor space at a 1978 price of 125,000 pesos (US$3,200). One-room houses with 19.5 square meters were begun at Las Calamares with a saving of perhaps 20 percent. Finishing and fixtures were rudimentary, but the foundations were there for expansions. A cost estimate was given in Chapter 5.

ICT was moving in the direction of anticipating expansion and remodeling by the occupants. In certain of its two-story dwellings, called *cepillos* or "brushes," steep roofs came down to make up part of a second-story wall. Occupants commonly raised the roof to a more obtuse angle to gain floor space on the second story. If such houses were properly designed, the change would not impair lighting and ventilation. Some architects worried about the waste involved in building components of houses only to have amateurs destroy them. Others deplored the increased costs because of lack of building skill and inability to buy materials wholesale.[2] They seemed to miss the point that poor families could bear these costs but not the risk of mortgaging their assets in a formal arrangement with the building industry.

Case histories of ICT housing

The scarcity of housing and finance, especially when offered at subsidized rates, causes pressures that modify the housing stock and assign it to occupants other than those designated by social nonmarket criteria. Low-income housing filters up to the well-to-do who then upgrade it in the various ways described earlier. Alternatively, the poor subdivide and over-crowd housing that would otherwise have brought one household up to socially prescribed minimum, but overly expensive, standards. These patterns and variations can be illustrated by cases from the ICT.

When the centrally located slum of Chambacú was eradicated, some of its occupants were resettled 7 kilometers to the west in the República de Venezuela section. Here they received 63-square-meter three-room houses on 96-square-meter lots. The dockworker who occupied one of these in our sample traveled ninety minutes back and forth to work instead of thirty minutes. Through subdivision and a slight extension, he had added a room to accommodate some additional relatives. Seven adults and five children now occupied the house which they called a *cajita de fósforos* (little matchbox).

In nearby Chiquinquirá even smaller (about 50-square-meter) houses cost 60,000 pesos in 1974 (180,000 1978 pesos, US$4,600). Within two years the construction foreman, who had acquired the house, had spent 50,000 pesos to add two rooms, increasing the size to 92 square meters. Five adults—four with jobs—and three children occupied this house.

A similar ICT Chiquinquirá house was originally occupied by the family of a jewelry repairman and that of his brother. Antagonism between the wives caused the families to put up a wall that divided the house and the patio. The jewelry man, his wife (who had married him at the age of 13), and their three children were now left with a 21-square-meter dwelling without kitchen or bathroom. The family cooked outside and used the bathroom of the husband's mother who lived a block away.

In the Paraguay development, ICT had given another family a lot after eviction from Chambacú and a 20,000-peso loan for a three-bedroom house. Apart from installing better windows and doors, this family of four adults and two children had made no further improvements and planned none. The husband was a guard at a Mamonal plant, and the wife worked in a fish-packing enterprise. Together they earned 10,000 pesos monthly. Three nearby non-Chambacú families earned half as much but had added rooms, gutters, a terrace, a flat ceiling, had plastered and painted, and were planning further changes.

Houses in the Gaviotas development were similar in size and price to those at Chiquinquirá, adjusted for inflation, and were being constructed and occupied during 1977–78. Four households turned up in our sample. Their average income of 16,700 pesos monthly was 2.7 times that of the Chiquinquirá and República de Venezuela households. They included a highly skilled petrochemical worker, a denture maker, a dentist-physician couple, and a bus driver. To the 150,000-peso cost of their house, the dentist-physician couple immediately added 90,000 pesos to get a better kitchen, bathroom, windows, doors, roof, walls, and floors than those specified by ICT. The regular ICT contractors did the work. The money was borrowed from friends. The petrochemical worker and the denture maker used savings to make extensive changes in their ICT house before moving in. They had walls plastered and painted and additional rooms built on, and substituted better materials here and there. Two of these families replaced the asbestos cement sheet roof with flat reinforced concrete to allow later installation of a second story.

Only the bus driver with his monthly income of 9,000 pesos could not afford to make changes before moving in. But as soon as he had done so, he and his sons began making improvements on weekends: plastering and painting the walls, making a partition to separate the kitchen from the living room, and building more solid and higher patio walls. As soon as money would be available, he planned to put in tile floors, to improve the bathroom, and to add more rooms. With seven members, his was the largest Gaviotas household sampled, and at age forty he was the oldest household head. Perhaps he was also the only genuine member of the ICT target income group. Given their incomes, the other three families were not really prepared to move into the sort of house that ICT was offering.

Upgrading houses during construction is probably not as efficient as beginning with a better design in the first place, but for the buyers these inefficiencies were more than offset by the benefits of subsidized credit.

The government was subsidizing H3 dwellings for young households that were only temporarily in the F3 income category. Soon they would have F4 incomes and would live in H4 housing. The fact that richer families spent their income on local labor and building materials—instead of on luxury goods with a high import content—must, however, be counted as gain to the local economy.

An Improved House in El Socorro

Not enough detailed cases can be presented in a short study to give an accurate portrait of a city, but presentation of only statistics on hundreds of cases also gives an incomplete view. A few cases can show what is behind the numbers. This one concerns a small family with an average Cartagena income of around 10,000 pesos (US$260) monthly living in an ICT house in El Socorro.

The father, Augusto, a photographer, had been abandoned by his first wife and lived with his teenage son and new common-law wife. Thirty years ago, Augusto had moved from Montería to Cartagena as a boy when his own father had abandoned his family and the mother had decided to move in with a sister. There were five sons and a daughter. As the years passed the family stayed together but moved from the Canapote-LeMaitre district in the North, to Getsemaní in the Center, to Pie de la Popa further east, and finally to an ICT corner house in Blas de Lezo in 1967. By this time several sons were married. The Blas de Lezo house was expanded to five rooms and equipped with a front porch and a large louvered picture window. The front was plastered with decorative granite chips, and a side window was enlarged to make one room a small grocery store.

After seven years in that house, the brothers decided to split up into several nuclear families and sold the Blas de Lezo house to an owner of small commercial boats. The house rented for 2,500 pesos monthly in 1978. When the house sold for 135,000 pesos in 1974, a 10,000-peso balance had to be paid to ICT plus seven years of accumulated real estate tax.

Augusto used part of his share of the proceeds to make a down payment of 6,000 pesos on the 40,700-peso El Socorro house when he won an ICT drawing. The new house consisted of 84 square meters of floor space in two stories on an 84-square-meter lot. His monthly mortgage payments were 375 pesos in 1978 and 394 pesos in 1979. Monthly payments were 159 pesos for electricity, 80 pesos for water, 15 pesos for sewerage service, 30 pesos for garbage collection (every other day), and 42 pesos for police protection and street planting—a total of 326 pesos. Real estate taxes were an additional 100 pesos monthly.

Within four years, Augusto had plastered his house inside and out and had painted it turquoise. His front door was beautifully carved and had an elaborate lock. For 6,000 pesos he had a large louvered window installed in front, together with several 1-inch plumbing pipes as bars to secure the window against burglars. With 9,000 pesos in materials, Augusto added two rooms in the back, one above the other. Prefabricated beams supported the concrete panels that made up the second story. Built-in closets had been added to the upstairs rooms. The patio was then too small for a garden and was, therefore, cemented in completely. With such a small family and an inexpensive ICT loan, Augusto had enough income left over during these years to buy a television set and refrigerator. He estimated the value of his house as 275,000 pesos, more than double his original investment, even after tripling that to allow for inflation. He had brought it from H2 to almost H4, from below the stock-user matrix diagonal to almost above.

Rental Housing

Twenty-two percent of the dwellings in our sample were rented, and few tenants had any idea about the year of construction or subsequent improvements. Most had been occupants for only two or three years. Often they even lacked clear knowledge about who the owner or rental agency was and where they were located. Some families simply knew that once a month someone came by to collect rent. The prevailing view was that landlords never made improvements.

A Brief Survey

We chose a quarter of the rented dwellings, all those with fairly intelligible addresses for owners or agencies, and made a brief survey. Seventeen dwellings were involved: ten handled by agencies and seven by the owners themselves. In three cases the agencies claimed to have no record of the particular dwelling. Three of the owners' addresses were unhelpful. One address did not exist at all. Another produced a relative in charge of collecting rent, not the actual owner. A third person at first admitted to being the owner and then changed his mind. Useful information came from the remaining seven agency houses and four owners.

The average rent collected by the agencies was 3,900 pesos (US$100) monthly. The owners who handled their rented dwellings personally, mostly elderly people, collected an average of 3,400 pesos (US$86). The four dwellings that they rented out were thirty years old and were estimated to be worth an average of 688,000 pesos (US$17,600). Thus monthly rent was claimed as 0.5 percent of the value of the dwelling. One owner had just sold the dwelling in question, so the stated value of 1 million pesos may be considered the actual market value. In his case the rent reported by owner and tenant coincided at 6,000 pesos. The tenant, however, was willing to pay 8,000 pesos for this 720-square-meter house in an excellent neighborhood.

The level of rent as reported by the agencies coincided with that reported by tenants in four of the seven cases. In the other three, the agencies claimed that rent was one-quarter less. Two of the managing owners agreed with tenants on the amount of rent: one claimed to collect less, and the other more. Half of the tenants willing to comment on the issue were willing to pay 40 percent more rent than they reported paying. The other half were satisfied with things as they were, but would not pay more. The typical tenant had been there two and one-half years, and none had been there more than four, so the rate of turnover was high. Some tenants had been dislodged from their previous dwellings, and one was currently protesting an attempt to raise the rent by 25 percent and was making his payments to an escrow account in a bank, as prescribed by the Colombian rent control law.

Improvements

Given inflation and rent control laws, owning dwellings was profitable only if tenants voluntarily agreed to periodic increases or if they were dislodged through a variety of legal stratagems. While the dwellings were empty, landlords authorized improvements. Four types of improvements had been made in the average dwelling in our sample. Owners using agencies had authorized only two or three types of improvements; managing owners had authorized six types. Painting and plastering was naturally the most widespread type of improvement, followed by hooking up to the public sewerage system when possible—a compulsory measure. The frequency of improvements was:

Improvement	Frequency
Paint and plaster	9
Connect with sewerage system	8
Improve windows or doors	6
Improve floors	4
Improve kitchen; improve roofing	3
Add rooms, water connection, terrace and railing; finish ceiling	2
Replace walls	1

The average income of this group of tenants was 18,600 pesos monthly, and the median income was 13,000 pesos, a relatively high level. Tenants with lower incomes typically had less education and were less able to give accurate landlord addresses.

Problems of Landlords

One function of the real estate agencies was to spare the owners all the irritations of dealing with tenants and with the government in the presence of unrealistic rent controls. The law dates back to the mid-1950s, but its enforcement was strengthened in the mid-1970s at the very time that accelerating inflation made its effects more damaging to the rational use of the housing stock. Colombians who worked abroad, including the many in Venezuela, preferred to leave their house vacant or in free occupancy by guarding friends rather than become involved with rental legislation. Even when occupants voluntarily agreed to rent increases that matched inflation, they could change their mind after some years and recover all the excess from the landlords through the courts.

Occupants could be dislodged only if they failed to make payments for two months or if the owner needed the house for himself. In this latter case, the tenant could challenge the owner's sincerity in the courts, and the process of eviction would take at least four months and possibly up to a year. In this frustrating situation, many owners preferred to have as little to do with their property as possible and to leave everything to the agencies. These guaranteed payment of monthly rent on schedule and would use the funds to make various tax, school, and other payments for the owners. The infrequency of long-term tenancy indicated that, after inflation had eroded the real value of rental payments, owners did take the necessary steps to restore their incomes even if it meant selling the property.

The best landlord-tenant relations existed when there was some kind of direct personal understanding between the two, regardless of laws. This was the case among the elderly couples whose extra houses were their investment and hedge against inflation for old age. Under these circumstances the most improvements were undertaken. We found this interest and willingness among landlords both in fashionable Bocagrande and in poor sectors. In Bocagrande we found a landlord who rented the other floor of his own house and who had built a second rental unit toward the side of his property. He had made more improvements than anyone.

A poor landlord, who had taught band music in a high school, lived in a wooden shack and had lodgers in other shacks at the back of his property. Open sewers ran past these shacks. Nearby was another house that he had built as a rental unit in 1938. Among the improvements on this house were a new straw roof and a latrine. The current occupant dropped in for a visit during the interview with the landlord. She supported herself and three children by selling contraband from Venezuela, earning 6,000 pesos monthly. She had been in the house less than a year. Eight types of improvements had been made on her house before she came.

One managing landlord who owned several units of low quality had made comparatively few changes, but one of these was interesting and significant. He had installed his own sewerage system, which emptied into a creek that flowed into the Cienaga de la Tesca o Virgen. Unfortunately sewerage from unconnected dwellings of others at higher levels still flowed into his terrain. This characteristic and the lack of serviceable streets led him to claim that the unit in the sample could be sold for only 250,000 pesos—not the 553,000-peso assessed value.

The Government as Landlord

Government agencies usually make the worst landlords. In Cartagena this tendency was illustrated by two dwellings in Barrio Militar, a quarter for noncommissioned officers at the northern tip of the city, located in angle between the runway of the airport and the Caribbean. Both units were intermediate 135-square-meter dwellings with one bathroom, built on 200-square-meter lots in 1966 for 94,500 pesos. Since Cartagena construction costs had sextupled since then, their 1978 replacement cost was around 600,000 pesos

Initially the Navy had planned to sell these dwellings to its personnel, but soon found that some families would have resold them and moved out. Title was, therefore, given to a Fondo Rotario de la Armada, and rents were put at such a low level that the temptation to move out was gone. A sergeant in his twenties earned 5,700 pesos monthly and paid only 250 pesos (US$6.40) in rent—4.4 percent of his income. Another sergeant in his forties earned 12,000 pesos and paid 800 pesos (US$21) rent or 6.7 percent. Both paid an approximate 600 pesos for services.

No improvements or additions had been made in either dwelling, a failure that is most unusual in Cartagena. When asked how much of a monthly payment a house of this quality was worth, the younger sergeant said 1,100 pesos, and the older 1,500 pesos. They compared it with Basic ICT four-room dwellings currently offered at Nuevo Bosque. But these have only 61 square meters on 126-square-meter lots and sell for 235,000 pesos. The implication may be that the Barrio Militar houses had lost half their value through deterioration. Both owners complained that they still had septic tanks instead of sewers and that streets had never been paved. The city thought that the Navy should pay for these, but the Navy was leaving it to the city. The Navy made up some of its losses on housing by not providing the customary transport for the 6.5-kilometer daily trip to the base.

Rooms for Rent in the Ancient Center

Dwellings tell the story of both particular families and entire cities. During the early 1950s people feared that the ancient center would be designated a hopeless slum to be demolished. The railway and nearby parts of La Matuna were in fact demolished, and values of structures fell everywhere in anticipation of more destruction. At this time a young clerk cashed in her retirement fund and bought a two-room house for herself and her mother for 8,500 pesos (US$3,800, 1978). Enough money was left over to add four other rooms in the back, to make repairs, to plaster and paint, to improve the kitchen, and to install better windows and doors.

In time, the mother, who had only one year of schooling in her hometown of Sincelejo, retired from her job at the Hospital Santa Clara, and the daughter found a husband in 1971 and moved out. At this time water and a better bathroom were installed for 6,000 pesos (US$725, 1978), and the mother, aged seventy-one, began renting three of the rooms to tenants, single men, especially students. Another room went to a servant who helped in various ways, including selling soft drinks to the lodgers. The daughter, as owner, did not charge rent to her mother, thus foregoing possibly 5,000 pesos monthly. The 1978 value of the structure was estimated as 500,000 pesos (US$12,800). The mother said her total income from her pension, the lodgers, and petty sales was 6,500 pesos. Electricity, water, and public services cost 500 pesos monthly.

Summary

The average Cartagena homeowner had made three types of changes on his dwelling, including addition of a room. From 1973 to 1975 the average dwelling expanded from 3.3 to 4.1 rooms. The total number of rooms, amount of floor space, and value per square meter were significantly associated with income and the number of adults in a household, but the number of rooms added or amounts spent on improvement were not. Need and feasibility came together in various ways at different income levels. With self-help many poor and intermediate-income households rapidly brought themselves up to and beyond the stock-user matrix diagonal. Regressions, cross-tabulations (Appendix C), and case studies elaborate on these generalizations.

Tenants generally occupied housing that was on or below the stock-user matrix diagonal. They were unaware of improvements on their dwellings, but interviews with landlords showed that improvements had nevertheless been made, usually when units were vacant. Some analysts have concluded that expanding and remodeling for tenants by landlords is a desirable way to expand low-cost housing (Appendix E).

Colombian housing authorities have gradually moved away from slum eradication toward a policy of providing upgradable semifinished housing of smaller and smaller dimensions. Such physical designs must be complemented by guaranteed loans that are not too risky for households with low and fluctuating incomes that wish to upgrade their dwellings. Selling building materials at a discount may be the best way to help the poor after roads, drainage, and piped water have been installed. During the 1960s and 1970s Cartagena dwellings with indoor piped water were improved to an extent that cannot be explained by the cost of the water installation itself, by the income level of occupants, or by the general quality of a district. Water, like security of tenure, released a zeal to expand and transform.

Notes to Chapter 6

1. W. Paul Strassmann, "Housing Policy and Improvements by Owner Occupants: A Comparison of Neighborhoods in Lima, Peru" (East Lansing: Michigan State University, September 1981; processed).

2. Nicolás Rueda García, Centro de Planificación y Urbanismo, University of the Andes, quoted in El Tiempo (August 19, 1978).

7

The Housing Market

THE WAY SUPPLY AND DEMAND INTERACT in the overall housing market is too complex to be summarized briefly and accurately: brevity without omissions and oversimplifications is impossible. Dwellings from shacks to mansions are built, improved, converted, and demolished. Neighborhoods change in quality and access to the rest of a city. Households are created through formal or informal marriage, then the members move away from or toward relatives, change occupations, have children, accumulate assets, and die. Each change can make a dwelling unsuitable. Households can consist of lodgers, tenants, owners, or landlords. Governments influence decisions by controlling use of land, providing infrastructure, charging taxes, limiting rents, guiding credit, and changing the rate of inflation.

Housing Used by Four Income Groups

A summary for Cartagena must at least distinguish four income levels. Twenty-two percent were the poor with jobs such as domestic service, street selling, messengers, dockworkers, and other unskilled work of a type that will largely disappear in the course of economic development. These F0 and F1 households earned less than 4,000 pesos (US$103) monthly, and half lived in the Southeast Zone. Only 12 percent were tenants renting waterless huts that were somewhat smaller than the 100,000-peso (US$2,600) houses that most would eventually acquire or build. The typical household contained six persons. Nearly half had relatives working in Venezuela.

The lower-middle group with incomes between 4,001 and 8,000 pesos (F2) had the most households, 36 percent of the total. Mechanics, shopkeepers, office workers, and drivers were in this category. The 21 percent who were tenants lived in three-room H2 houses with their families of six or seven members. Few dwellings had sewerage system connections. As households grew to eight and nine members, often through doubling up with adult siblings or adult children, they became owners and added a room, usually with self-help but rarely if indoor piped water could not be installed. Thirty percent of owners in this income range, with households averaging 7.8 members, had not expanded their dwellings to four rooms or beyond the substandard H1 level in quality because of the lack of indoor water. Low value was not simply due to the mere absence of a water facility in itself; nor was small size due to lower need (smaller families) or lower per capita income (larger families).

Half of the ICT-financed dwellings had reached the higher levels of the F2 income group, usually in connection with some past eradication. These houses were designed to be expandable. The F2 households lived throughout the city, from the higher elevations of the Southeast Zone to others in Getsemaní apartments.

The upper-middle group (F3) consisted of highly skilled workers in mechanical, chemical, or electrical tasks, foremen, cashiers, bank clerks, private teachers, and people with fairly responsible positions in business or government. They earned between 8,001 and 16,000 pesos, not all from wages and salaries of one worker, and they were all above the median income level. They made up 28 percent of households. New households in this income range avoided waterless dwellings with latrines and were likely to rent until they inherited a house or could afford to buy something adequate. Hence, a large proportion were tenants (27.5 percent) and had two or three fewer members than households of owners. The household size for owners was 8.4 persons: 10.4 persons for households below the diagonal and 7.7 elsewhere. Hence lower per capita income had prevented expansion for some. The household size for tenants was 5.8 persons. Rents were disproportionately higher than rents at lower income levels.

As the head of an F3 household reached his mid-thirties, he acquired either an old house or a new expandable one with an ICT loan. Both tenants and owners were likely to move every five years, either because the landlord reclaimed his property or later because the owned dwelling could be sold for a better one. After all, dwellings on small lots cannot be expanded beyond a certain point. Houses could also be turned into rental property. After a room was added, still with much self-help, the average dwelling acquired by F3s was transformed into an H3 or H4 dwelling of four to six rooms with indoor water and sewerage connection, worth 300,000 pesos (US$7,700). Apart from taxis and tools, it was the family's best investment opportunity. Households in this income range typically lived in the ICT and Lomas zones, but they could be found anywhere, except perhaps in the Southeast.

Finally, some 14 percent of households earned over 16,000 pesos (US$410) monthly and were the upper class, unless that term is reserved for the 2.7 percent who received more than 32,000 pesos or those with distinguished family names. This F4–F5 group consisted of people such as owners of businesses, plant superintendents, doctors, and lawyers, much of whose income came from investments. If one of these households acquired a new dwelling, it was probably custom-designed and financed with family assets or a loan through the Banco Central Hipotecario or a Corporación de Vivienda. These households insisted on living in Coastal Zone 1 or Turbaco and were willing to occupy a small unit to make that possible. Hence 31 percent were tenants who paid fairly high rents when first moving into a unit and thus did not necessarily acquire a suitable H4 or H5 good-to-excellent unit on the diagonal. All nevertheless had water and flushing toilets. Accelerating inflation and rent control invariably brought rents down to bargain levels after a year or two, and that encouraged repossession by landlords and conversion to other commercial uses in Bocagrande. Conversion or expansion in the historical center was forbidden unless the dwelling remained white Spanish Colonial and in some areas not even then.

Thus the housing shortage in Cartagena, given incomes, was greatest for the rich and the poor. Most of the rich owners had tried to add a room, bringing the number of rooms to six, the same number as the size of the family. (Two persons per room was the average in all lower income groups.) The unfulfilled demand or high prices for excellent housing created a possibility for cross-subsidization from rich to poor, and for a while ICT tried to exploit that possibility by building profitable luxury apartments in the area where the slums of Chambacú had been eradicated. After pilings for 1,400 apartments had been hammered in, however, the land had to be sold, as previously discussed.

The major drawback of the preceding discussion is that it compartmentalizes the population into four income classes. It gives the impression that if new households joined one of the classes as tenants and then became owners and upgraded their dwelling, they still would stay within the class. If the data base had not been a cross-section but a time series of several decades, we could have reported the movement up from one class to the next. Illiterates have trouble moving up, and doctors begin high, but in between, earnings do rise with experience, promotions, and property accumulation.

Income also depended on the changing number of working adults, not just the career of one person. The median Cartagena household had three adults and four children under eighteen, some of them working. Ill health and accidents often brought early retirement, however, and many

Table 7-1. *Income, Rent, and Dwelling Value per Adult*
in Households with Different Numbers of Adults

Number of adults, excluding servants	Income per adult (pesos)	Rent per adult (pesos)	Dwelling value per adult (pesos)
1	13,100	1,830	563,000
2	4,900	1,090	182,000
3	3,000	690	137,000
4	2,500	510	93,500
5	1,700	240	59,600
6+	1,700	140	86,600

Source: Cartagena household survey, 1978.

adults, such as wives with small children, the aged, and invalids, were unemployed and thus had no earnings. Yet about two-thirds of households had more than one working member, as might be expected when two-thirds have three or more adults present. Income per adult fell sharply as the number of adults per household increased, mainly because second workers had worse jobs but partly because the poor were more likely to double up. Rent per adult and dwelling value per adult also fell as the number of adults per household rose, as can be seen in Table 7-1. Compared with households of two adults, households with only five adults had one-third the income per adult, and the dwelling value per adult was also only one-third as high. As discussed in Chapter 2, family structure in Cartagena was complex, and the patterns and prospects for doubling up and undoubling can only be guessed at without a study aimed primarily at that issue.

The Southeast Zone and Squatters

Throughout the study, conditions in the Southeast Zone have been compared with other zones and with those in the city as a whole. The Southeast population of 85,000 was one-fifth that of the city. Its average household size of 7.0 was the same as the entire city; but the average income of 5,500 pesos monthly was less than half that of others. Here 68 percent of dwellings were less than eleven years old, and 65 percent of occupants had lived in them less than eleven years. For the city as a whole, the same proportion—68 percent—had occupied a dwelling for less than eleven years. Those who rented paid an average of 860 pesos in the Southeast, less than half of the 1,960 pesos paid in the city. This represented 13.6 percent of their income instead of 18 percent. The greatest difference was in the value for nonrental housing: 418,000 pesos for the city and only 113,000 pesos for the Southeast, 27 percent. Excluding the Southeast, income in the rest of the city averaged 11,200 pesos and housing 503,000 pesos. The Southeast's income was 49.1 percent as high, but its housing was valued at only 22.5 percent of the value of the city's other housing. Half of Cartagena's H0 and H1 housing was there. Since demand patterns appear similar, the housing in this area was below a level explicable by poverty alone—a failure of supply due to the inability or reluctance of occupants to upgrade their dwellings.

In the Southeast 68 percent of households obtained water from water sellers or from public standpipes, compared with only 29 percent for the city. Sanitary facilities were latrines or less in 71 percent of housing in the Southeast, compared with 32 percent for the city. The income elasticities of demand for number of rooms in the Southeast was 0.935; for floor space, 0.431; for value per square meter, 0.562; and for total value, 1.123 (given family size and the life cycle stage)—all close to those for the entire city. When it came to housing, the inhabitants of the Southeast were not different, just poorer. Most of the analysis in this report has, therefore, been by income group, not by location. Specifically, density of settlement, lot size, distance from work, or real estate taxes did not seem to be an important influence on housing decisions. Future research might explore the threshold population size that makes these factors important, and how the transition comes about.

The number of poor households who occupied terrain without legal title is unknown. Part of the problem was that many of these households obtained the land themselves by filling in marshes so that sites were never illegally "invaded." Moreover asking about legality of tenure was a sensitive issue among people who clearly remembered the massive eradication at Chambacú. In our survey we decided not to probe for documents of legality. The 1976 census by ICT of the Boston-Tesca sector of the Southeast Zone did ask for documentary proof, and interviewers encountered much antagonism: "Very few showed ownership documents; most simply said that they had this or that document and displayed much suspicion and hostility in answering the question."[1]

Tenure among the 1,064 households was said to be documented as follows:

Document or type of tenure	Percentage of households
Owners; *escritura* (deed)	19.1
Owners; *minuta* (certificate of occupancy)	28.0
Receipt or certificate of sale	2.6
Certificate of inspection	0.6
None	32.0
Dwelling granted or lent without charge	4.0
Tenant	13.7
Total	100.0

With this information, one can only proceed with a variety of conjectures. If 33 percent of households in Boston-Tesca were without title or legality, perhaps the proportion was the same in the rest of the Southeast Zone. In that case, 4,000 households could be classified as squatters in this area. If an equal number was squatting throughout the rest of the city along the Juan de Angola Channel, at El Milagro, around El Pozón, and so forth, the total would come to 8,000 households, exactly the number estimated to be in H0 temporary dwellings. If 20 to 25 percent of occupants of H1 substandard dwellings were squatters, the total might come to 10,000 to 11,000 households or 73,000 persons, perhaps 17 percent of the population. Since a policy of no eradication (unless ICT land was invaded) and legalization of tenure was underway, no matter how the land had been originally acquired, the legal concept of squatting had less meaning than the physical characteristics of dwellings. Knowledge about this policy, however, diffused slowly. According to the 1976 survey, 88 percent of households had no members that belonged to any type of communal organization, and 34 percent had either not heard of the Southeast Zone upgrading program or "expressed a low opinion of the government and ICT and believed they would be evicted like those of Chambacú."[2]

The current policy amounted to a tacit understanding that, after thirty days, squatters would not be disturbed except for the possible construction of public facilities such as roads, drainage systems, and markets. Giving title involved an expense since it required surveying and drawing up legal documents. Depending on the amount of surveying and demarcation already carried out as part of civil engineering work, titles could be processed for 1,000 to 2,000 pesos each. In 1978 ICT had a 12.1-million-peso program to regularize land tenure in this manner. Households qualified if they had lived two years or longer at a site and if they were able to repay the cost over fifteen years at 14 percent, including insurance. Plans to extend water and sewerage systems to other dwellings in an area were also reassuring to those who could not yet afford connections. The more explicit such programs become and the more they are supported by small loans or below-cost sales of materials, the faster H0 and H1 housing will be transformed into something better.

The Overall Housing Matrix for 1978

The main 1978 stock-user matrix (Table 5-2) showed the way households with various incomes occupied houses of various grades. For example, 6,130 households (36 percent) in the 8,001 to 16,000-peso income range of F3 occupied H3 housing worth 160,000 to 320,000 pesos or 2,000 to 4,000 pesos in monthly rent. To repeat, such housing typically had four rooms, piped water, and a septic tank or sewerage connections. If it was built by ICT, it was called "basic," and one of the rooms was supposed to be added by the owner.

A striking characteristic of the matrix was the proportion of households in cells above the diagonal, 41.1 percent, with 13.3 percent substantially above, or two cells to the right. Only 29.1 percent were below the diagonal, with 10.8 percent substantially below. This variation can be quantified by ranking a position on the diagonal as 100, a position to the left as 50, and one to the right as 200. This corresponds to the doubling in value from one column to the next but remains relative to income or capacity to pay. According to this system, a weighted index for all Cartagena housing, except that of F0 households, gives a value of 157, a number that is unusually high compared with findings elsewhere.[3] It shows that for every household that is on the diagonal in the kind of housing that on the average it would be willing to pay for on unsubsidized market terms, another is in housing twice as good. The household can afford to be in that kind of housing because it has been upgraded by self-help and with remittances from Venezuela, among other sources. The lag of building costs behind inflation may also have shifted demand in this direction more than might have been expected.

The diagonal of the matrix is defined as representing where the average household would prefer to live. If more households in any income range prefer to be above than below (or vice versa), that is due either to market imperfections or to an improper choice of income or housing price ranges for the matrix. The ranges should reflect the income elasticity of demand: the percentage change in preferred housing expenditures at given prices that results from a percentage change in income.

Actual expenditures can hardly be trustworthy guides to income elasticities untinged by market imperfections, since spending takes place in the world as it is. The physical characteristics of each of the six housing types can be related, however, to new construction costs of each type and that can be related to monthly payments over fifteen years plus a realistic interest rate. In what income range would households be willing to make the monthly payments that fit each type? Would households earning twice as much be willing to pay double for a dwelling built with twice as much labor and materials? Would they want something still better? Market imperfections, shortages, and overbuilding make payments (actual or implicit) vary from this level. Clues about imperfections can be found through statistical techniques, through noting the extent of rent control and credit rationing, by examining distortions in land markets and utility allocation, by comparing price trends in different parts of the economy, and perhaps by naively asking questions directly. All these techniques were used, and they pointed toward an elasticity of about unity. This means little more than that 0.7 is definitely too low and 1.3 too high. An unduly low elasticity would put an incredible number of households above the diagonal at high income levels and too many below at low income levels. An unduly high elasticity would have the reverse effect.

Descriptions, interpretations, and policy conclusions of this study are not, however, sensitive to having ascertained perfectly what the true income elasticity of demand for housing is, hence the matrix diagonal. A poorly set up matrix would still show that improvements and expansions have put many households in cells to the right of ones that they would otherwise occupy. The widespread willingness and ability to improve housing at all income levels is the important finding about Cartagena. In making projections to a future year, it is more important to keep boundaries between income and value ranges unchanged than to worry about minor errors in the implied income elasticity. One can specify a goal of keeping housing conditions from deteriorating for households in any income range without being sure whether initially one-fifth or one-third were out of equilibrium. A correctly specified diagonal is analytically attractive and, like a Gini coefficient, makes it possible to compare one city with another at a different stage of development. For policy purposes it is needed if the goal is undefined except to maximize housing welfare under an investment constraint. Then one tries to move as many households as close to the diagonal as possible, and a wrong diagonal would be misleading. But if the housing targets have been determined in some other manner, then a correct diagonal is not critical.[4]

The stated willingness of both tenants and mortgagors to pay more for their premises than they were being charged does not necessarily prove the existence of market imperfections. In a competitive market with many homogeneous buyers, sellers, and commodities, only a few are at the margin, unwilling to pay a penny more for benefits received. The price was lowered to bring in these marginal buyers, and everyone else thereby received "consumer surplus."

Such market conditions obviously do not prevail in housing. At best, competition is monopolistic with great differentiation among buyers, sellers, and dwellings. No doubt, some tenants or buyers may gain by paying little for premises that have been vacant unduly long in the opinion of owners. But the cases we encountered were otherwise. Controls and inflation had made rents and mortgage payments less than households were willing to pay; information was imperfect at the time of contracting, and payments did not vary with market conditions. A different case applied to some tenants who paid more than they considered reasonable for their current dwelling but less than they would have been willing to pay for something larger and better. In this case, the supply response was faulty.

As can be seen in Table 7-2, the index of housing quality in Cartagena in 1973 was probably between 93 and 115—not bad, given income levels, but much below the 1978 index of 157. The great upsurge in home improvement since 1973 was due to a combination of factors. It began from a low physical base, after policy was reoriented because of the Chambacú eradication, and at the same time as the increased migration to and remittances from Venezuela began after the first OPEC price increase.

Upgrading and housing transformation was carried on by everyone, but especially by F1 and F2 households earning between 2,001 and 8,000 pesos monthly. Consequently, these reached an index level of around 185, compared with 125 for those in the 8,001-to-16,000-peso range. Thus, housing was distributed more equally than was income. The Cartagenian housing Gini was 0.305, whereas the income Gini was 0.419. By contrast, urban Sri Lanka in 1971 had an income Gini of 0.408 and a housing Gini of 0.551. San Juan and Ponce, Puerto Rico, in 1970 had income Ginis of 0.480 and 0.516, but these cities benefited from all the U.S. housing and urban development programs. So their housing Ginis were merely 0.196 and 0.320.[5]

The Cartagena housing Gini was brought down partly by the inability of high-income tenants to find suitable housing at sufficiently low initial rents. Highest income families may also have understated the value of their premises more than that of their income, although we have no special reason to suspect that.

From 1973 to 1978 the average value of Cartagena housing, owned and rented combined, increased from 183,000 pesos (US$4,700) to 275,000 pesos (US$7,000)—a growth rate of 8.5 percent, perhaps three times that of household income. Since this increase in value is in real terms, it may not be typical of developing countries. Linn notes:

> In the aggregate the supply of housing, as reflected by the rate of increase in dwelling units due to new construction and renovation, has generally not expanded by more than 1 to 3 percent per annum (Grimes, 1976), but that at unchanged prices demand for housing would be expected to increase by 8 to 10 percent a year ... Real housing prices will tend to rise in the rapidly growing cities of the developing countries.[6]

In Cartagena, the average house still under amortization was worth 308,000 pesos (US$7,900) and had three rooms, whereas owner-occupied houses without mortgages were worth 480,000 pesos (US$12,300) and

Table 7-2. *Distribution of the Occupied Housing Stock, 1973*
(percent)

Household income (pesos per month)	Dwelling type						Σ_F	Index
	H0 (temporary)	H1 (substandard)	H2 (minimal)	H3 (basic)	H4 (intermediate)	H5 (excellent)		
F0 (0–2,000)	<u>9.6</u>						9.6	100
F1 (2,001–4,000)	6.3	<u>14.2</u>					20.5	85
F2 (4,001–8,000)		8.8	<u>24.9</u>				33.7	87
F3 (8,001–16,000)			3.1	<u>20.0</u>	1.4		24.5	99
F4 (16,001–32,000)					<u>7.6</u>	1.8	9.4	119
F5 (32,001+)						<u>2.2</u>	2.2	100
Σ_H	16.0	23.0	28.0	20.0	9.0	4.0	100.0	93

Note: Since there were about 50,000 households, the actual distribution in thousands is equal to half of the percentages given in the table. Distribution of the housing stock was adapted from the census of 1973, as in Tables 5-4 and 5-5. The 1973 median income level of 6,660 (1978) pesos was found by assuming a 2.4 percent growth rate. Dispersion around the median in percentage terms was assumed to be as in 1978. The distribution shown in the table is simplified into a net presentation with the assumption that no richer household lives in worse housing than any poorer household. It was derived by knowing the dispersion of incomes and that of households but not the actual cross-tabulation. This procedure introduces a margin of error, and the actual distribution could have had an index around 115. Using this method the 1978 distribution would have had an index of only 127.

Source: 1973 census.

142

had four rooms. Owner-occupied dwellings five years old or less were worth 230,000 pesos (US$5,900), and those between twenty-one and thirty years old were worth 605,000 pesos (US$15,500).

These increases in value did not seem to be due to the rising amount or value of land and transport advantages. A distance from work of 2 to 3 kilometers was not significantly associated with incomes or density of settlement. Indeed the sign is wrong, and the longer commuters had smaller lots. What mattered for site value was not the size or distance of the lot, but whether or not it had water and public sewerage service and whether or not it was located in a prestigious district. When families in a given income range lived in more valuable housing, it was usually a physically better structure with better sanitary and water facilities.

The combination of new construction, maintenance, upgrading, and public works during 1973–78 was financed by savings, remittances from Venezuela, self-help, taxes, and subsidies. The share of the top three housing categories (H3, H4, and H5) rose from less than one-third to one-half, and that of the top two housing categories doubled from 13 to 26 percent.

The share of substandard and temporary housing, H0 and H1, fell from 39 to 30 percent, but this figure still represents some 18,000 dwelling units. These were dwellings worth less than 80,000 pesos, mostly shacks with latrines or no sanitary facilities whatsoever. The Southeast Zone had 48 percent of these dwellings. Clearly much remained to be done. What could be done, and what had already been accomplished must be judged in terms of income levels and what a city could afford.

Projections to 1990

Since dwellings and urban facilities are durable, policies to promote upgrading or new construction must look at least a dozen years ahead. During those years few dwellings will be demolished, but households will proliferate, incomes will grow, and the two will interact. It is a fairly plausible assumption that the population of a city like Cartagena will continue to grow at no more than 4.4 percent a year, that household income will grow 2.4 percent per year, and that the inequality of income distribution will remain about the same, that is, the dispersion around the median. Thus the median level of income rises gradually over the years, but, within an income range of from 20 percent below to 20 percent above the median income, the same percentage of households will be found. In the absence of convincing information to the contrary, such persistence must be expected since it is in line with experience elsewhere.

Whether estimated by quintiles, deciles, Gini coefficients, or some other measure, patterns of inequality change little in most geographic units. If manufacturing, tourism, and government continue to be the economic base of Cartagena and expand in proportion, then the structure of employment and incomes in these primary, as well as in secondary, activities is not likely to change much. A great expansion in residential construction and the manufacture of building materials could modify the distribution toward less dispersion on the low side of the median. But such an expansion is not likely to be as great in Cartagena as it might in other cities, since the conditions for transforming housing have already been relatively favorable.

With all those assumptions, the fraction of households earning less than 4,000 pesos monthly will fall from 22 to 11 percent by 1990 and will even decline in absolute numbers (Table 7-3). The 4,001-to-8,000-peso group will also fall relatively from 36 to 23 percent but will rise in absolute numbers. Households earning more than 8,000 pesos monthly will rise from 41 to 65 percent and will grow rapidly in numbers. The poorest subsector of households earning less than 1,000 pesos will fall most rapidly and will dwindle to 2,000 or 3,000 difficult or temporary cases. Since 1,000 pesos are equivalent to only US$25 (1978), achieving no

Table 7-3. *Income Distribution in 1978 and 1990*

Monthly income per household (pesos)	Number of persons (thousands)		Percentage distribution	
	1978	1990	1978	1990
0–1,000	6	3	1.4	0.4
1,001–2,000	19	18	4.4	2.5
2,001–4,000	70	60	16	8
4,001–8,000	155	165	36	23
8,001–16,000	117	241	27	33
16,001–32,000	50	159	12	22
32,001+	12	75	2	10
Total	429	721	100	100
Median income, pesos	7,500	9,300	—	—

Note: The income distribution is assumed to be as in our 1978 sample. Population growth from 1978 to 1990 is assumed to be 4.4 percent annually. Income growth is assumed to be 2.4 percent. The parameters of the income distribution around the median and the extent of doubling up are assumed as unchanged.

— Not applicable.

Source: Cartagena household survey, 1978.

more than that would hardly be reassuring. At the high end of the range, more than 32,000 pesos monthly, the number of households should rise sixfold or from 2 to 10 percent of the total. This pattern has been common throughout the world.

Although housing problems have usually grown worse in the course of economic development, the demographic and income pattern just described implies that the worsening has been unnecessary. Housing should become more manageable as the chance for cross-subsidization from the more-than-8,000-peso group to the less-than-4,000-peso group rises. The numerical ratio of these two groups goes from about 2:1 to 6:1. More or less stable in between these two groups are the 4,001-to-8,000-peso (US$100 to US$200) households that should continue to be supplied with semifinished, expandable, minimal housing.

Building to Meet the Demand

Let us not attempt to predict what will be built, but, rather, to estimate what should be built if housing conditions for each income level are to remain about what they were in 1978. Assume that all F5 (more than 32,000 pesos monthly) households will occupy luxury H5 housing. At all other income levels, assume that the index of housing welfare will be 150, meaning half on the diagonal and half of one cell to the right in housing twice as good. Let us assume, optimistically, that maintenance keeps all 1978 H2 to H5 housing from deteriorating and that none needs to be demolished for nonresidential use. Subtracting this remaining stock from what will be needed in 1990 produces the number of dwellings that have to be built (Table 7-4): 5,140 H2s, 10,770 H3s, 18,480 H4s, and 19,200 H5s. Including infrastructure cost, but not the site, these dwellings would each cost approximately 110,000 pesos, 220,000 pesos, 440,000 pesos, and 920,000 pesos, respectively. The pure site value is assumed to be 8 percent. Total construction cost would come to 38,682 million pesos over the twelve-year period, or 3,224 million pesos annually. This amount is 7.9 times as much as the 409 million pesos that was spent for licensed residential construction in 1977 measured in 1978 pesos.

All of these figures are to be understood as orders of magnitude that could vary substantially with different assumptions. If licensed construction by commercial contractors were to supply all the dwellings needed to keep housing conditions as they were in 1978 for each income group, it would have to grow at an annual rate of about 33 percent. Sharply different but still plausible assumptions could not bring that figure down by a great deal. Hence, the needed volume of building must continue to

Table 7-4. *Stock-User Matrix for 1990, Showing Minimal Construction Needed to Preserve Housing Conditions as in 1978* (thousands of units)

Household income (pesos per month)	Dwelling type						Σ_F	Index
	H0 (temporary)	H1 (substandard)	H2 (minimal)	H3 (basic)	H4 (intermediate)	H5 (excellent)		
F0 (0–2,000)	1.9	1.9					3.8	150
F1 (2,001–4,000)		5.2	5.2				10.3	150
F2 (4,001–8,000)			11.0	11.0			22.0	150
F3 (8,001–16,000)				15.7	15.7		31.3	150
F4 (16,001–32,000)					12.6	12.6	25.2	150
F5 (32,001+)						12.7	12.7	100
Σ_H	(1.9)	(7.1)	16.2	26.7	28.3	25.3	105.3	144
Remaining, H_j 1990	(8.0)	(10.4)	11.0	15.9	9.8	6.1	53.6	
Build, D_j 1978–90	(−6.1)	(−3.3)	5.1	10.8	18.5	19.2		

Note: The assumptions are that households will grow at an annual 4.4 percent and incomes at 2.4 percent. Maintenance keeps housing from deteriorating. In each income bracket, except for the highest, half of the households are on the diagonal and half are one cell to the right. Dwellings without the site cost 110,000 pesos for H2, 220,000 pesos for H3, 440,000 pesos for H4, and 920,000 for H5. All F5 households are assumed to be in H5 housing. Since durability should not be assumed for temporary and substandard dwellings, numbers for these are put in brackets.

Source: Cartagena household survey, 1978.

146

come, as it has in recent years, to a great extent from upgrading and self-help construction in a variety of ways—some informal, others partly commercial. Government policy should, therefore, continue to concentrate on facilitating this process by expanding the infrastructure, by building expandable housing, and by providing credit and guarantees for small improvement loans.

The absolute number of households earning less than 4,000 pesos monthly may hardly change from around 14,000 households. That this amount will be only 13 percent, not 23 percent, of the total is no consolation for those in that bracket. By 1990 some of the original 18,000 H0 and H1 housing units will have been improved to the level of better housing types, and others will have collapsed. Many of the original 14,000 households will have moved on to higher income brackets, and others will have dissolved through death and perhaps emigration. A strong tendency will exist for new poor households to raise new unsanitary, unsafe shacks. It would not cost much to bring these households up to the H2 level through heavily subsidized sales of sites and materials. The cost of 14,000 H2 dwellings would be 1,540 million pesos, less than half of what would otherwise be needed for residential construction in a single year, or about 3.8 percent of the total building program. If the poor can be brought to save half and to pay that much, the cost to others would be less than 2 percent of the building program. If such a small amount is set up as a target, a variety of programs could be the mechanism for mobilization. The 25-billion-to-30-billion-peso volume of H4 and H5 building could be tapped in part for cross-subsidies, as ICT and the Caja de Vivienda Popular (CVP) of Bogotá were already planning to do.

Housing problems in a city like Cartagena cannot be expected to disappear in a dozen years. Nevertheless, a normal amount of income growth will make the problem more manageable in relative terms. The poor will be a smaller share of a richer community. Their temporary and substandard shacks without water or sanitary facilities can be replaced with decent minimal housing at a comparatively modest annual cost. A large amount of self-help and informal upgrading must nevertheless be sought, not only from the poor, but also from households in the middle-income categories. Experience in Cartagena shows that under favorable circumstances people are willing to make that effort.

Notes to Chapter 7

1. Instituto de Crédito Territorial, "Censo de Propietarios en la Zona Suroriental, Sector II" (Cartagena, 1976; processed), p. 6.

2. Ibid., p. 55.

3. For other areas the indexes were as follows: Urban Sri Lanka (1971), 57: Tunis (1975), 81; and Lima (1970–71), 81. For Mexico, indexes were estimated for two years, 1960 and 1970: Mexico City, 68, 65; Monterrey, 68, 66; Puebla, 72, 68; Chihuahua, 73, 72; and Morelia, 75, 75. W. Paul Strassmann, "Alternative Housing Strategies for Sri Lanka," *Marga Quarterly Journal*, no. 2 (1977), p. 30. Agency for International Development, Office of Housing, *Tunisia: Shelter Sector Assessment* (Washington, D.C., January 1979), p. 49. Jesus Yañez Orviz, "Optimal Allocation of Housing Investment in Five Mexican Cities, 1960–70, 1970–85," Ph.D. dissertation, Michigan State University, East Lansing, 1976, pp. 116–23. The Lima estimate is unpublished work by the author.

4. W. Paul Strassmann, "Housing Priorities in Developing Countries: A Planning Model," *Land Economics* (August 1977), pp. 310–27.

5. A Gini coefficient of 1.0 indicates perfect inequality with one recipient having all and the rest nothing. When all share equally, the Gini is zero. Lower Ginis mean greater equality. Estimates were made with U.S. census data and with data from Marga Institute, *Housing in Sri Lanka* (Colombo, 1976).

6. Johannes Linn, *Cities in the Developing World: Policies for Their Equitable and Efficient Growth* (New York: Oxford University Press, 1982).

8

Lessons from Experience

UNEMPLOYMENT, POVERTY, AND POOR HOUSING CONDITIONS reinforce one another in virtually all developing countries. The poor cannot be employed formally to build housing because more than half of the urban population cannot afford a commercially built dwelling with standard low-cost specifications. National housing institutions and international donors, including the World Bank, have therefore turned toward providing housing cores, serviced sites, and loans for upgrading substandard housing as an alternative approach. Dwellings would be built or improved by the occupants in a comparatively informal manner. Much evidence supports the belief that this strategy has worked well and should be expanded. What is uncertain is the form that additional support should take: whether more resources should be better controlled to avoid waste, or whether constraints, including rent control, should be removed to generate resources from the building and occupying population. Either way, can programs to improve dwellings be self-expanding or replicable?

Review

This study has attempted to explore these issues in the context of the entire urban housing market under the assumption that there is no separate, insulated housing sector for the poor. The housing market may be too fractured to justify a sophisticated neoclassical equilibrium model, but still no part can be understood without reference to the whole. In this study specific issues have been illustrated with experience in Cartagena.

Housing needs in terms of mere numbers of units can be derived from population growth and average household size. For Cartagena, a population growth of from 429,000 to 721,000 between 1978 and 1990 would mean the addition of at least 44,000 dwellings. Their minimum quality, however, can only be socially—not physically—determined. Actual standards will depend on income and access to finance, land, and public utilities. The most likely income distribution is log-normal with a Pareto tail; and with a substantial variance, the income elasticity of demand is likely to be close to unity. In Cartagena, median income in 1978 was 7,500 pesos (US$192), but log-normality and the Pareto tail brought the average up to 9,900 pesos (US$254). The apparent income elasticity of demand of observed payments and values was 0.8 for tenants, 0.9 for mortgagors, and 1.2 for all owners. Adjustments for market disequilibrium seemed to bring all three groups closer to unity.

On the supply side, the housing stock was divided into the usual six categories: temporary, substandard, minimal, basic, intermediate, and excellent. In Cartagena, the share of the top three categories rose from one-third to slightly over one-half of the housing stock during 1973–78. Still only one-third had both piped water and a connection to the sewerage system. Wherever such infrastructure was lacking, self-help improvements were considered less worthwhile by owners, and housing values were correspondingly lower. The average house was worth 275,000 pesos (US$7,000) and had a floor space of 145 square meters divided among four rooms. In recent years about one-half had been built by the owner, more or less informally; and one-quarter had been supplied by the ICT with highly subsidized credit. Nearly 90 percent of owners had made improvements on their dwellings, usually three different types of changes. On the average they had added 0.8 rooms, an amount that is confirmed by comparing sizes in 1978 with those of the 1973 census. Two other types of improvement had also been made, usually within two years of moving in. This high rate of improvement explains why Cartagena owner-occupants generally had better dwellings than could be explained on the basis of income alone.

Becoming an owner of a relatively adequate dwelling was easier for poorer families who were willing to squat and build for themselves or for middle-income families who had access to subsidized credit than for richer families. Hence the average monthly income of tenants, 12,800 pesos, was 36 percent above the 9,500 pesos of owners without mortgages. Tenants spent 18 percent of their income on rent, but for every two households that lived in housing they considered appropriate for their income level, three households lived in less adequate housing. Since tenants were willing to pay 50 percent more for their current premises if necessary, and still more for something better, their inadequate housing may have been, as in so many other countries, the effect of rent control. Making a tenant move by selling or reoccupying premises oneself temporarily was the only sure way for an owner to raise rent in Colombia. This cumbersome technique and others were used so often that tenants moved twice as much as owners. Only 16 percent of tenants had lived more than five years at a site, compared with 58 percent of others. Interviews with a small subsample of landlords suggested that they made about as many different types of changes as owner-occupants whenever their property was vacant. Improved housing supplies and more construction employment would result from removing constraints on landlords of all types.

For new housing, construction costs in 1978 ranged from 2,000 pesos (US$51) per square meter for minimal housing to 3,000 pesos (US$77) per square meter for intermediate housing, not including the cost of the site, site improvement, development, and sales promotion. Site costs varied from 35,000 to 70,000 pesos and amounted to 20 percent of the costs of intermediate housing and 40 percent of minimal housing. Without subsidies, the most minimal 20-square-meter unfinished housing could have been sold for perhaps 80,000 pesos (US$2,000). If monthly incomes of 4,000 pesos were considered the minimum for financing such an amount, 78 percent of Cartagena households could have afforded this quality of new house or better. If costs proved to be one-third higher, only 67 percent of households could afford that much. The remainder had to depend on self-help, upgrading, or filtering.

Lack of reliable data at the national, urban, enterprise, and household level made it difficult to assess the effects of alternative housing strategies on employment. One source, however, estimated that on-site employment to build single-family housing required eighteen man-hours per square meter and 29 percent of construction costs. Another made the share 31.5 percent. A third study put the share at only 22 percent and concluded that an 80-square-meter dwelling would generate 1.5 work-years of work on the site. The employment share is less partly because larger and better housing is less labor-intensive. For any type, about half the work would be unskilled.

Small builders in residential construction had subcontractors hire more than two-thirds of the workers used and did not really know how many masons, helpers, or diggers were employed. Nor did self-help builders keep track of how long each family member worked on what. At least it can be stated that the labor intensity of this sector had been preserved, and that its costs had risen at a rate only half that of the cost of living. All this had been accomplished without remarkable innovations. Experiments with sulfur bonding, however, suggest that construction costs could be dramatically reduced by one-quarter if the price of sulfur stays low and workers learn the technique.

In Appendix D, conditions in Cartagena are illustrated with cross-tabulations of households and housing, called stock-user matrixes. These show the characteristics of household-dwelling combinations for six income ranges and six rent or value ranges. In Chapter 7 rental and value matrixes were combined in a single set and were projected to 1990. Such matrixes have shown, first, the share of the population in each cell and, second, other characteristics of the households and dwellings. If the income and value categories have been set up to reflect the income elasticity of the demand for housing, the combinations on the diagonal can be used as the standard for housing welfare, adjusted for relative economic capacity. Thus we found that, because of upgrading, owner-occupants were unusually well off—and tenants not so well. Projections of these conditions under alternative assumptions would be a worthwhile subject of future research.

Households in different cells varied greatly in size. In general, tenants had smaller households. For dwellings we reported floor space, number of rooms, number of rooms added, adequacy of materials, type of water source, type of plumbing facility, and the like. Thus one can see why dwellings in a certain cell happened to be in that value range and what type of household tended to prefer these characteristics. Some of the results were further tested with multiple regressions and logit analysis. Among other things, a strong association was found between indoor piped water and home improvement. More adults in a household raised the number of rooms and floor space occupied but reduced the value per square meter. Household size was negatively associated with both value and rent, but not at a highly significant level. By life cycle, new and old households tended to spend more on housing than those with many children, at least among owner-occupants.

In most cities in developing countries, residential construction lags behind other output, income, and demand, with the result that rents and dwelling prices rise more than inflation. In Cartagena during 1973–78 the reverse appears to have been true: dwelling prices rose less than others, and construction (especially informal upgrading) expanded to such an extent that the real value of the stock rose for the average household. The Gini coefficient showed more equality in housing consumption than income, and the stock-user index of housing quality rose from about 93 to 157. If this level is to be retained to 1990, the city must amplify such policies as regularizing land tenure, extending utilities networks, building small but expandable dwellings or sanitary cores, and selling building materials with small loans or matching grants. Rental of rooms should also be encouraged as a way to raise capital and expand the housing stock.

What has happened in Cartagena on a large scale has been observed elsewhere for individual projects. Madavo, Haldane, and Cameron reviewed serviced-site and slum upgrading projects assisted by the World Bank and concluded that:

Houses are being built and built quickly. Once lots are serviced and allocated, virtually all families entitled to take out materials loans do so and usually take out the full amounts they are entitled to. . .

Participants also appear to build their houses more quickly when left to organize their own construction efforts and to choose the mix of self help, group or mutual help, and hiring artisan contractors from the informal sector. . . The use of small contractors in the projects has been one unanticipated but important result of site and services and upgrading. . .

Another important finding has been that the houses coming up on site in almost all projects are very substantial structures, more substantial than anticipated. . . . Some of them can mobilize substantial savings of their own, not revealed by their monthly income flows, or of family and friends. It also seems that most families accept a much tighter budget than normal during the short period of construction. . . . Individual households appear to be carrying on improvements beyond the project requirements. In Jamaica, roughly 70 percent of the houses provided under the project are being extended. In Zambia and Botswana, where the reticulation supplying the stand-pipes was planned to provide up to 50 percent of the households with individual connections, many residents have hooked up their own individual connections.[1]

Surveying the same experience, Linn reported that the important constraints on low-income shelter construction were building codes, zoning requirements, rent control, lack of collateral for loans, capital rationing due to submarket interest rates, and insufficient accessible serviced land. Actual construction could be carried out by families and hired artisans at a cost of from 20 to 50 percent below that of similar work using normal government contracting methods, as reported for Manila:

In the case of the first urban development project in Manila financed by the World Bank, it was found that building materials loans contributed significantly to the stimulation of private housing investment. In the same project, it was furthermore found that with regularization of land titles and basic services provision considerable amounts of informal capital (from relatives, friends, and so forth) became available to finance land acquisition charges and shelter construction costs.[2]

Finally, a number of issues turned up for further exploration. For example, 17 percent of owner-occupied households were headed by women. Average value of their dwellings was only 216,000 pesos (an H3 basic), less than half that of H4 intermediate dwellings headed by men and worth an average of 458,000 pesos. Were the female-headed households less able to organize improvements, and are they therefore good candidates for assistance? Or were they also in a different income and life cycle stage? Absence of a male head of household generally removes one source of income and presumably lowers the total. Households with only one source of income occupied housing worth an average of 349,000 pesos, whereas those with multiple sources occupied housing worth 48 percent more or 516,000 pesos.

Obstacles to Transformation

What inhibits the transformation of housing for and by the poor? Their poverty is the main factor, but to build for oneself is to become less poor, and growth can begin with a few more concrete blocks and pipes here and there. What factors besides poverty frustrate expansion?

To begin, the poor build less and less well than they could because of ignorance and fear that is often well founded. Ignorance results in less building because of excessive costs due to improper designs. Architects say that plumbing could be arranged more conveniently, that foundations could be simpler, and that prestressed beams could save ceiling costs. Unfortunately, where building has to be clandestine, official channels for advice on better designs are not likely to be set up or used. Knowledge of and access to conventional materials does not seem to be a problem. Technological difficulties are minor.

More important is the fear of losing one's investment. The catalytic effects of giving squatters title to their land, if at all possible, are now well known, and programs to eradicate slums have become anachronistic throughout the world. Nowadays the poor are more afraid of losing their investment if they are unable to make regular payments on their debts. One does not borrow for an improvement like an added room if bad luck on the job can jeopardize ownership of an entire house. Even if the equity is repaid by the creditors, fears are that a similar house without the improvement cannot be bought with that amount. A flexible, sensitive, and generous insurance system is needed to prevent unnecessary hardship from default.

Opportunities are also missed not only because fears are generated, but because hope is not aroused. Access to water and public sewerage systems fosters confidence in the future of a district and in the yield from housing improvements. It therefore inspires upgrading activities. If households doubt that their neighborhoods will shortly or ever be included in utility network expansion, the transformation of housing through self-help will be discouraged. Public utility networks thus generate benefits not only from water and waste disposal, but from externalities in the form of other construction and employment. Delays in network expansion have a cost.

Another fear of the poor is that investment in improvements may be lost because their structure may violate some regulation. Since the poor do not like to build physically unsafe and unsanitary buildings, the regulations that threaten them are likely to have other objectives. One of these is that new buildings must come up to minimum standards of space and quality in other respects. At this point conflict arises between the wishes of the poor and those of groups in power with whom they must deal.

That elite groups find slums unaesthetic and would rather see something else is well known, possibly understandable, but this preference is no longer a threat to the shelter of the poor, as mentioned above. A more real threat is an attitude that may be called "gap mentality." Those with this attitude feel that there is a gap between decent and less-than-decent housing, and that this gap can only be narrowed by progressively building more and more decent housing; anything less will not help to close the gap. Such an attitude often has little relation to what a country can afford in macroeconomic and demographic terms. As economic sophistication spreads among those in public authority, gap mentality vanishes.

Closely related, however, is paternalism, the attitude that the poor do not really know what is good for them, and that priorities must be established for them through regulations. Each regulation of that type may inhibit the flow of credit, the generation of savings, the speed of granting permits, and will generally get in the way of what would otherwise be happening. No one treats the clothing of the poor that way, however, and they manage to sew and tailor for themselves quite satisfactorily.

Finally, there is outright suspicion of the poor—that they must be carefully supervised and controlled or they will do evil things like exploiting one another. They may build housing to rent to each other at excessive prices. That these prices reflect the shortage of housing and may well incite a supply response is often ignored. After all, the government agencies are doing the best they can to supply housing. Recipients of government housing at bargain terms, according to this view, should not benefit by subdividing their dwellings to let other families share space or to operate a workshop or store. Was not the housing program set up to bring housing prices down and to eliminate overcrowding? One can see that suspicion easily merges with gap mentality. Whenever market pressures are such that some poor nevertheless remodel their houses to have a shop or to take in tenants, this activity is forbidden and has to be undertaken in a clandestine fashion. Naturally there will be less of it as a result, and it will receive no official support in the form of credit and technical assistance. Some public housing may even be deliberately designed so that expansion and subdivision for shops and tenants is difficult. Such policies should be reversed.

Housing Prospects

The prospects for housing transformation are different for the poor, the well-off, and those in between. All can benefit from better incentives for building, but for the poor these incentives should include a carefully designed transfer of resources from the top group. The middle group can be fully self-supporting. The next sections will give the reasons.

For the Poor

A fully self-supporting, replicable urban program of any type is unrealistic for those with an income of less than 4,000 pesos (US$100) monthly. The humanitarian gains and economic externalities from clean water and safely disposed sewerage are such, however, that subsidies for these services are fully justified. Convenient access roads and adequate drainage are also investments that probably raise productivity in proportion to costs, or more. A program of well-designed serviced sites is therefore logical. As mentioned above, programs should not mean large-scale destruction of existing assets, although these may seem like slums to outsiders. Now almost everyone knows that.

Whatever savings can be mobilized from this poor sector and whatever supporting labor can be generated are a gain for the program. To insist on mobilizing them to a fully self-financing level, however, amounts to giving up. Assistance to the poor should have realistic goals and should be justified in the context of the entire urban program and its possibilities for cross-subsidization. If small loans can be extended to the poor and conveniently collected through neighborhood institutions, fine. But if not, a system of matching grants against prior savings is worth a try. If the grants are paid in the form of building materials, it amounts to selling materials at a loss, hardly a replicable program. Nevertheless, it is worthwhile in the total urban context. Subsidized sales can stimulate savings better at that level than can subsidized credit, and they both amount to the same thing in principle. The difference is simply the ratio of subsidy to the recipient's contribution—which, inevitably, would be higher for the poor. The main problem is to avoid fraud by making sure that materials bought are indeed incorporated in the purchaser's dwelling. If not, that household should receive no more bargain sales.

A further gain would arise if the recipient of subsidized materials sales were required to help produce and distribute the materials as well as work on urban infrastructure in his own neighborhood. The actual contributions would still not make the total program financially viable in a narrow sense. Justification of the plan depends on its external effects, and among these, the educational effects of participating responsibly must be included, although they are hardly quantifiable. ICT has had such programs jointly with SENA, the vocational training agency, in Combeima near Ibague, Tolima, and in Venadillo, Tolima, and that experience should be studied carefully. The training of local leaders through the extensive *Acción Comunal* system is also a good example worth expanding. In Esperanza, district 7, a communal materials shop was being planned in 1978 with the idea of paying workers in blocks, not money. A problem was finding someone with collateral to back the credit for the initial installation. International support could take the form of underwriting the probable losses of an insurance or guarantee system, such as the one organized for Bogotá.

All programs of subsidies are rightly viewed with skepticism. But two reassuring elements exist. One is that within a dozen years, in countries that have reached the income level of Colombia, the target population is very likely to decrease. In Cartagena it should fall from around 95,000 to 81,000 or from 22 to 11 percent of the population. The other element comes from our survey: the astonishing zeal with which poor households improve housing. One grandmother said *"rellenar o comer"* (to fill in earth or to eat) was almost a daily decision that often went in favor of rellenar. Some observers have even feared that the poor build at the expense of their health, but that seems a little extreme: building as the "opium of the people."[3]

For the Middle-Income Group

The large group with incomes of from 4,001 to 8,000 (1978) pesos can afford minimal semifinished housing without subsidies. At the low end of the range, households seem willing to pay from 801 to 1,000 (1978) pesos monthly for housing and simply need terms and maturities that will bring a dwelling worth from 80,001 to 100,000 pesos within range— not an unreasonable condition. Since such a dwelling is not likely to exceed 20 square meters plus kitchen and washroom, it must be expandable. Payments must rise annually at as close to the rate of inflation of building costs as possible; and for families who cannot meet that rate because of some misfortune, the mortgage maturity must be extended. On the same terms, three-bedroom, semifinished dwellings can be sold for 160,000 pesos to households at the top of the income range. Given population growth, transport costs, and the need for increased density, the introduction of low-rise multifamily housing is farsighted. But multistory housing must be expandable and improvable. Once architects made their reputation by including everything in their plans; now they need to be able to leave things out in an ingenious way. A few models already exist in ICT housing at Rio Negro near Medellín. If housing policies in Cartagena had not been relatively successful in stimulating upgrading in the past at this level, not as many families would be in dwellings above the diagonal. As the city grows, that activity must be encouraged in new ways.

For the Upper-Income Group

Since households with incomes below 4,000 pesos need subsidies, and since those with incomes between 4,001 and 8,000 pesos can only be selfsustaining, the households earning more than 8,000 pesos must provide the surplus capital needed. They could do so in a general way through higher taxes, or they could have that contribution linked to the acquisition of better housing. Much can be said about the theoretical welfare advantages of unlinked taxation. In practice, tax collections or induced savings can be generated most easily when linked to benefits or permits disbursed by collecting institutions. Currently, urban housing policies in Colombia and other countries do the reverse and subsidize upper-income families by letting them acquire capital gains from general urban improvement, and by giving them subsidized loans. About half of the ICT mortgagors in our sample were at this high income level and were receiving public loans at negative real interest rates. The fact that they had not been in that high range when the mortgage was signed proves that their payments could have risen faster than the 5 percent annual rate. They should have taken out price-indexed mortgages with the Banco Central Hipotecario or one of the Corporaciones de Vivienda.

The advantage of multiple lending systems is competition; the disadvantage is that surpluses from institutions for one tier are not readily transferred to those for another. This barrier was to be avoided by programs like the ICT redevelopment of Chambacú for those with incomes greater than 25,000 monthly, by charging a 50 percent markup. Presumably, enough families can be found to pay that much for such a convenient location and ingenious designs. If several lending agencies cover most of the range of incomes, then all can be involved in cross-subsidy programs for the poor and can compete with one another. In Bogotá, ICT and cvp are already competing and learning from one another. Both do a little cross-subsidizing.

But if upper-income groups are to pay more, perhaps they should also be granted some conveniences in exchange for their contributions. Perhaps finance for selling used housing should be made more easily available, so that they would have the liquidity to seek the new housing that generates the surpluses. Rent control should be abandoned. It destroys maintenance incentives and therefore much of the old housing stock. In Cartagena it absurdly forces landlords to pretend to reoccupy premises to evict recalcitrant tenants. If the rich could buy and sell and move around as their needs changed, they could benefit more from the part of the housing stock that is theirs. They could, of course, be charged for the privilege. They should pay a bit more than the full cost of sites, roads, and services.

Completing the Circle

After we had talked to all the officials, read their documents, and reviewed our own sample of interviews of households, all of the ideas expressed above gradually emerged. To check them one more time, we returned to Fredonia, the poorest and the most distant part of the Southeast Zone, where Caño Calicanto and the last road merged into a swamp of sewerage. The cab driver took us as far as he could go and said be careful and not stay too long. Municipal officials had told us that only two former Franciscan nuns and university volunteers were helping this sector, and that it was simply beyond their own range and resources. They had enough problems elsewhere. But we had begun our interviews here, and so it seemed appropriate to finish here, to see it now in a different perspective, and to compare ideas with the former Franciscans, Sister Amparo and Cruz Elena Ramirez.

No, said Sister Amparo, a system of loans would not work here. People had other priorities, some worthwhile, others not. They would not repay loans, even small ones on the grounds that *"El gobierno o el obispo tiene plata. Nosotros somos pobres."* (The government or the bishop have money. We are poor.) Matching prior savings for building materials with an equivalent amount had possibilities. Some communal work on roads and ditches might even be induced with such an incentive. Without incentives some people would always shirk their duties, and the rest would become demoralized. Nothing could get done that way. If it could, these paths would not be such a morass.

We walked past a makeshift school with bamboo walls that provided a strip of shade. In it a line of small boys did calisthenics under the direction of a college student. Sister Amparo showed us where a German Catholic charity was helping to build a new school on the newest island salvaged from the marsh. Construction lagged because clean water for making concrete blocks had to be trucked in on a little causeway financed by the Germans. Anyway, Fredonia had not been totally neglected by the outside world. Sister Amparo hoped that a playground for children would rise out in the marsh where the herons now stalked among the mangroves.

As we left the area, a young woman came to us, and asked if our clipboards meant we were some kind of officials taking reports. A drunken neighbor had broken down the bamboo fence between their yards and had beaten her. Now he was in there with her children and would not leave. No one was at the small police station on Calle 32B. We showed her the house where she could find Sister Amparo.

Notes to Chapter 8

1. Callisto Madavo, Donna Haldane, and Sally Cameron, "Site and Services and Upgrading: A Review of World-Bank-Assisted Projects," Urban Projects Department (Washington, D.C.: World Bank, January 1978; processed), pp. 15–18.

2. Johannes Linn, *Cities in the Developing World: Policies for Their Equitable and Efficient Growth* (New York: Oxford University Press, 1982).

3. *El Tiempo*, August 19, 1978, quotes the architect Nicolás Rueda García as insisting on a distinction between the capacity to save and the capacity for self-deprivation. According to him much autoconstruction comes "with a sacrifice of vital necessities."

Appendix A

The Sample

THE AIM OF THE SURVEY OF CARTAGENA was to study 300 cases, about 1 for every 1,400 people or for every 200 households. To allow for unsuccessful interviews, a larger sample than 300 was actually drawn. Consequently 340 interviews were attempted, and 293 were successful. The distribution was:

Successful interviews	293
Competent adults absent	23
Refusals	13
Nonresidential use	4
Vacant site	4
Contradictory or incomplete	3
Total	340

The sample was drawn on the basis of population density. Gustavo Pacheco, demographer of the University of Cartagena and the Municipal Planning Commission, had divided the city into twenty-three districts, with an average of six subdistricts, and had estimated the population for each. We allocated our sample according to these densities but omitted a few subdistricts:

1. The fishing village of La Boquilla seemed too cut off from the rest of the area.
2. The naval bases and their barracks were hardly part of the housing market.
3. District 23 beyond Alberto Sierra was too remote and rural.

For any subdistrict with 7,000 inhabitants, five streets would be chosen at random, an easy matter in Colombia since streets are numbered. Then the block, the side of the street, and the house would be chosen at random: for example, the third house in the second block on the left side.

For most districts we obtained the planned number of interviews. Since we completed only thirty-eight of the planned forty-seven interviews in Bocagrande, Centro, and Manga (districts 1, 2, 6), high-income households are underrepresented in the sample. Twenty-one of the failures occurred here. Since we oversampled the area somewhat, expecting nonresponses, the net loss was only nine.

We also expected lack of cooperation in Esperanza, district 7, because this first sector in the Southeast Zone had been studied often but had received little help, causing cynicism and hostility toward any interviews. Thirty-nine interviews were attempted, and thirty-one were completed, so that we had four more than the twenty-seven that would have been in proportion to population. After that experience, we limited our interviews to the maximum number needed for any subsector, but made sure that attempts were evenly distributed within the area. Nevertheless, we were two interviews short in district 13 where the ICT development of Los Calamares was still uninhabited.

The Preliminary Questionnaire

Although the questionnaire had been developed as carefully as possible, using models of similar efforts and showing the results to colleagues for revision, actual trial led to surprises. No answers were possible at all in the first modest dwelling sampled in the Esperanza quarter of the Southeast Zone. A grandmother who was taking care of three children was amiable but said, frankly, she had no idea how much anything cost or what was planned. She did not even know the whereabouts of her son, the father of the children. The four of them were supported by remittances from the mother who worked as a maid in Caracas, Venezuela.

The head of the second household nearby was another grandmother who worked as a maid herself in the fashionable Bocagrande section, receiving meals and 1,800 pesos monthly. Her house was a rather large (170 square meter) concrete block single-story structure without windows, but it opened toward a 35-square-meter courtyard in back that was surrounded by an assortment of lumber. This lumber had made up two walls of the shack in which the family had lived for a dozen years until the father died. With the retirement pay that the mother received at his death, the family bought concrete blocks and enlarged the shack. The two walls that would now have been an interior division were dismantled and used for the backyard fence. A new latrine was installed and equipped with a porcelain toilet bowl. But the house still lacked sewerage connections, and water was bought from a neighbor. Apart from the mother, who was forty-five years old, four of her children lived in the house, including an unmarried daughter with three children of her own. Furniture consisted of straw mats for sleeping and boxes for sitting. The floor was dirt. The only decoration was a sign, "Viva el Socialismo." Few of the answers resembled our precoded ones, but after more trials, we knew some revisions that would be helpful.

The Final Questionnaire

The questions are divided into thirteen groups by topics: A. General Information, B. The Dwelling, C. Additional Rooms, D. The Kitchen, E. Water, F. Sanitary Facilities, G. General Questions about Dwelling Improvements, H. Finances, I. Moves, J. The Household, K. The Head of the Household and Employment, L. Transport, and M. Income. The sequence was determined by interviewing effectiveness rather than by logic in subsequent analysis. If respondents are told that information about improvements is sought, one had better get around to that subject quickly, as soon as the occupant and owner have been identified and the principal characteristics of the structure have been noted. Five sections (C–G) cover improvements and their cost. The section on finances (H) goes back to considering the dwelling as a whole. Value, monthly payments, and household income (M) remain the basic coordinates of any economic analysis of housing. But income, as the most touchy matter, is best left for last.

Value and income belong in some context. Neighborhood effects and location are explored in the sections on moves and transport (I,L). In between is the demographic section about the household (J) and the section about employment, unemployment, age, education, and so forth (K). If incomes and costs do not explain behavior, knowing these characteristics may be helpful.

The basic cross-tabulation involves monthly income (question 100) and monthly rent (question 42) or current market value of the dwelling (question 54). Other information either modifies this relationship or is related separately to either income or value. A closer examination of the questionnaire and its interpretation should, therefore, begin with questions 100 and 54/42.

In only three cases out of 296 were interviews rejected from the sample because of unreliable income information. The rejects all were in the highest income category and lived in the better residential districts. In one case the nominal head of the household was a sixteen-year-old girl who had been sent to study in Cartagena by her rich physician-rancher father. Four brothers and sisters and two servants shared the 3-million-peso (US$77,000) dwelling and received a monthly allowance of 20,000 pesos, but upkeep and improvement of the dwelling did not really come out of that. In two other cases income levels were given that were unrealistically low and inconsistent with other answers. Five other high-income households simply declined to be interviewed. There were eight other refusals in the rest of the city. Still other failures occurred, as noted above, simply because no one was present or because the address turned out to be nonresidential, including one house of prostitution.

In some cases respondents preferred to limit themselves to indicating the range in which their income fell in question 99. In such cases the midpoint was inserted in question 100. For the category of more than 16,000 pesos, 27,000 pesos was used since that was the typical income given by respondents who did answer. Only one household fell in the category of less than 700 pesos. Question 97 about the different sources of income was supposed to make the respondents think of sources other than salaries. Detailed information on each source would not have been forthcoming from many respondents and would have been very time-consuming to explore and to straighten out. The relative importance is therefore assessed only by question 98, which asks if any source accounted for more than half of the household income. Workers who received meals on the job usually came close to agreeing with the 1,000-peso estimate that was used. Employers and government officials thought a substantial variance around 1,000 pesos existed, but roughly an equal number thought it was too high or too low. The figure does put the 1,000-peso income of domestic workers on a par with the 2,000-peso wages of unskilled workers. Imputed income from owner-occupied housing was not counted in question 100.

Rental information (question 42) was checked with a small sample of landlords (see Chapter 6) and seems comparatively devoid of problems. However, tenants were not interested in the market value of their dwelling (54). It was important to note how long they had been on the premises (4) and if their rent had risen (43) in spite of rent control. Utility charges are paid by the tenant, not the landlord. Sixty-eight dwellings, about one-fourth of the sample, were rented and had to be analyzed separately. The tenure breakdown (question 5) is:

Type of tenure	Number of cases	Percent
Owner-occupied, with a mortgage	53	18.1
Owner-occupied, no mortgage	154	52.6
Rented	65	22.1
Granted, lent without charge, and so forth	21	7.2
Total	293	100.0

Analysis

Apart from household income, the current market value of a dwelling is the principal characteristic around which the analysis is built for 228 cases or 77 percent of the sample. Value can be obtained either by using the owner's estimate of the current situation or by applying a price index to past expenditures. In a high share of cases the two approaches gave almost identical results. If anything, respondents were better at appraising the current market (54) than at remembering past construction costs and values. In a few cases the construction cost index for Barranquilla-Cartagena did give a substantially higher current value than the owner's estimate. We then checked whether age and lack of education or other factors might have impaired the respondent's understanding of accelerating inflation. Alternatively, the dwelling might be unimproved or deteriorated (40) and unsuitable for the neighborhood (64). In clear cases of underestimation, the cost-indexed amount was substituted in question 54. Apparent overestimates were far more unusual and were usually related to a change in the value of the site, for example, in the neighborhood to which the municipal market, Bazurto, was transferred.

The first objective of the interviews, therefore, was to assess in monetary terms the current household-dwelling combinations in Cartagena. Next comes association of households by income category with other household characteristics, such as family size, number of children, changes in family size, age and education of the family head, number of workers, and type of occupation, sections J and K.

Similarly the value or monthly rent of the structure can be related to its age, manner of construction, area, basic materials, number of rooms, type of kitchen, and plumbing facilities, sections A–F.

At a more complex level, combinations of size and value in structures can be related to combinations of income and family size in households. Both of these can be separated further by district in Cartagena. Various other permutations are also possible and will not be listed here.

Most important to this study, however, is explaining the types of improvements in a dwelling—those already carried out, those planned, and those needed but beyond the capacity of the occupants. In cross-tabulations each of these changes can be related to dwelling type by value, type of household by income level, and combinations of income and value. The number of combinations rises to 100 if there are ten categories of income and ten of value, as in questions 47 and 99. On the one hand, there is the average number and cost of changes that improving households undertake; and, on the other, there is the percentage of all households that undertake some kind of improvement. The average actual change for the total population (*A*) is equal to the average change among improvers (*C*) times their percentage, a kind of probability (*p*). $A = p\ C$.

Most of the statistical analysis, however, has been concerned with simply determining the characteristics, question by question, of the housing stock and the occupants in various subgroups. Regressions can be used to explain the value of changes, the rent levels, total value, and income. Shares of rent or mortgage payments in income can be found (42 or 46 divided by 100). Income elasticities of demand can also be estimated (42, 46, or 54 and 100) for families of varying sizes and stages in the life cycle (section J).

In a similar manner, neighborhood and locational elements (sections I and L) can be related to housing values and income levels. One can expect that in a medium-size but rapidly growing city like Cartagena these have not had overriding importance. Far more important has been the uneven and partial availability of water and a public sewerage system. Correction of these deficiencies does not, however, depend on household behavior and, as discussed in the text, seems to be fairly well under way with the help of various national and international loans.

Appendix B

Questionnaire for the Housing Survey in Cartagena, 1978

Interviewer number ____   Interview number _____
District, name _____ number ____
Address ——

A. General Information

1. Type of dwelling (One answer only)

    a. ____ Single family, one floor
    b. ____ Single family, two or more floors
    c. ____ Multifamily, one to two floors
    d. ____ Multifamily, three to five floors
    e. ____ Multifamily, six or more floors
    f. ____ Rooms in outbuildings

2. Name and sex of the respondent

    _____

3. Name of the head of the household (household is considered to be persons who eat and live together)

    _____

    a. ____ Male
    b. ____ Female

4. How many years have you lived at this site? ____

5. Tenure of the dwelling (One answer only)

    a. ____ Owner-occupied with a mortgage
    b. ____ Owner-occupied no mortgage

   c. ____ Rented

   d. ____ Granted or lent without charge

   e. ____ Family property

   f. ____ Other (explain)

6. If the house is not yours, what is the name and address of the owner or rental agency?

_____

B. The Dwelling

7. How many years ago was this dwelling built? ____

8. Who built this dwelling? (One answer only)

   a. ____ The household; self-help

   b. ____ Workers paid by the head of the household; a direct arrangement

   c. ____ A contractor; using one of his own plans chosen by the head of the household

   d. ____ A contractor; using a plan designed for the head of the household

   e. ____ A private developer; this is the first occupant

   f. ____ ICT designed and built

   g. ____ Mutual aid or communal effort

   h. ____ Dwelling not new; another household had previously occupied it

   i. ____ Other (explain)

9. Area of the lot:

____ meters by ____ meters = ____ square meters

10. Floor space:

____ meters by ____ meters = ____ square meters

11. Wall materials (If several, choose the principal material)

   a. ____ Reinforced concrete

   b. ____ Concrete blocks

   c. ____ Clay bricks (tiles)

   d. ____ Wood

   e. ____ Adobe

    f. ____ Metal sheets
    g. ____ Asbestos cement sheets (Eternit)
    h. ____ Impermanent industrial materials—cardboard,
         burlap, plastic, and so forth
    i. ____ Impermanent plant material—palm thatch,
         bamboo, and so forth
    j. ____ Stones
    k. ____ Other

12. Roofing materials (If several, choose the principal material)

    a. ____ Reinforced concrete
    b. ____ Concrete blocks
    c. ____ Clay bricks (tiles)
    d. ____ Wood
    e. ____ Adobe
    f. ____ Metal sheets
    g. ____ Asbestos cement sheets (Eternit)
    h. ____ Impermanent industrial material—cardboard,
         burlap, plastic, and so forth
    i. ____ Impermanent plant material—palm thatch,
         bamboo, and so forth
    j. ____ Stones
    k. ____ Other

13. Number of rooms (exclude kitchen, toilet, or bathroom) ____

C. Additional Rooms

14. How many rooms have been added by this family? ____

15. How many rooms have been abandoned or lost, if any? ____

16. How was (were) the new room(s) made? (One answer only)

    a. ____ Subdivided an existing room without enlarging the
         house
    b. ____ Added on at ground level
    c. ____ Added on and subdivided the remaining structure
    d. ____ Added on the roof
    e. ____ Other (explain)

17. How many years ago was the room built? ____

18. How many pesos did the room(s) cost? ____

19. How many days of work did it take? ____

20. Why did you add the room(s)?

    a. ____ Had additional children
    b. ____ Gained additional relatives
    c. ____ Could afford more space; had higher income
    d. ____ Wanted to earn rent from lodgers
    e. ____ Wanted a workshop or store
    f. ____ Wanted a long-term investment
    g. ____ Other (explain)

D. The Kitchen

21. With what type of fuel do you cook?

    a. ____ Wood
    b. ____ Charcoal or coal
    c. ____ Gasoline or kerosene
    d. ____ Bottled gas
    e. ____ Electricity
    f. ____ Other (explain)

22. Where do you cook?

    a. ____ Outside
    b. ____ Inside without a kitchen
    c. ____ Share kitchen with another household
    d. ____ Have own separate kitchen

23. (If chose 22c. or 22d.) How many years ago was this kitchen installed? ____

24. (If chose 22c. or 22d.) How much did the installation cost? ____ pesos

E. Water

25. What is your source of water? What type of facility do you have? (If several, mark the most important)

    a. _____ River, spring
    b. _____ Rain, cistern
    c. _____ Well
    d. _____ Public standpipe
    e. _____ Water wagon
    f. _____ Neighborhood vendor
    g. _____ Faucet, shared with another family (public service)
    h. _____ Faucet, private, but no shower or bath
    i. _____ Shower
    j. _____ Complete bathroom
    k. _____ Two or more bathrooms

26. (If chose 25h.–25k.) How many years ago was this source installed? _____

27. (If chose 25h.–25k.) How many pesos did the installation cost? _____

28. (If chose 25h.–25k.) How many days of work did it take? _____

29. Is there running hot water?

    a. _____ Yes
    b. _____ No

F. Sanitary Facilities

30. What kind of sanitary facilities does this household have? (If several, mark the best)

    a. _____ None
    b. _____ Pit latrine
    c. _____ Toilet shared with others; communal
    d. _____ Septic tank

e. _____ Toilet connected to public sewerage system
f. _____ Two or more toilets connected to the public sewerage system
g. _____ Other (explain)

31. How many years ago was this facility installed? _____

32. How many pesos did the installation cost? _____

33. How many days of work did it take? _____

34. Today:

a. _____ The toilet works
b. _____ The toilet does not work
c. _____ The toilet does not work because there is no water
d. _____ Other

G. General Questions about Dwelling Improvements

35. When you acquired the dwelling, which of the changes that you have already made did you plan to make definitely?

a. _____ Additional room(s)
b. _____ Better kitchen
c. _____ More convenient water
d. _____ Better toilet
e. _____ Improved basic wall materials
f. _____ Improved roofing materials
g. _____ Plaster and paint
h. _____ Improved flooring
i. _____ Better windows or doors
j. _____ Earth fill
k. _____ None, the dwelling was finished
l. _____ Others, not specified
m. _____ None, although some were needed
n. _____ Terrace or railing
o. _____ Finished inside ceiling
p. _____ Connection with the public sewerage system
q. _____ Total reconstruction
r. _____ Other (explain)

36. Are you planning to make other changes soon? If so, what changes?

    a. ____ Additional room(s)
    b. ____ Better kitchen
    c. ____ More convenient water
    d. ____ Better toilet
    e. ____ Improved basic wall materials
    f. ____ Improved roofing materials
    g. ____ Plaster and paint
    h. ____ Improved flooring
    i. ____ Better windows or doors
    j. ____ Earth fill
    k. ____ None, the dwelling was finished
    l. ____ Others, not specified
    m. ____ None, although some were needed
    n. ____ Terrace or railing
    o. ____ Finished inside ceiling
    p. ____ Connection with the public sewerage system
    q. ____ Total reconstruction
    r. ____ Other (explain)

37. These other changes have not been made because:

    a. ____ Lack of money
    b. ____ Regulations
    c. ____ Lack of space
    d. ____ Value of the dwelling would not increase
    e. ____ Lack of time
    f. ____ Other (explain)

38. How did you finance the improvements in your dwelling? (Mark the most important)

    a. ____ Financing by the owner in rented dwellings
    b. ____ Self-help labor, cash for the materials
    c. ____ Self-help labor, credit from the materials supplier
    d. ____ Self-help labor, credit from ICT or other sources
    e. ____ Savings or sale of property
    f. ____ Advanced retirement funds
    g. ____ Inheritance, insurance, or other death benefits
    h. ____ Loans for everything from the ICT

     i. ____ Loans for everything from the BCH or a CAV
     j. ____ Loans from relatives or friends
     k. ____ Other (explain)

39. What other type of work does your house still need?

     a. ____ Additional room(s)
     b. ____ Better kitchen
     c. ____ More convenient water
     d. ____ Better toilet
     e. ____ Improved basic wall materials
     f. ____ Improved roofing materials
     g. ____ Plaster and paint
     h. ____ Improved flooring
     i. ____ Better windows or doors
     j. ____ Earth fill
     k. ____ None, the dwelling was finished
     l. ____ Others, not specified
     m. ____ None, although some were needed
     n. ____ Terrace or railing
     o. ____ Finished inside ceiling
     p. ____ Connection with the public sewerage system
     q. ____ Total reconstruction
     r. ____ Other (explain)

40. How would you compare the condition of the dwelling now with its condition when you acquired it?

     a. ____ Much better
     b. ____ Somewhat better
     c. ____ Same
     d. ____ Worse
     e. ____ Much worse

41. To keep it in this condition how many days of maintenance per month are needed? (The minimum is 1.) ____

H. Finances

42. How many pesos do you pay for rent each month? ____

43. How many months ago did it increase? ____

44. How many pesos do you pay for utilities each month? ____

45. How many pesos do you pay in real estate taxes each year? ____

46. How many pesos do you pay for the loan or mortgage each month? ____

47. When you acquired the dwelling, how many pesos was it worth (including lot)?

    a. ____ Less than 5,000
    b. ____ 5,000–10,000
    c. ____ 10,001–20,000
    d. ____ 20,001–30,000
    e. ____ 30,001–40,000
    f. ____ 40,001–60,000
    g. ____ 60,001–80,000
    h. ____ 80,001–160,000
    i. ____ 160,001–320,000
    j. ____ More than 320,000

48. Exactly how many pesos is the dwelling (including lot) worth now? Exact value (if possible) ____

49. When you acquired the lot, how many pesos was it worth (more or less)? ____

    a. ____ Less than 5,000
    b. ____ 5,000–10,000
    c. ____ 10,001–20,000
    d. ____ 20,001–30,000
    e. ____ 30,001–40,000
    f. ____ 40,001–60,000
    g. ____ 60,001–80,000
    h. ____ 80,001–160,000
    i. ____ 160,001–320,000
    j. ____ More than 320,000

50. Exactly how many pesos is the lot worth now? ____

51. How many pesos was the down payment? ＿＿

     a. ＿＿ Less than 5,000
     b. ＿＿ 5,000–10,000
     c. ＿＿ 10,001–20,000
     d. ＿＿ 20,001–30,000
     e. ＿＿ 30,001–40,000
     f. ＿＿ 40,001–60,000
     g. ＿＿ 60,001–80,000
     h. ＿＿ 80,001–160,000
     i. ＿＿ 160,001–320,000
     j. ＿＿ More than 320,000

52. Exact amount of the down payment ＿＿ pesos

53. How many years did you have to pay off the mortgage? ＿＿

54. If you wished to sell your house today, how many pesos do you think you could sell it for? ＿＿

     a. ＿＿ Less than 5,000
     b. ＿＿ 5,000–10,000
     c. ＿＿ 10,001–20,000
     d. ＿＿ 20,001–30,000
     e. ＿＿ 30,001–40,000
     f. ＿＿ 40,001–60,000
     g. ＿＿ 60,001–80,000
     h. ＿＿ 80,001–160,000
     i. ＿＿ 160,001–320,000
     j. ＿＿ More than 320,000

55. What share of your household income (including gifts, pensions, and so forth) are your monthly payments or your rent? (Use percentages) ＿＿

56. Before deciding to buy or to build, did you receive some special income, advanced retirement benefits, inheritance, and so forth?

     a. ＿＿ Yes
     b. ＿＿ No

57. If you got a loan, who lent the money?

    a. _____ ICT
    b. _____ BCH
    c. _____ CAV, or other banks
    d. _____ Relatives or friends
    e. _____ Employer or company
    f. _____ Other (explain)

I. Moves

58. What was the main reason you moved here? (One answer only)

    a. _____ To be close to work
    b. _____ To have better public utilities
    c. _____ To have a better neighborhood in other ways
    d. _____ To become an owner
    e. _____ To pay less
    f. _____ To have a bigger dwelling
    g. _____ To have a better quality dwelling
    h. _____ To have a shop, store, or office
    i. _____ To move away from relatives
    j. _____ To move closer to relatives
    k. _____ Other (explain)

59. What were other important reasons for moving here?

    a. _____ To be close to work
    b. _____ To have better public utilities
    c. _____ To have a better neighborhood in other ways
    d. _____ To become an owner
    e. _____ To pay less
    f. _____ To have a bigger dwelling
    g. _____ To have a better quality dwelling
    h. _____ To have a shop, store, or office
    i. _____ To move away from relatives
    j. _____ To move closer to relatives
    k. _____ Other (explain)

60. Are you now thinking of moving?

    a. _____ Yes
    b. _____ No

61. If yes, what is the main reason?

      a. ____ To be close to work
      b. ____ To have better public utilities
      c. ____ To have a better neighborhood in other ways
      d. ____ To become an owner
      e. ____ To pay less
      f. ____ To have a bigger dwelling
      g. ____ To have a better quality dwelling
      h. ____ To have a shop, store, or office
      i. ____ To move away from relatives
      j. ____ To move closer to relatives
      k. ____ Other (explain)

62. How many pesos would you be willing to pay for a dwelling of this quality? ____

63. If another household occupied this dwelling before yours, were they:

      a. ____ Much richer
      b. ____ Somewhat richer
      c. ____ About as well off as your family
      d. ____ Somewhat poorer
      e. ____ Much poorer

64. How would you rate your neighbors in this street according to income?

      a. ____ Much richer
      b. ____ Somewhat richer
      c. ____ About as well off as your family
      d. ____ Somewhat poorer
      e. ____ Much poorer

J. The Household

65. How many households live in this dwelling? ____

66. When you moved here, how many minors (seventeen years old or less) were part of your household? ____

67. When you moved here, how many adults (eighteen years old or more) slept here, including servants? ____

68. Now how many children up to five years old? ____

69. Now how many minors, six to thirteen years old? ____

70. Now how many minors, fourteen to seventeen years old? ____

71. Now how many adults (eighteen years old or more)? ____

72. How many servants (adults and minors) are in the household? ____

73. Now how many renters or lodgers (adults, minors, or children) are in the household? ____

K. The Head of the Household and Employment

74. How old is the head of the household? ____

75. Was the head born in Cartagena?

    a. ____ Yes
    b. ____ No

76. How many years ago did he or she migrate to Cartagena? ____

77. How many years of schooling did the head receive? (99 means "none" or "illiterate") ____

78. Is the head currently employed?

    a. ____ Yes
    b. ____ No

79. Has anyone in this household ever worked in Venezuela?

    a. ____ Yes
    b. ____ No
       Explain:

80. What is the occupation of the head of the household?

    a. ____ Unskilled worker
    b. ____ Skilled worker
    c. ____ Highly skilled worker
    d. ____ Office worker
    e. ____ Foreman
    f. ____ Technician, semiprofessional
    g. ____ Professional
    h. ____ Street vendor
    i. ____ Other salesperson
    j. ____ Owner of a store or business
    k. ____ Domestic service
    l. ____ Other personal services
    m. ____ Other (explain; includes retirement)
    n. ____ Police or military
Write the name of the job _____

81. What is the occupation of the spouse?

    a. ____ Unskilled worker
    b. ____ Skilled worker
    c. ____ Highly skilled worker
    d. ____ Office worker
    e. ____ Foreman
    f. ____ Technician, semiprofessional
    g. ____ Professional
    h. ____ Street vendor
    i. ____ Other salesperson
    j. ____ Owner of a store or business
    k. ____ Domestic service
    l. ____ Other personal services
    m. ____ Other (explain; includes retirement)
    n. ____ Police or military
Write the name of the job _____

82. What is the occupation of the first other worker, if any?

    a. ____ Unskilled worker
    b. ____ Skilled worker
    c. ____ Highly skilled worker
    d. ____ Office worker
    e. ____ Foreman

    f. ____ Technician, semiprofessional
    g. ____ Professional
    h. ____ Street vendor
    i. ____ Other salesperson
    j. ____ Owner of a store or business
    k. ____ Domestic service
    l. ____ Other personal services
    m. ____ Other (explain; includes retirement)
    n. ____ Police or military
Write the name of the job _____

83. What is the occupation of the second other worker, if any?

    a. ____ Unskilled worker
    b. ____ Skilled worker
    c. ____ Highly skilled worker
    d. ____ Office worker
    e. ____ Foreman
    f. ____ Technician, semiprofessional
    g. ____ Professional
    h. ____ Street vendor
    i. ____ Other salesperson
    j. ____ Owner of a store or business
    k. ____ Domestic service
    l. ____ Other personal services
    m. ____ Other (explain; includes retirement)
    n. ____ Police or military
Write the name of the job _____

84. What is the occupation of the third other worker, if any?

    a. ____ Unskilled worker
    b. ____ Skilled worker
    c. ____ Highly skilled worker
    d. ____ Office worker
    e. ____ Foreman
    f. ____ Technician, semiprofessional
    g. ____ Professional
    h. ____ Street vendor
    i. ____ Other salesperson
    j. ____ Owner of a store or business
    k. ____ Domestic service

l. ____ Other personal services
m. ____ Other (explain; includes retirement)
n. ____ Police or military
Write the name of the job _____

85. How many unemployed workers live here? _____

L. Transport

86. Where does the head of the household work?
(Name of district) _____
(Number) ____

87. How many kilometers must the head of the household travel
to work? (If unknown, insert later from table) ____

88. How many minutes does it take for the head of the household
to travel to work? ____

89. Before moving, how many minutes was the trip? ____

90. How does the head of the household travel to work?
a. ____ Works here
b. ____ Foot
c. ____ Bicycle
d. ____ Motorcycle
e. ____ Automobile
f. ____ Bus
g. ____ Transport provided by the employer
h. ____ Other (explain)

91. Where does the spouse or other major worker work?
(Name of district) _____

92. How many kilometers must he or she travel to work?
(Use table) ____

93. How many minutes does it take for him or her to travel to
work? ____

94. Before moving, how many minutes was the trip? ____

95. How does he or she travel to work?
    a. ＿＿＿ Works here
    b. ＿＿＿ Foot
    c. ＿＿＿ Bicycle
    d. ＿＿＿ Motorcycle
    e. ＿＿＿ Automobile
    f. ＿＿＿ Bus
    g. ＿＿＿ Transport provided by the employer
    h. ＿＿＿ Other (explain)

M. Income

96. How many persons receive meals (paid for by others) away from home? ＿＿＿

97. What are the sources of funds that members of this household can spend?
    a. ＿＿＿ Wages and salaries
    b. ＿＿＿ Sales or work on one's own account
    c. ＿＿＿ Rent from lodgers who live here
    d. ＿＿＿ Other rent, property income, interest, or dividends
    e. ＿＿＿ Pensions
    f. ＿＿＿ Aid in cash from family members who do not live here
    g. ＿＿＿ Aid from others
    h. ＿＿＿ Other (explain)

98. Does one of these sources of income produce more than half (more than 51 percent) of the income of all the rest combined?

    ＿＿＿

99. What was the total income (pesos) from all these sources for your household during the past month? (If meals were received at work, add 1,000 pesos for each recipient. Explain to high-income respondents that we only need these very broad categories.)
    a. ＿＿＿ Less than 700
    b. ＿＿＿ 700–1,000
    c. ＿＿＿ 1,001–2,000
    d. ＿＿＿ 2,001–3,000
    e. ＿＿＿ 3,001–4,000

f. _____ 4,001–5,000
g. _____ 5,001–6,000
h. _____ 6,001–8,000
i. _____ 8,001–12,000
j. _____ 12,001–16,000
k. _____ More than 16,000

100. Exact amount _____ pesos

Note: The survey was administered in Spanish.

Appendix C

Value, Income, and Housing Characteristics

DETAILS ABOUT HOUSING CHARACTERISTICS and their association with housing value or with the income of occupants can be shown in stock-user cross-tabulations, such as Table C-1. Numbers in the cells show the average number of rooms. Houses worth less than 40,000 pesos occupied by households earning less than 2,000 pesos (the upper-left cell) have 2.5 rooms. Looking down the column, one can see that households in higher income ranges occupying lowest-value housing also have 2.5 rooms. But the average number of persons per household rises from 4 to 6.5 to 8 in the higher income ranges. There is more income and more crowding. A slightly lower percentage—71 not 86 percent—is made of inferior materials as income rises, but none have piped water, and 79 percent have no type of sanitation (not even latrines).

Other ranges of housing value show a similar pattern. A more prosperous household in a given value range will not occupy more rooms than a poorer household. At the same time the higher income is associated with a larger family size. The extreme case is that of occupants of H2 housing, with 4.5 family members in the F0 range and 10.5 in the F3 range.

The higher income—or larger family size—is, however, associated with better materials. Few households that earn more than 8,000 pesos occupy housing made of inferior materials, and no H4 or H5 housing is built with them. The same applies to any type of housing that puts its occupants considerably to the right of the matrix diagonal. Within an income range, these are likely to be smaller households. Housing above the diagonal is likely to have both more rooms and be made of better materials. By the same token, housing below the diagonal has fewer rooms, a higher proportion is made of worse materials, and most are occupied by larger families. Extra family members bring in more income but not enough to prevent a deterioration of housing conditions. Table C-2 shows the number of persons per room in different cells of the matrix. Table C-3 gives household size per cell for tenants.

Table C-1. *Number of Rooms, Family Size, and Percentage with Inferior Materials, by Income and Dwelling Value, for Owner-Occupied Housing* (N = 220)

Household income (pesos per month)	Dwelling value (pesos)						
	H0 (0–40,000)	H1 (40,001–80,000)	H2 (80,001–160,000)	H3 (160,001–320,000)	H4 (320,001–640,000)	H5 (640,001+)	Σ_F
F0 (0–2,000)	2.5, 4, 86	3, 7.5, 57	4.5, 4.5, 0				3, 5.5, 63
F1 (2,001–4,000)	2.5, 6.5, 80	3, 6.5, 36	4, 5, 11	3.5, 5, 14	6, 4.5, 0		3.5, 6, 35
F2 (4,001–8,000)	2.5, 8, 71	3.5, 7.5, 43	4, 9, 7	4, 7.5, 7	5, 7.5, 0	4.5, 5.5, 0	4, 8, 14
F3 (8,001–16,000)		4, 10, 0	4, 10.5, 27	4, 7.5, 0	5, 7.5, 0	6, 8.5, 0	4.5, 8.5, 5
F4 (16,001–32,000)				4, 4.5, 0	7, 8.5, 0	6, 6.5, 0	6, 6.5, 0
F5 (32,001+)			4, 4, 0	4, 6, 0		5, 4, 0	4.5, 4.5, 0
Σ_H	2.5, 6, 79	3.5, 7.5, 38	4, 8.5, 14	4, 7, 5	5.5, 7.5, 0	6, 7, 0	4, 7.5, 17

Note: The first figure is the number of rooms, the second is family size, and the third is the percentage of dwellings in the cell made of wood, metal sheets, or impermanent materials. Numbers are rounded to the nearest half unit.

Source: Cartagena household survey, 1978.

Table C-2. *Persons per Room, by Income and Dwelling Value, for Owner-Occupants*
(N = 220)

Household income (pesos per month)	Dwelling value (pesos)						Σ_F
	H0 (0–40,000)	H1 (40,001–80,000)	H2 (80,001–160,000)	H3 (160,001–320,000)	H4 (320,001–640,000)	H5 (640,001+)	
F0 (0–2000)	<u>1.6</u>	2.5	1.0				1.8
F1 (2,001–4,000)	2.6	<u>2.2</u>	1.3	1.4	0.8		1.7
F2 (4,001–8,000)	3.2	2.1	<u>2.3</u>	1.9	1.5	1.2	2
F3 (8,001–16,000)		2.5	2.6	<u>1.9</u>	1.5	1.4	1.9
F4 (16,001–32,000)				1.1	<u>1.2</u>	1.1	1.1
F5 (32,001+)				1.5		<u>0.8</u>	1.0
Σ_H	2.4	2.1	2.1	1.8	1.4	1.2	1.9

Note: Housing of higher value is progressively less crowded until the number of persons per room has fallen by half. However, by income level crowding rises to a peak in the middle categories with incomes between 4,001 and 16,000 pesos. These are also the ranges with the largest household sizes (from eight to nine persons), with many households living below the diagonal. Extra adults bring in more earnings but not enough to make better housing affordable, given the extra children.

Source: Cartagena household survey, 1978.

187

Table C-3. *Household Size, Income, and Dwelling Value for Tenants*
(N = 65)

Household income (pesos per month)	Dwelling rent (pesos)					
	H0 (0–500)	H1 (501–1,000)	H2 (1,001–2,000)	H3 (2,001–4,000)	H4 (4,001+)	ΣF
F0 (0–2,000)						
F1 (2,001–4,000)	5.0	6.5				5.9
F2 (4,001–8,000)	5.6	7.6	8.0	2.5		6.6
F3 (8,001–16,000)		5.3	5.6	6.9	4.0	5.8
F4 (16,001–32,000)				7.0	4.2	5.1
				3.7		
F5 (32,000+)						
ΣH	5.5	6.6	7.3	5.6	4.4	6.0

Note: Housing categories for tenants are as in Table 4-9. Single observations in four cells are omitted.
Source: Cartagena household survey, 1978.

A similar pattern can be observed with respect to water sources and sanitary facilities. Table C-4 shows only the absence of piped water and all sanitary facilities (including latrines), but matrixes for other plumbing characteristics have been worked out, and they confirm this pattern. When families within a given income range live in housing above the diagonal, they usually have better sanitary and water facilities. In fact, access to these inspires the improvements that bring the dwellings above the diagonal. Those who live below the diagonal are more likely to have latrines or nothing and to buy water in lard cans from neighbors.

These results may be interpreted as follows. A larger family makes it easier to improve the materials of a given structure but makes it harder to acquire a larger dwelling with much better plumbing and access to utilities. In only one out of eleven cells above the diagonal is the average family size equal to eight or more persons. Two out of six diagonal cells have family sizes of eight or more, as do three out of eight below the diagonal. Income can put families in housing above the diagonal, provided it is not needed to feed and clothe a larger number of people. This negative association of value with household size is analyzed in Chapter 4 with multiple regressions.

Tables C-5 through C-8 are cross-tabulations of income with dwelling value and with rent, and show floor space, number of rooms, and rooms added in the appropriate cells. The summary rows show the average number of rooms for different income ranges, and the columns show different value or rental ranges. The lower right corner gives the overall averages. Rental houses have 3.8 rooms with 145 square meters, whereas others have 4.2 rooms with 143 square meters. Rental dwellings below the diagonal usually have less floor space and fewer rooms, but the difference is less for upper-income groups and more expensive housing.

Among owned dwellings the increase in floor space, although irregular, is also clear from positions below to those above the diagonal. The number of rooms increases from two to three for the poor in the upper left to from five to seven for the rich in the lower right. But, except for H1 dwellings and the richest and poorest households, the rise is not consistent.

Irregularity is greatest, as might be expected, for the number of rooms added. F1 families added the most rooms (0.9), an activity that puts 14 percent of them into H3 housing. But the most added-on housing type is H4. Here an average of 1.2 more rooms has brought the housing size up from 4.2 to 5.4 rooms. Particularly energetic were F2 families, who increased 3.5 rooms to 5.1 rooms and F4 families who had increased 5.2-room houses to 7.0 rooms. These two income ranges occupied 58 percent of H4 housing other than rentals.

Table C-4. Percentage of Households without Piped Water and without Sanitary Facilities, by Income and Dwelling Value, for Owner-Occupants (N = 219)

Household income (pesos per month)	H0 (0–40,000)	H1 (40,001– 80,000)	H2 (80,001– 160,000)	H3 (160,001– 320,000)	H4 (320,001– 640,000)	H5 (640,001+)	Σ_F
			Dwelling value (pesos)				
F0 (0–2,000)	100, 71	86, 43	0, 0				75, 50
F1 (2,001–4,000)	100, 90	73, 36	67, 22	29, 14			65, 40
F2 (4,001–8,000)	100, 71	57, 14	40, 13	16, 0	0, 0		27, 10
F3 (8,001–16,000)		75, 25	0, 0	4, 0	7, 0	0, 0	7, 2
F4 (16,001–32,000)				0, 0	0, 0	0, 0	0, 0
F5 (32,001+)				0, 0	0, 0	0, 0	0, 0
Σ_H	100, 79	70, 31	32, 11	13, 2	3, 0	0, 0	29, 17

Note: The first number is the percentage who buy water from a neighbor or a water wagon or who use a public standpipe or share a faucet of a neighbor. The second number is the percentage without any sanitary facilities, not even a pit latrine.
Source: Cartagena household survey, 1978.

Table C-5. Average Floor Space (in Square Meters), by Income and Dwelling Rent (N = 62)

Household income (pesos per month)	Dwelling rent (pesos)					Σ_F	N
	H0 (0–500)	H1 (501–1,000)	H2 (1,001–2,000)	H3 (2,001–4,000)	H4 (4,001+)		
F0 (0–2,000)	24.0					24.0	1
F1 (2,001–4,000)	66.7	126.0				100.6 (53.7)	7
F2 (4,001–8,000)	116.1	128.0	213.8	60.0		138.5 (102.6)	20
F3 (8,001–16,000)		102.0	136.0	153.7	226.0	140.5 (76.7)	22
F4 (16,001–32,000)		125.0		234.0	248.0	229.1 (120.8)	8
F5 (32,001+)			100.0	165.0	160.0	147.5 (48.6)	4
Σ_H	94.3 (70.6)	118.2 (51.1)	163.1 (107.2)	153.3 (79.7)	231.5 (133.7)	145.4 (93.8)	62

Note: Standard deviations are in parentheses.
Source: Cartagena household survey, 1978.

Table C-6. *Average Floor Space (in Square Meters), by Income and Dwelling Value*
(N = 225)

Household income (pesos per month)	Dwelling value (pesos)						Σ_F	N
	H0 (0– 40,000)	H1 (40,001– 80,000)	H2 (80,001– 160,000)	H3 (160,001– 320,000)	H4 (320,001– 640,000)	H5 (640,001+)		
F0 (0–2000)	67.6	79.5	(82.0)				74.3 (37.0)	15
F1 (2,001–4,000)	55.2	69.8	102.6	111.1	(69.0)		81.3 (45.5)	38
F2 (4,001–8,000)	71.1	85.9	123.0	152.3	177.0	265.8	142.5 (99.7)	80
F3 (8,001–16,000)		141.2	205.5	161.3	132.5	200.3	167.6 (117.7)	61
F4 (16,001–32,000)				138.3	347.5	213.9	225.3 (142.6)	27
F5 (32,001+)			(100.0)	(60.0)		(60.0)	70.0 (25.8)	4
Σ_H	63.8 (31.2)	88.6 (52.0)	137.1 (112.3)	149.2 (107.5)	174.9 (132.9)	207.3 (108.7)	143.1 (109.8)	225

Note: In the summary columns parentheses enclose standard deviations. In the cells they enclose averages based on only one or two observations.
Source: Cartagena household survey, 1978.

192

Table C-7. Number of Rooms, by Income and Dwelling Rent
(N = 65)

Household income (pesos per month)	Dwelling rent (pesos)					Σ_F	N
	H0 (0–500)	H1 (501–1,000)	H2 (1,001–2,000)	H3 (2,001–4,000)	H4 (4,001+)		
F0 (0–2,000)	2.0					2.0	1
F1 (2,001–4,000)	2.3	3.8				3.1	7
F2 (4,001–8,000)	2.6	3.6	4.2	3.0		3.4	22
F3 (8,001–16,000)		2.8	4.1	4.4	5.0	4.0	22
F4 (16,001–32,000)		3.0		6.0	5.2	5.1	8
F5 (32,001+)			4.0	4.7	6.0	4.8	5
Σ_H	2.5	3.4	4.2	4.5	5.3	3.8	65

Note: N = 11 for H0, 19 for H1, 13 for H2, 14 for H3, and 8 for H4.
Source: Cartagena household survey, 1978.

Table C-8. *Number of Rooms and Rooms Added, by Income and Dwelling Value* (N = 231)

Household income (pesos per month)	Dwelling value (pesos)						Σ_F	N
	H0 (0-40,000)	H1 (40,001-80,000)	H2 (80,001-160,000)	H3 (160,001-320,000)	H4 (320,001-640,000)	H5 (640,001+)		
F0 (0-2,000)	2.6 (0.3)	2.9 (0.4)	4.5 (0)				2.9 (0.5)	16
F1 (2,001-4,000)	2.3 (0.6)	3.2 (0.5)	3.9 (0.1)	3.4 (1.0)	6.0 (0.7)		3.4 (0.9)	40
F2 (4,001-8,000)	2.3 (0.8)	3.4 (0.4)	3.9 (0.5)	4.2 (0.7)	5.1 (1.6)	4.7 (0.5)	4.1 (0.8)	81
F3 (8,001-16,000)		3.8 (1.4)	4.2 (0.6)	4.0 (0.9)	5.0 (0.7)	5.9 (0.6)	4.5 (0.8)	62
F4 (16,001-32,000)				3.7 (1.0)	7.0 (1.8)	6.3 (0.4)	6.1 (0.7)	28
F5 (32,001+)			4.0 (0)	4.0 (0)		5.0 (0.5)	4.5 (0.3)	4
Σ_H	2.4 (0.6)	3.3 (0.6)	4.0 (0.4)	4.0 (0.8)	5.4 (1.2)	5.9 (0.5)	4.2 (0.7)	231

Note: N = 25 for H0, 30 for H1, 39 for H2, 67 for H3, 33 for H4, and 37 for H5. Rooms added by the occupying household are given in parentheses. Standard deviation for the sample mean is 1.065 for rooms added; 1.692 for number of rooms.
Source: Cartagena household survey, 1978.

Table C-9. *Share of Households Receiving Primarily Wage Income or Having Relatives in Venezuela, by Income and Dwelling Value, for Owner-Occupants*
(N = 220 for the income source; 203 for relatives in Venezuela)

Household income (pesos per month)	Dwelling value (pesos)						Σ_F
	H0 (0–40,000)	H1 (40,001–80,000)	H2 (80,001–160,000)	H3 (160,001–320,000)	H4 (320,001–640,000)	H5 (640,001+)	
F0 (0–2,000)	0.286 (0.200)	0.286 (0)	0 (0)				0.250 (0.083)
F1 (2,001–4,000)	0.500 (0.571)	0.636 (0.400)	0.333 (0.375)	0.714 (0.714)	0.667 (0)		0.550 (0.471)
F2 (4,001–8,000)	0.571 (0.600)	0.571 (0.143)	0.267 (0.467)	0.452 (0.571)	0.643 (0.214)	0.333 (0)	0.468 (0.417)
F3 (8,001–16,000)		0.251 (0.500)	0.818 (0.400)	0.739 (0.364)	0.455 (0.273)	0.222 (0)	0.586 (0.304)
F4 (16,001–32,000)				0 (1.00)	0.250 (0.250)	0.500 (0)	0.423 (0.115)
F5 (32,001+)				1.00 (0)		0 (0)	0.333 (0)
Σ_H	0.458 (0.471)	0.483 (0.269)	0.432 (0.400)	0.578 (0.517)	0.531 (0.226)	0.382 (0)	0.491 (0.33)

Note: Share with relatives working in Venezuela is given in parentheses.
Source: Cartagena household survey, 1978.

Possibly important for housing improvement was temporary income, the kind that is more likely to be saved. Three-quarters or more of housing improvements were financed by funds generated internally by the family, that is, without involving the government or borrowing from others. What kind of household is most likely to receive unexpected income flows? One might hazard a guess that it is not those with primarily wage income, and, as Table C-9 shows, such households are more likely to live below the matrix diagonal. It is most typical of the 8,001-to-16,000-peso income range, however, the same group that has the high 1.6 income elasticity of demand that is also the best statistical fit for any range.

Another possible source of temporary income was relatives sending remittances from Venezuela. But for owner-occupants, it turned out that 44 percent of those below the diagonal had such relatives, compared with only 28 percent of those above. That does not fit. What does fit is that 33 percent of all owner-occupants had such relatives compared with only 19 percent of tenants. The regressions reported in Table 6-8 did not support these propositions, however.

Appendix D
Housing Models and Density of Settlement

CHOICE OF RESIDENTIAL LOCATION was worked out during the early 1960s in terms of journeys to work through areas of increasing density of settlement to a central business district. Important factors such as the heterogeneity and durability of dwellings, the difficulty of modifying them, and consequent effects on demand and stock adjustment were ignored. The models were only partial equilibrium solutions. They ignored neighborhood effects, ethnic preferences and prejudices, and interactions with local governments. A realistic model must also incorporate the different behavior of owner-occupants and landlords. For example, the two groups may be taxed differently or perceive housing as unlike blends of investment and consumption components. Each of these complications involves elements more complicated than distance and density. In measuring and testing urban models, problems of aggregation and disaggregation arise in a manner that is especially baffling.

The safe and usual procedure is to complicate models by no more than one or two elements at a time. For example, Richard Muth has incorporated age of the dwelling unit in a residential location and income model and has found it an unimportant factor.[1] Most analysts had assumed that the flow of housing services gained from a given dwelling unit falls steadily as the unit ages and that it will from time to time be transferred to families with successively lower incomes, that is, filtered down. Unanticipated immigration of poor families would accelerate the filtering process. But this theory has had to be reconciled with the fact that some neighborhoods remain with high income groups for long periods while others are transferred rapidly.

More important than age is the decision to maintain and even to rehabilitate and to improve a dwelling. According to William C. Wheaton, that decision is not much influenced by the interplay of demand for low density versus that for proximity to work. Those two effects almost cancel each other so that the rich barely outbid the poor for peripheral locations. In San Francisco, California, for example, it is by less than 10 percent. What the richer families really seek in deciding on location are the externalities of less noise, less pollution, less crime, and lower taxes compared with public services, a choice possible due to urban political and fiscal fragmentation in the United States. Measures of these elements may be found in the pupil-teacher ratio, tax rates, crime rates, percentage of the population on welfare, and so forth.

On the supply side, most of the standard complications come from imperfections in the capital market and from variations in the price of land. Labor and materials are usually in elastic supply and can be lumped together as nonland inputs. If their elasticity of substitution for land is below unity, the land cost share of housing will be higher near the city center. This model obviously does not allow for high-rise solutions. Single-family housing can be more elastically supplied further from the center of the city in part because there is more vacant land. Speculators with distant land probably have more risk preference than those who still hope for further improvements in potential uses near the center. The vacancy rate together with price is what motivates entrepreneurs to build or not, here or there.

Upgrading and Conversion

Filtering implies downward transfers, but upward transfers are also possible when incomes and demand rise faster than new construction of better units. Such upward transfers are typically accompanied by increased investment in the old dwelling units. Usually one thinks of investment in old dwelling units as maintenance and repair—steps that are supposed to prevent a decrease in value. But rehabilitation, improvements, and expansion to increase value can be as important, especially in fast growing cities. Housing theorists have usually omitted or postponed analysis of improvements because their tasks were already complex enough without adding that.

Moreover, an assumption of sharply decreasing returns to scale in maintenance and conversion implies that it is hard to prevent or to slow down deterioration, let alone foster improvements. This assumption seems to be widely held, but it needs to be questioned, especially for the rudimentary housing of poor people in developing countries. Abstractly, and with a simulation that roughly fits rented apartments in Boston, the assumption has been relaxed and the implications explored by Gregory Ingram and Yitzhak Oron.[2] Their paper illustrates the difficulties of rigorous theorizing in this complex field. Apart from complexity one runs into rigidities, interdependence, externalities, uncertainties, and other market failures.

The Ingram-Oron Model

In the Ingram-Oron model, landlords maximize profits and house-holds maximize utilities by changing the flow of housing services from an existing housing stock. Some of these services come from accessibility and neighborhood quality, and these characteristics cannot be changed in the model. Landlords can vary operating inputs and housing capital. This capital consists of extremely durable structure capital and of quality capital that depreciates in about ten years. Structure capital is the foundation and shell, their size, materials, and plumbing. Quality capital can be varied through changing repairs, decorations, and minor appliances. In their critiques of the model, Rothenberg and Steele charge that the most important types of conversion are omitted, meaning either expansion of the shell or its subdivision into additional rooms—the very changes that are of primary concern in developing countries. Ingram and Oron treat such conversions as a type of new construction that competes with other new building since it produces brand new units.

With conversion cost C_{ij} landlords will change a unit of structure type i to type j if the sum of discounted net revenues V_j from type j is bigger than $(V_i + C_{ij})$, which also must be less than building costs of a new unit of type j. The present value V depends on gross rent per unit R, the volume of operating inputs O_t and their prices P_o, the amount of maintenance M_t and its unit price P_m, and fixed costs apart from financing F_t plus the interest rate r

$$V = \sum_{t=0}^{\infty} [R_t - P_o O_t - P_m M_t - F_t] \frac{1}{(1 + r)^t} .$$

If this framework is to be applied to upgrading by owner-occupants or landlords with a few lodgers in poor countries, one must assume that they have clear expectations about the volume and unit prices of inputs used and services obtained. Almost as much information is required for the types of decision that Ingram and Oron consider: choice of the volume of operating inputs and of maintenance or quality investment.

The landlord presumably knows how gross rents will vary with changes in operating inputs, and he chooses a volume to satisfy the first-order conditions

$$\frac{dR\,(O;\,K,\,t)}{dO} = P_o .$$

The price of a unit of capital flow P_k gives the first-order conditions for an equilibrium level of capital in the housing unit:

$$\frac{d\,(R - P_oO)}{dK} = P_k.$$

P_k for a unit of quality capital is P_m, the price of a unit of maintenance, which must be converted to a flow basis with the depreciation rate d and the interest rate r:

$$P_k = P_m\,(d + r).$$

Maintenance expenditures are set to bring the capital per unit from the current level, $K\,(1 - d)$, to the optimal level K^* within, say, five years. In a dynamic framework with changing expectations, a stationary state will never be attained, and the five-year interval rolls along, always with redefined objectives.

Ingram and Oron show that, even with further drastic simplifications, such a model cannot be easily applied to a concrete case. Only two types of neighborhood and two types of structure are considered: good and bad; high-rise and walk-up apartments. For each type, eight quality levels are possible. Rent per room is used as the index of capital quality, although rent actually reflects the combined vagaries of both supply and demand, including variations in location and neighborhoods.

Landlords are assumed to maximize their returns by varying mainte-nance (quality capital) and operating expenditures in accordance with a CES production function. The distribution and substitution parameters of this function are plausible inventions by the authors, which their discussants were inclined to reject, even reversing relative magnitudes. Rothenberg would not even accept the assumption of constant returns to scale. For one thing, the greater the amount of maintenance and conver-sion, the higher will be the opportunity cost of lost revenue from units made temporarily vacant by being worked on. New construction is not subject to that loss.

Implications of the model are sought with a simulation that assigns 200 hypothetical dwelling units to 200 households in six income categories. Rents for structural and neighborhood attributes are changed with each iteration, and quality capital is augmented or allowed to deteriorate until the market is cleared. The long-run equilibrium capital stock has then been reached. The overall implication is that incremental investment in quality capital is often a superior alternative to new construction, a con-clusion that follows from the assumption of constant returns to scale.

In spite of much ingenuity, little general significance can be attributed to any specific numbers or orders of magnitude that Ingram and Oron found. Some criticism of the model focuses on its neglect of neighbor-hood quality as endogenous, as well as on assumptions about the trade-offs that rich and poor will make for that neighborhood quality, meaning the cross-elasticity of demand. Steele suggests that if structural conver-sion or adding rooms were given full status as a fifth housing option (in addition to structure type, quality, accessibility, and neighborhood), then conversion would look better compared with neighborhood quality than the authors believe and would absorb a larger share of possible federal housing allowances. It would make these more palatable to voters. Taxpayers want the poor to have better shelter, not just to bid up real estate values in better neighborhoods.

Similarly, Rothenberg approves of the idea of adding an intermediate supply adjustment to those of the very long and the very short run for housing. But he has the reservations that have already been mentioned, as well as others involving distinctions among tenure classes, market structure, and neighborhoods. The exclusion of capital market imperfec-tions, tax effects, and the difficulty of prediction, of knowing what is "in the works" by others in this long-gestation sector all may cause serious biases. Perhaps analytical rigor and simulation elegance can only be at-tained at excessive cost. The pioneering analytical efforts made so far should be welcome as simply points of reference for exploring the very different setting of housing in a developing country.

Notes to Appendix D

1. Richard F. Muth, "The Influence of Age of Dwellings on Housing Expenditures and on the Location of Households," in *Residential Location and Urban Housing Markets*, ed. Gregory K. Ingram (Cambridge, Mass.: National Bureau of Economic Research, 1977), pp. 3–22; "Comments" by William C. Wheaton, pp. 23–26. See also, William C. Wheaton, "Income and Urban Residence: An Analysis of Consumer Demand for Location," *American Economic Review* (September 1977), pp. 620–31. Since the income elasticities of demand for land and time appear "remarkably similar," their interaction or "the long-run theory of urban land markets is empirically an unimportant determinant of income spatial patterns in American cities."

2. Gregory K. Ingram and Yitzhak Oron, "The Production of Housing Services from Ex-isting Dwelling Units," in *Residential Location and Urban Housing Markets*, ed. Gregory K. Ingram (Cambridge, Mass.: National Bureau of Economic Research, 1977), pp. 273–314, followed by "Comments" by Jerome Rothenberg and Marion Steele, pp. 315–25.

Appendix E

Subdivision and Expansion
in Ciudad Kennedy, Bogotá

Subdivision and expansion often occur together, as has been shown in a detailed study of landlords and renters in Ciudad Kennedy, a suburb of Bogotá.[1] The low-cost houses and apartments had been sold at below-market terms in 1963 by the ICT to families that presumably owned no other housing. In 1975 a random sample of 594 of these dwellings showed that 160 had been subdivided and rented to tenants. Detailed information was available on 136 of the subdivided dwellings. Seventy-one percent had been remodeled. On the average 2.2 rooms had been added, and two-thirds of the remodeled units had a new kitchen or bathroom. In 92 percent of cases the landlord continued to share the dwelling.

Family income of the landlords—4,470 pesos monthly, including rent—was only 42 percent above that of the tenants' average 3,140 monthly. Average rent was 736 pesos or 16.5 percent of the landlords' income (23.4 percent of the tenants' income). Tenant families were newer and smaller (3.9 members) than landlord families (7.3 members), and, therefore, actually had a higher per capita income of 813 pesos monthly than the landlords' 508 pesos. More than half of the landlords had themselves lived as renters in a subdivided house before coming to Ciudad Kennedy. Some 11.5 percent had previously owned other houses.

Only 4 out of the 160 subdivided dwellings were apartments, so one may conclude that apartment construction discouraged such initiatives, reduced flexibility in the housing stock, and made life harder for some newly formed, low-income families. Raising the value of their property was the main reason that owners let in tenants (56 percent), followed by a desire for other goods and services (28 percent).

Remodeling was financed with personal savings and retirement funds in 58 percent of the cases. Loans from banks or employing firms accounted for 29 percent of sources, and 13 percent used personal loans.

The gross yield from remodeling was estimated to be about 26 percent, and the net yield ranged from 3 percent for those who used personal loans at 24 percent annually to 20 percent for owners who used their own savings. These returns were viewed by the authors of the study as being in line with other investment opportunities available to the landlords.

In general, Zorro and Reveiz concluded that renting rooms in subdivided dwellings was a relatively satisfactory way to provide low-cost housing in a country at Colombia's stage of development. Instead of opposing the landlords' capitalization of their housing subsidies, the government should encourage and anticipate that activity. Dwellings should be designed to facilitate future remodeling, and potential landlords should perhaps be the only recipients of subsidized housing instead of being regarded as unsavory profiteers, a group to be excluded if possible.[2]

Notes to Appendix E

1. Carlos Zorro Sánchez and Edgar Reveiz Roldán, *Estudio sobre Los Inquilinatos (Vivienda Compartida en Arrendamiento) en Bogotá* (Bogotá: Centro de Estudios sobre Desarrollo Económico, University of the Andes, Etapa I February 1974 and Segunda Parte June 1976).

2. Ibid., Segunda Parte, pp. 114–15.

Appendix F

A 1970 Survey
of the Southeast Zone

A 1970 SURVEY BY HUMBERTO TRIANA Y ANTORVEZA found that 30 percent of housing in these four southeast districts (7, 8, 9, 10) needed partial rebuilding, and 45 percent needed total rebuilding.[1] Twenty-three percent of dwellings were occupied by more than one family, and 4 percent by three families or more. In addition, 69 percent of families kept dogs, cats, pigs, chickens, ducks, pigeons, and other animals and birds. More than half of the households consisted of from five to ten members: one to four persons, 28 percent; eleven and more persons, 16 percent; and sixteen or more persons, 6 percent.

The extent of overcrowding can be seen by the finding that 70.5 percent of dwellings had only one or two rooms (16 and 54.5 percent, respectively). Sixteen percent had three rooms, 11 percent had four, and 2.5 percent had five rooms. The average number per bed or hammock was 2.2.

Household income was mainly in the range of from 501 to 1,000 pesos per month. Less was earned by 32 percent, and more by 21 percent. If these earnings are compared with the classification of Cortés, the inhabitants of the southeast sectors become not only poor, but the poorest of the poor.[2] That is why they have been surveyed so often that future interviewers may encounter skepticism and resistance.

Notes to Appendix F

1. Humberto Triana y Antorveza, *Cultura del Tugurio en Cartagena* (Bogotá: Impresa en Italgraf for UNICEF, 1974). Owners were 82 percent, renters 15 percent, and uncharged guarding occupants 3 percent. Housing was 20 percent of the budget.

2. Lácydes Cortés Diás, *Familia y Sociedad en Cartagena* (Departamento de Investigación Económica y Social, Universidad de Cartagena, July 1971).

Appendix G

A 1976 Census of the
Southeast Zone: Boston-Tesca

In 1976 a census of 1,064 dwellings occupied by 5,118 people was conducted in district 8 by ict.[1] About 46 percent of the population were children under sixteen years old. Forty-seven percent were between sixteen and fifty years of age, and only 7 percent were fifty-one or older.

Among the economically active population between the ages of sixteen and fifty, 28 percent were unemployed, that is, 682 out of 2,419. Merchants and street sellers were the leading occupational group (30 percent). Then came domestic servants (17 percent) and building workers (13 percent). Others were drivers, unskilled labor, and public employees. Income distribution was:

Monthly income (pesos)	Percent
None	1.9
80–1,000	19.5
1,001–2,000	15.2
2,001–3,000	19.8
3,001–4,000	9.4
4,001–5,000	10.0
5,001–6,000	7.8
6,001–7,000	5.8
7,001–8,000	3.1
8,001–9,000	1.8
9,001–10,000	0.9
10,001+	4.7

Only 55 percent of dwellings were occupied by single families. Another 26 percent were occupied by two families, 12 percent by three families, 4 percent by four families, and 2.4 percent or thirty-five dwellings by five families. Since 23 percent of dwellings were occupied by from ten to nineteen persons and 55 percent by from five to nine persons, undoubling was a critical housing need.

In this district 13.7 percent of households were tenants, and 4.0 percent occupied the premises of others without charge. The lots of owners were typically 200 square meters in area; those of tenants 150 square meters. Rental property was owned by 3.7 percent of households, with about 80 percent within the same district. The rest were in neighboring districts. ICT classified 21.4 percent of dwellings as being in bad condition, consisting of one room built out of inferior materials with no floor and no latrine. Only 18.1 percent were classified as good, with at least four well-finished rooms, water, and connection to the sewerage system.

The average owner with a deed had lived in the area ten years and nine months, but only 9.6 percent of tenants had occupied their premises more than five years. From one to five years had been the length of stay of 48.6 percent of tenants, and 41.7 percent had been there less than a year.

Note to Appendix G

1. Instituto de Crédito Territorial, "Censo de Propietarios en la Zona Suroriental, Sector 2" (Cartagena, 1976; processed).

Appendix H

A 1978 Study of Employment
in the Southeast Zone: Esperanza

A SURVEY OF 160 FAMILIES living in 140 dwellings was made in early 1978 by SENA (Servicio Nacional de Aprendizaje), the national vocational training institution.[1] In general this group found that so many studies had been made in "La Esperanza" that people had become hostile to any official concern about them. They felt like guinea pigs who gained nothing from such attention. What was most needed, according to the authors, was to train people with leadership talent in a way that would not dissipate into mere politics.

The survey found that 83 percent of dwellings were occupied by their owners, 75 percent by single families, and that 63 percent were physically inadequate. Some 53 percent of families had been in the area for more than a decade. The first settlers had come in 1916, putting up houses along the shores of creeks. Some land was bought from rich Cartagena families named Dadger, Badel, and Román; whereas the land of the Granger family was simply appropriated by squatters who illegally sold parcels to others. In the Pescadores (Fisherman) sector, land had been reclaimed from the lagoon. With rising pollution, the fish were disappearing and becoming genetically deformed.

Income levels per occupation corresponded to those we found five months later. Full-time employment is assumed in these figures.

Occupation	Earnings (pesos)	Share of employment (percent)
Domestic servant	1,000	32
Construction worker and unskilled labor	1,800	15
Driver	2,500	8
Dressmaker	3,000	5
Carpenter	3,500	6
Salesman	6,000	25
Others	2,000	9
Total		100

One may assume that the domestic servants approximately doubled their income through meals and other benefits received on the job. Hence 1,800 pesos was something like the minimum effective wage. The relatively high level that salesmen earned explains the attraction of opening a small shop or selling in the street as a way of beginning.

Since the SENA survey did not include income from pensions, rent, food on the job, transfers from absent family members, and the like, as did our survey, income levels per family were naturally lower.

Income level (pesos)	Percentage of families
0–1,000	28.1
1,001–2,000	30.6
2,001–3,000	15.0
3,001–4,000	10.6
4,001–5,000	9.3
5,001–6,000	6.4
Total	100.0

A problem with this distribution is that a quarter of the labor force was reported as being salesmen, earning 6,000 pesos if fully employed. If any other family members were employed, a category higher than 5,001–6,000 pesos would be needed. But the income distribution only included earnings of heads of families.

Note to Appendix H

1. Gloria Amparo Gomez de Gongora, Aura Miranda de Hernández, and Edgar Galofre Vega, "Diagnóstico Socio-Económico del Barrio 'La Esperanza' " (Cartagena: SENA, February 1978; processed).

Appendix I

Housing in Latin American
Budget Surveys

WITHOUT EXAMINING THE WAY HOUSING has been specified, one can easily misinterpret budget surveys. Organizers of the Latin American surveys sponsored by the Brookings Institution during 1966–75 (Estudios Conjuntos sobre Integración Económica Latinoamericana—ECIEL) were thoroughly aware of this problem.[1] For owner-occupants housing was specified in alternative ways: either as all of the imputed rent or as half of actual mortgage payments (regardless of the proportion of interest and amortization components). The second specification assumes arbitrarily that half of housing payments are saving. Changing the specification in this manner turned out not to actually matter much unless the effects of age or life-cycle on the relation between consumption and income were being studied. The propensity to save does, however, appear to be less for renters than for owner-occupants (in ten cities in Venezuela, Colombia, Ecuador, Peru, and Chile), even if all imputed rent is treated as consumption and the increased equity is disregarded. The dwelling is the asset owned by the greatest number of households, often the only significant asset. Total consumption was not affected by whether a dwelling was a house or apartment, nor by its materials of construction. But households of a given size that occupied more rooms had a higher propensity to consume. Subtracting imputed rent from the consumption and income of older households makes them appear more thrifty than might have been expected—that is, their spending does not exceed income, as in industrialized countries. Imperfections in the capital market and inflation may cause this pattern.

Expenditures on Housing as a Share of Income in Four Colombian Cities

During 1967–68 information on housing expenditures (among others) was collected under the direction of Rafael Prieto D., Centro de Estudios sobre Desarrollo Económico (CEDE) of the Universidad de los Andes.[2] The four cities covered were Bogotá, Medellín, Cali, and Barranquilla. Households were defined as the group of people inhabiting a dwelling unit, but excluded were units with three or more lodgers and the institutional population. Interviewed were 2,014 households, some only once, but 876 repeat interviews took place. The findings are reported in some detail here because of their similarity to our data from Cartagena a decade later.

The share of income spent on housing averaged 22.4 percent: Bogotá 25.1 percent, Medellín 22.8 percent, Cali 17.9 percent, and Barranquilla 16.9 percent (see Table I-1). The share seemed to vary with city size and altitude (inversely with temperature). Over time the share of housing rose most in the larger and higher-income cities. In this respect it did not seem to matter much that one city (Bogotá) had a somewhat more equal distribution of income than the other (Medellín). These assertions may be checked by comparing Tables I-2 and I-3. Around 0.6 percent of income, or 2.6 percent of housing expenditures, went for maintenance.

Households in the lowest quartile of the income distribution (0–3,200 pesos quarterly [US$523, 1978]) spent 18.51 percent on housing, followed in the other quartiles by 21.80 percent (3,201–5,270 pesos); 24.09 percent (5,271–8,970 pesos); and finally 25.28 percent (8,971+pesos [US$1,467, 1978]). The rising share seems at first glance to indicate an income elasticity of demand above unity. Actually that elasticity was estimated as 0.92, including maintenance and expenses on secondary dwellings (a mere 0.04 percent of spending on housing). Without these, the elasticity fell to 0.85. The elasticity of spending on maintenance was 0.99, an amount not significantly different from unity. All of these are elasticities with respect to total spending, estimated with multiple regres-

Table I-1. *Spending Share of Housing, by Social Class*
(percentage of income)

City	High	Medium	Low	Total
Bogotá	25.2	25.7	24.5	29.1
Barranquilla	25.2	19.3	14.4	16.9
Cali	23.4	22.3	15.5	17.9
Medellín	28.7	25.5	21.8	22.8
Total	25.4	24.4	21.2	22.4

Source: Rafael Prieto D., "Gasto e Ingreso Familiar Urbano en Colombia," *Ensayos* ECIEL (August 1977), pp. 45–120.

Table I-2. *Share of Housing in Expenditures for Comparable Groups in Four Colombian Cities, 1953, 1967–68, and 1970*

City	DANE 1953, total	CEDE 1967–68		DANE 1970, $5,001–$10,000 income range
		Total	Middle class	
Bogotá	20.3	25.1	25.7	27.0
Barranquilla	18.8	18.5	19.3	20.2
Cali	21.7	19.6	22.3	22.2
Medellín	19.0	24.3	25.5	26.2

Source: Same as Table I-1.

Table I-3. *Income Distribution According to the Income of the Family Head and Gini Coefficients in Four Colombian Cities, 1967–68*

Income level (pesos per trimester)	Bogotá	Barranquilla	Cali	Medellín	Total
Income share (percent)					
0–3,200	18.3	28.8	34.4	29.5	25.2
3,201–5,270	22.3	28.7	25.3	27.5	24.9
5,271–8,970	29.2	21.5	19.0	22.3	24.7
8,971+	30.1	21.0	21.3	20.7	25.2
Gini coefficient	0.472	0.463	0.479	0.499	0.473
Income (pesos)	9,450	7,530	7,220	7,930	8,033[a]
Share of top 10 percent	37.6	37.3	38.6	41.8	38.8
Bottom 40 percent	13.8	12.7	13.5	12.8	13.4

a. Unweighted average.
Source: Same as Table I-1.

sions that include other variables discussed below. The figures in Table I-1 suggest that the spending elasticity for housing was higher in the poorer, warmer cities, Cali and Barranquilla. Their upper classes spent as large a share on housing as in the other cities, but their poor spent much less.

Other Determinants of Housing Expenditures

Some variables affected housing expenditures much less than might be expected. For example, larger families tended to crowd up or spend less on quality, compared with space, to an extent that their housing share actually fell slightly, from 22.9 percent for from three to five members, to 21.7 percent for from six to eight members, or 21.3 percent for households with nine or more members. This decline of 1.6 percent roughly matches the rise of 1.8 percent spent on food and drink. Households with from one to two members spent the largest share on housing, 27.6 percent. Put differently, households without children spent 26.0 percent; those with one or two spent 21.9; with from three to five, 21.0 percent; and those with six or more, 21.1 percent. The same 21 percent applies to the middle stages of the life cycle, compared with 27.9 at the beginning and 33.0 at the end. Alternatively, when the head of the household was more than sixty-four years old, the share was 32.9 percent.

Education had little effect on spending for housing. When the head of the household had university, primary, or no education, 22 percent was spent. Only when the head of the household had secondary education was a bit more spent (23.9 percent). A similar factor that made little difference was type of occupation. The share did fall slightly, to 19.5 percent, if the wife was employed, showing that more of her income had to go for other things. Such households made up about 10 percent of the sample.

Owner-occupants spent 25.2 percent, or substantially more than renters (21.4 percent). The owners' share included 1.0 percent on maintenance or 3.9 percent of spending on housing. By contrast, renters left maintenance to landlords, adding only 0.04 percent to their rental payments. Basically, becoming an owner meant multiplying the value of one's maintenance decisions by ten. About 5.6 percent of households lived in dwellings that were neither owned nor rented, and they paid only 2.9 percent of their income for these, including 14.0 percent of that on maintenance.

The ECIEL study did not explore the extent to which the variations in spending on housing might have been due to the general demographic situation of a city, its size, and rate of growth. Thus we find that Cali grew more than 8 percent during the 1940s and 6.3 percent annually during 1951–64. Medellín grew at a similar rate of 6 percent. By the years 1965–70 the rate of immigration to Bogotá and Cali had reached 3.4 and 3.6 percent, respectively, whereas Medellín had 2.6 percent and Barranquilla only 1.6 percent. These rates must be weighed together with those of employment and unemployment. In Medellín the unemployment rate was lowest (14.5 percent), and in Barranquilla it was highest (18.4 percent). Cali had the lowest male unemployment rate (11.1 percent) and one of the highest female rates (22.3 percent).

Notes to Appendix I

1. Philip Musgrove, "Determinants of Urban Household Consumption in Latin America: A Summary of Evidence from the ECIEL Surveys," *Economic Development and Cultural Change* (April 1978), pp. 441–65.

2. Rafael Prieto D., *Estructura del Gasto y Distribución del Ingreso Familiar en Cuatro Ciudades Colombianas, 1967–68* (Bogotá: CEDE, 1971); Rafael Prieto D., "Gasto e Ingreso Familiar Urbano en Colombia," *Ensayos* ECIEL (August 1977), pp. 45–120. This study was part of the ECIEL Program of Joint Studies on Latin American Economic Integration. See Philip Musgrove, *Income and Spending of Urban Families in Latin America: The* ECIEL *Consumption Study* (Washington, D.C.: Brookings Institution, 1978).

Appendix J

CVP Housing Projects in Bogotá

SOME ICT POLICIES were influenced by the experiments of the Caja de Vivienda Popular of Bogotá (CVP), so a brief description of that program follows.

After building 291 minimal houses in the Manuelita neighborhood of Bogotá during 1972–73, the CVP undertook a new project of 2,697 dwellings at Las Guacamayas. The size of minimal units was raised from 11 to 12 square meters and the lot size from 54 to 64 square meters. This last change and the new hexagonal honeycomb layout for groups of lots lowered the density from eighty-two to fifty-two housing units per hectare. Money was saved, however, by letting the occupants build a temporary shed around the sanitary outlet instead of building a brick structure for them. Moreover, the outlet was moved from a corner of the lot to its center, where the bathroom of the final dwelling would be. Pipes to the main sewerage line would no longer have to be relocated. Minor changes were also made in the suggested layout of the ultimate two-story, six-room house.

Occupants did not have to expand their dwellings according to CVP designs. They could use different materials, for example, concrete blocks instead of the recommended bricks, and they did not have to follow any predetermined set of priorities. Expansions needed approval to ensure structural soundness and to prevent impinging on neighbors. But such approval could be obtained in written form without delay from one of the three architects who were part of the seven-person CVP staff on the site. Visits to model units and training programs for new occupants were, however, expected to channel construction into preferred forms.

The greater size of Guacamayas and its greater distance from shopping areas did promote a larger number of shops and stores in dwellings than had been the case at La Manuelita, and the CVP welcomed this change. Several units had been converted to rental use, however, a change that CVP disapproved of because it seemed to be unfair to profit from public subsidies and to perpetuate the sort of overcrowding that CVP wanted to correct. The institution had a minimal occupancy requirement of two years, but it did not really want to police the occupants rigorously, to set up disagreeable mechanisms of control and eviction, or even to put substantial resources into such work when more dwellings could be built instead. Rather, it chose to evaluate Guacamayas with a sixty-four-item questionnaire that might identify the kind of family most or least tempted to convert its dwelling into a rental unit.

Officials of CVP acknowledged that even Guacamayas solved only a small portion of the growing housing deficit among the poor. Though the housing was inexpensive, subsidies were still needed, so imitation of the project by large-scale private builders was unlikely. With other demands on the city budget of Bogotá, the best way for CVP to mobilize additional resources seemed to be to construct expensive apartments in the richer northern parts of the city. In 1978 construction of 500 62-square-meter units costing from 500,000 to 600,000 pesos began. At the same time very rudimentary rental units costing only 200 pesos monthly had been built at Los Laches. They consisted of one room, outside cooking facilities, and communal plumbing. Occupants were allowed to remain only two years and were supposed to save enough to qualify for something like the Guacamayas project. The forty-eight units of this project were still considered experimental.

References

The word *"processed"* indicates works that are reproduced by mimeograph, xerography, or similar means; such works may not be cataloged or commonly available through libraries, or may be subject to restricted circulation.

Agency for International Development, Comptroller General. *Agency for International Development's Housing Investment Guaranty Program.* Report to Congress. Washington, D.C.: U.S. General Accounting Office, September 6, 1978.

Agency for International Development, Office of Housing. *Tunisia: Shelter Sector Assessment.* Washington, D.C., January 1979.

Ahumada Sulbaran, Regulo. "A Medias Quedó el Censo de Cartagena." *El Espectador* (August 11, 1978).

Araud, Christian, Gerard Boon, Victor Urquidi, and Paul Strassmann. *Studies on Employment in the Mexican Housing Industry.* Development Center Studies, Employment Series no. 10. Paris: OECD, 1973, pp. 80, 163.

Asociación Nacional de Industriales. *Monografia Industrial de Cartagena, 1976.* Cartagena, 1977, pp. 22–23.

Bureau of Educational Research. "The Residents of Umoja Housing Estate." University of Nairobi, March 1978. Processed.

Burns, Leland S., and Leo Grebler. *The Housing of Nations: Analysis and Policy in a Comparative Framework.* London: Macmillan, 1977.

CAMACOL. *Empleo Generado por la Construcción en Colombia* (Bogotá, October 1977), p. 5.

Cameron, Sally. "Local Participation in Bank-Supported Urban Development Projects." Washington, D.C, World Bank, Urban Projects Department, 1978. Processed.

Cardona, Ramiro. *Migración y Fuerza de Trabajo en el Departamento de Bolivar,* vol. 1 and 2. Bogotá: Consorcio de Ingenierías e Investigaciones, Consultores, August 1977, p. 71.

Cebrecos Revilla, Rufino. "Construcción de Vivienda y Empleo." Lima, Departamento de Económia, Pontificia Universidad Catolica del Peru, April 1978, p. 39. Processed.

Centro Nacional de Estudios de la Construcción (CENAC). *Deficit de Vivienda en Colombia 1964–1973 y Proyecciones 1974–1980.* Bogotá, December 1976. Processed.

_____. *La Construcción en Cifras.* Bogotá, January 1977, October 1977, February 1978, May 1978. Processed.

Churchill, Anthony A., and Margaret Lycette. *Shelter.* Poverty and Basic Needs Series. Washington, D.C.: World Bank, 1980.

Collier, David. *Squatters and Oligarchs: Authoritarian Rule and Policy Change in Peru.* Baltimore, Md.: Johns Hopkins University Press, 1976.

Cortés Diáz, Lácydes. *Familia y Sociedad en Cartagena.* Departamento de Investigación Económica y Social, Universidad de Cartagena, July 1971.

DANE. *Indice de Precios.* Bogotá, 1977.

_____. *La Vivienda en Colombia, 1973.* Advance sample of the fourteenth national census. Bogotá, 1978. Processed.

Departamento Nacional de Planeación. *Posibilidades de Reducción de Costos de Edificación,* vol. 2. Bogotá, November 1972.

Drakakis-Smith, David. "Low-Cost Housing Provision in the Third World." In *Housing in Third World Countries.* Edited by H. S. Murison and J. P. Lea. New York: St. Martin's Press, 1979.

Farrell, Robert V., and Lácydes Cortés. "Four Walls Are Not Enough: A Case Study of Education and Housing in Cartagena, Colombia." *International Journal for Housing Science and Its Applications,* vol. 4, no. 5 (1980), pp. 425–26.

Gallin, Bernard. *Hsin Hsing, Taiwan: A Chinese Village in Change.* Berkeley, Calif.: University of California Press, 1966.

Gómez de Gongora, Gloria Amparo, Aura Miranda de Hernández, and Edgar Galofre Vega. "Diagnóstico Socio-Económico del Barrio 'La Esperanza'." Cartagena, SENA, February 1978. Processed.

Greene, David, and W. Paul Strassmann. "Peruvian Construction Statistics and Productivity Changes." *Journal of Development Studies* (January 1971), pp. 189–95.

Grimes, Orville F. *Housing for Low-Income Urban Families.* Baltimore, Md.: Johns Hopkins University Press, 1976.

Gutierrez de Gomez, Marta Isabel. "Politica Tarifaria y Distribucion de Ingresos." Bogotá, National Planning Department, 1975. Processed.

Gutierrez Pineda, Virginia. *Familia y Cultura en Colombia.* Bogotá: Ediciones Tercer Mundo, 1968.

Ingram, Gregory K. "Housing Demand in the Developing Metropolis." Paper presented at the Econometric Society Meetings, Atlanta, Ga., December 1979.

Ingram, Gregory K., and Yitzhak Oron. "The Production of Housing Services from Existing Dwelling Units." In *Residential Location and Urban Housing Markets.* Edited by Gregory K. Ingram. Cambridge, Mass.: National Bureau of Economic Research, 1977.

Instituto de Crédito Territorial. "Censo de Propietarios en la Zona Suroriental, Sector 2." Cartagena, 1976. Processed.

_____. "Inventario de Zonas Subnormales de Vivienda y Proyectos de Desarrollo Progresivo." Bogotá, 1972. Processed.

Jellicoe, Marguerite. "Credit and Housing Associations among Luo Immigrants in Kampala." In *Urban Challenge in East Africa*. Edited by John Hutton. Nairobi: East Africa Publishing House, 1970.

Laquian, A. A. "Squatters and Slum Dwellers." In *Housing Asia's Millions*. Edited by Stephen H. K. Yeh and A. A. Laquian. Ottawa: International Development Research Center, 1979.

Linn, Johannes. *Cities in the Developing World: Policies for Their Equitable and Efficient Growth*. New York: Oxford University Press, 1982.

_____. "Urban Public Finances in Developing Countries: A Case Study of Cartagena, Colombia." Urban and Regional Report no. 77-1. Washington, D.C., World Bank, January 1975. Processed.

Lowry, Ira S., Mack Ott, and Charles Noland. "Housing Allowances and Household Behavior." Rand Corporation note prepared for the Department of Housing and Urban Development. Santa Monica, Calif., March 1973. Processed.

Madavo, Callisto, Donna Haldane, and Sally Cameron. "Site and Services and Upgrading: A Review of World-Bank-Assisted Projects," Urban Projects Department. Washington, D.C, World Bank, January 1978. Processed.

Marga Institute. *Housing in Sri Lanka*. Colombo, 1976.

Mazingira Institute. "Post-Habitat Evaluation Report on Human Settlements." Nairobi, July 1978. Processed.

Ministerio de Desarrollo Económico. "Zona Franca Industrial y Comercial de Cartagena: Una Vision Nueva de Una Region en Desarrollo." Cartagena, August 1976.

_____. "Zona Franca Industrial y Comercial de Cartagena: Area de Población y Medio Ambiente: Informe Final," vol. 1, Bogotá, December 1976. Processed.

Mohan, Rakesh. *Urban Economic and Planning Models: Assessing the Potential for Cities in Developing Countries*. Baltimore, Md.: Johns Hopkins University Press, 1979.

Muller, M. S. "House Building in Site and Services Schemes: Some Observations." University of Nairobi, Housing Research and Development Unit, June 1977. Processed.

Musgrove, Philip. "Determinants of Household Consumption in Latin America: A Summary of Evidence form ECIEL Surveys." *Economic Development and Cultural Change* (April 1978), pp. 441–65.

_____. *Income and Spending of Urban Families in Latin America: The ECIEL Consumption Study*. Washington, D.C.: Brookings Institution, 1978.

Muth, Richard F. "The Influence of Age of Dwellings on Housing Expenditures and on the Location of Households." In *Residential Location and Urban Housing Markets*. Edited by Gregory K. Ingram. Cambridge, Mass.: National Bureau of Economic Research, 1977.

Payne, Geoffrey K. *Urban Housing in the Third World*. London: Leonard Hill, 1977.

Prakash, Ved. *New Towns in India*. Durham, N.C.: Duke University Program in Comparative Studies on Southern Asia, 1969.

Prieto D., Rafael. *Estructura del Gasto y Distribución del Ingreso Familiar en Cuatro Ciudades Colombianas, 1967–68.* Bogotá: CEDE, 1971.

_____. "Gasto e Ingreso Familar Urbano en Colombia." *Ensayos* ECIEL (August 1977), pp. 45–120.

Quigley, John. "What Have We Learned about Urban Housing Markets." In *Current Issues in Urban Economics.* Edited by Peter Mieszkowski and Mahlon Straszheim. Baltimore, Md.: Johns Hopkins University Press, 1979.

Renaud, Bertrand. *National Urbanization Policy in Developing Countries.* New York: Oxford University Press, 1981.

Rosen, Sherwin. "Hedonic Prices and Implicit Markets: Product Differentiation in Pure Competition." *Journal of Political Economy* (January 1974), pp. 34–55.

Rueda García, Nicolás. Centor de Planificación y Urbanismo, University of the Andes, quoted in *El Tiempo* (August 19, 1978).

Serna Gomez, Humberto, and Francisco Rodriguez Urrego. *Area de Promoción Humana y Desarrollo Tecnológico, Informe Segunda Etapa.* Bogotá: Ministerio de Desarrollo Económico, September 1976.

Stevenson, Rafael. "Housing Programs and Policies in Bogotá: A Historical and Descriptive Analysis." Urban and Regional Report no. 79-8. Washington, D.C., World Bank, June 1978. Processed.

Strassmann, W. Paul. "Alternative Housing Strategies for Sri Lanka." *Marga Quarterly Journal,* no. 2 (1977), p. 30.

_____. "Employment in Core House Building: A Comparison of Estimates from Six Cities in Six Countries." East Lansing, Housing-in-Development Unit, Michigan State University, 1980. Processed.

_____. "Employment Generation through Residential Construction in Rio de Janeiro." Report for the U.S. Agency for International Development, Washington, D.C., October 1975. Processed.

_____. *Housing and Building Technology in Developing Countries.* MSU International Business and Economic Studies. East Lansing: Michigan State University, 1978.

_____. "Housing Policy and Improvements by Owner-Occupants: A Comparison of Neighborhoods in Lima, Peru." East Lansing: Michigan State University, September 1981. Processed.

_____. "Housing Priorities in Developing Countries: A Planning Model." *Land Economics* (August 1977), pp. 310–27.

_____. "Innovation and Employment in Building: The Experience of Peru." *Oxford Economic Papers* (July 1970), pp. 243–59.

Triana y Antorveza, Humberto. *Cultura del Tugurio en Cartagena.* Bogotá: Impresa en Italgraf for UNICEF, 1974.

Turner, John F. C. *Housing by People: Towards Autonomy in Building Environments.* New York: Pantheon Books, 1976.

Ward, Barbara. *The Home of Man.* Toronto: McClelland and Stewart, 1976.

Wheaton, William C. "Income and Urban Residence: An Analysis of Consumer

Demand for Location." *American Economic Review* (September 1977), pp. 620-31.

_____. "Monocentric Models of Urban Land Use: Contributions and Criticisms." In *Current Issues in Urban Economics.* Edited by Peter Mieszkowski and Mahlon Straszheim. Baltimore, Md.: Johns Hopkins University Press, 1979.

World Bank. *Housing.* Sector Policy Paper. Washington, D.C., 1975.

Yañez Orviz, Jesus. "Optimal Allocation of Housing Investment in Five Mexican Cities, 1960-70, 1970-85," Ph.D. dissertation, Michigan State University, East Lansing, 1976, pp. 116-23.

Zorro Sánchez, Carlos, and Edgar Reveiz Roldán. *Estudio sobre Los Inquilinatos (Vivienda Compartida en Arrendamiento) en Bogotá.* Bogotá: Centro de Estudios sobre Desarrollo Económico, University of the Andes, Etapa I February 1974 and Segunda Parte June 1976.

Index

The full range of World Bank publications, both free and for sale, is described in the *Catalog of World Bank Publications*; the continuing research program is outlined in *World Bank Research Program: Abstracts of Current Studies*. Both booklets are updated annually; the most recent edition of each is available without charge from the Publications Distribution Unit (Dept. B), World Bank, 1818 H Street, N.W., Washington, D.C. 20433, U.S.A.

W. Paul Strassmann is professor of economics and director of the Housing in Development Unit at Michigan State University and is a consultant to the World Bank.